SONGS FROM THE EDGE OF JAPAN: MUSIC-MAKING IN YAEYAMA AND OKINAWA

Songs from the Edge of Japan: Music-making in Yaeyama and Okinawa

MATT GILLAN
International Christian University, Tokyo, Japan

ASHGATE

Published by
Ashgate Publishing Limited
Wey Court East
Union Road
Farnham
Surrey, GU9 7PT
England

Ashgate Publishing Company
Suite 420
101 Cherry Street
Burlington
VT 05401-4405
USA

www.ashgate.com

British Library Cataloguing in Publication Data
Gillan, Matthew.
  Songs from the edge of Japan : music-making in Yaeyama and
  Okinawa. -- (SOAS musicology series)
  1. Music--Japan--Okinawa Island--History and criticism.
  2. Music--Japan--Yaeyama Islands--History and criticism.
  I. Title II. Series III. University of London. School of
  Oriental and African Studies.
  780.9'5229-dc22

Library of Congress Cataloging-in-Publication Data
Gillan, Matt.
  Songs from the edge of Japan : music-making in Yaeyama and Okinawa / Matt
Gillan.
     p. cm. -- (SOAS musicology series)
  Includes bibliographical references.
  ISBN 978-1-4094-2404-8 (hardcover) -- ISBN 978-1-4094-2405-5 (ebook)
  1. Music--Japan--Ryukyu Islands--History and criticism. I. Title.

ML3750.7.R9G55 2011
781.62'95605229--dc23

2011031830

ISBN 9781409424048 (hbk)
ISBN 9781409424055 (ebk)

Printed and bound in Great Britain by
TJ International Ltd, Padstow, Cornwall.

Contents

List of Figures   *vii*
List of Music Examples   *ix*
Acknowledgements   *xi*
A Note on the Romanisation of Japanese, Yaeyaman and Okinawan Words   *xv*
A Note on Transcriptions   *xix*

1   Island Treasures (*Sïma nu Takara*)   1

2   Islands of Song and Dance: Yaeyama and its Music   17

3   The Southern Islands –
     Yaeyama and Okinawa in the Japanese Cultural Imagination   45

4   Music for Gods, Ancestors and People –
     Yaeyaman Music in a Ritual Context   65

5   *Nama ni nukushōri* – Lineages and Preservation Groups   91

6   *Izu su du nusï* – The Singer is Master:
     Regional versus Individual Styles in the
     Performance of *Tubarāma*   127

7   The Okinawa 'Boom' – Local Music on the National Stage   149

8   Afterword   177

Appendix 1: Glossary of Japanese, Yaeyaman and Okinawan Terms   *183*
Appendix 2: Glossary of Place Names   *189*
Appendix 3: Glossary of Personal Names   *191*
Bibliography   *195*
Discography   *213*
Index   *217*

List of Figures

0.1   Map of East Asia   xvii
0.2   Map of Yaeyama   xviii

2.1   *Sanshin* and *tsume*   36

4.1   *Miruku* at 2002 Harvest festival in Hatoma   70

5.1   *Fushiuta* lineages   99
5.2   *Fushiuta* lesson with Ōsoko Chōyō   101
5.3   Concert by Kantō branch of YKMH, Tokyo 2009   103
5.4   Tonoshiro *koyō hozonkai* performing in 2002 at
       Tonoshiro's harvest festival (*on-pūrï*)   109
5.5   Collage of song monuments: *Basï nu turï bushi*; *Tubarāma*;
       Akanma bushi; *Hatoma bushi*   113
5.6   *Sanshin* lessons for tourists in Ishigaki   122
5.7   Tourist cart in Taketomi. The driver is playing a *sanshin*   122
5.8   Asadoya folk song bar   124

7.1   BEGIN performing in Ishigaki, 2002   154

List of Music Examples

2.1   *Shūritsï yunta*. Tonoshiro version as performed by
      Tonoshiro Kayō no kai   24
2.2   *Kunkunshi* (section) for the song *Tsuki ya pama bushi*   38
2.3   *Yunaha bushi*   40
2.4   Koizumi's four scale types: a) *miyako-bushi* scale; b) *ritsu* scale;
      c) *min'yō* scale; d) *ryūkyū* scale   40
2.5   *Asadōya yunta*. Tonoshiro *kayō no kai*, 2002   41
2.6   *Kuigusuku bushi*   42
2.7   Summary of movement between *ryo* and *ryūkyū* scale   43

3.1   Instrumental intro to *Hatoma bushi*: traditional version on *sanshin* (a)
      from Ōhama (1964); Miyara Chōhō's 1921 version on piano (b)   61

4.1   *Gaku* – instrumental melodies identifying a particular village
      (Hazama or Nakasuji) at Taketomi's *Tanadui* festival   85

6.1   Ishigaki village *Tubarāma*   137
6.2   Second phrase of the 'Mafutanē' *Tubarama* version   138
6.3   First phrase of the Kabira version of *Tubarāma*   138
6.4   Second phrase of Miyara Kōrin's version of *Tubarāma*   139
6.5   Comparison of three verses of Sakiyama Yōnō's 1934
      Tubarāma recording   140

7.1   *Kaze no donan*   166
7.2   *Shimanchu nu takara*   166

Acknowledgements

This book is the result of more than 10 years research into Yaeyaman and Okinawan music. During that time I have been incredibly fortunate to receive academic, financial and moral support from a large number of organizations and individuals. It would be impossible to list all of them here, and I apologise for any that have been inadvertently omitted.

The research on which this thesis is based was made possible through generous financial assistance from several bodies. The initial period of fieldwork between 2001 and 2002 was carried out as part of a PhD project funded by the British AHRB (AHRC). A further grant for a short research trip in Osaka in spring 2004 was provided by Osaka City University. Between 2005 and 2007 I was able to continue my research into Yaeyaman music as part of a post-doctoral research project at Okinawa Prefectural University of Arts under the sponsorship of the Japanese Society for the Promotion of Science. Since 2007 I have also made several short trips to Okinawa with financial assistance from International Christian University in Tokyo.

Throughout this project, I have been fortunate to receive advice and guidance from many prominent ethnomusicologists and researchers. Thanks must go first of all to David Hughes, my PhD supervisor at the School of Oriental and African Studies, without whom my career in ethnomusicology would not have begun, and who has provided consistent support since I began a masters degree in ethnomusicology in 1998. During my time at SOAS I received advice and assistance from several faculty members of the music department and fellow students. Particular thanks to Keith Howard, Steven Jones, Owen Wright, Rachel Harris, and Richard Widdess. Also in London, I have benefitted greatly from many conversations with the musician and Okinawa specialist Robin Thompson.

At Okinawan Prefectural University of Arts in Naha I am particularly indebted to Kaneshiro Atsumi for acting as my academic advisor both during my initial fieldwork research and again during a postdoctoral research project. Also at the Prefectural University of Arts, Kumada Susumu and Hateruma Eikichi have also been consistently positive towards my research, and tolerant of my frequent misunderstandings of issues surrounding Okinawan music. Shinjō Wataru and Takahashi Miki, both graduates of the university, have also provided numerous comments and introductions that have helped my studies progress. Also in the Okinawa mainland, the researchers Higa Etsuko and Ōshiro Manabu have also been helpful in providing contacts and information over the years.

In Tokyo, Sakai Masako has been continually supportive of my research and has generously shared many of her research results and recordings with me. James Roberson of Tokyo Jogakkan College, in addition to providing insightful comments as examiner for my original PhD thesis, has on several occasions enhanced my understanding of Okinawan pop music through informal conversations. At International Christian University in Tokyo, I have been fortunate to work since 2007 with a multi-disciplinary faculty who have broadened my scholarly horizons immensely. Particular thanks to Itoh Tatsuhiko in the music department for academic and moral support.

In the Yaeyaman musical community, I have been overwhelmed by the extent that people went out of their way to help me. Special thanks must go to Tominaga Hide, Yamazato Setsuko, and all the members of the Tonoshiro 'Kayō no Kai', who welcomed me into their midst, and the regular practice sessions on Tuesday evenings, as well as excursions to play ground golf, were among the highlights of my time in Yaeyama. Yamazato Setsuko also provided me with introductions to a number of performers and *koyō* groups in Yaeyama, and was an endless source of knowledge on many aspects of Yaeyaman culture. Special thanks also to my *fushiuta* teacher Ōsoko Chōyō who has been both a fount of knowledge on many aspects of Yaeyaman music, and a patient teacher to an erratic student. The veteran singer Yamazato Yūkichi took me under his wing from the very first days in Okinawa, and provided information about aspects of Yaeyaman music in the Okinawan mainland, as well as teaching me much about aspects of performance. I have also spent many happy evenings over the years in Asadoya, the folk song club owned by the performer Asato Isamu, who also took me on regular fishing expeditions around Yaeyama. In the Okinawan mainland, Ōtake Zenzō taught me much about *fushiuta* performance between 2005 and 2007. Tōyama Zendō also provided me with important insights on *fushiuta* performance and history on a number of occasions.

I have had extensive connections with Taketomi islanders, both those living in Ishigaki and in Taketomi itself. Ōyama Takeshi provided me with a number of introductions as well as much constructive advice, as well as organizing a leaving party at the end of my fieldwork that I will never forget. Ishigaki Hisao, president of the Yaeyama Bunka Kyōkai allowed me access to the practices of the Hazama Geinō Hozonkai in his home during the weeks before the Taketomi *Tanedori-sai*, as well as providing me with information about other Taketomi groups. The Yaeyaman scholars Ishigaki Shigeru and Ishigaki Hirotaka of the Yaeyama Bunka Kenkyūkai offered extensive information on many aspects of Yaeyaman song, particularly help with the many problems I faced understanding local dialects. The local writer and scholar Morita Son'ei gave me extensive advice on Yaeyaman lyrics, as well as providing information about the workings of the *Tubarāma Taikai*, and the *Yaeyama Mainichi Shinbun*-sponsored *sanshin* grade tests. Ōta Shizuo guided me on several occasions to ritual events around Ishigaki island, including a memorable music session in front of his family grave.

Finally, studying Yaeyaman music has constantly reminded me of the importance of family. Love and thanks to family members in my three *shima* of England, Yonaguni and Tokyo, without whom I would not have got this far.

Shikai tu nīfaiyū.

A Note on the Romanisation of Japanese, Yaeyaman and Okinawan Words

Romanisation of standard Japanese words follows the modified Hepburn system, with long vowels represented by a macron. The romanisation of Yaeyaman and Okinawan words presents specific problems, and it is often difficult to choose a single correct romanisation for many terms due to the large regional variations in pronunciation. Yaeyaman dialects are considerably different from the Shuri pronunciation usually used when romanising Okinawan terms (e.g. Kokuritsu Kokugo Kenkyūsho 1963), and dialect varies considerably even within Yaeyama. Yaeyaman dialects contain the same five vowel sounds as standard Japanese (*a, i, u, e, o*), although there are some slight differences such as the Yaeyaman *u*, which is pronounced with the lips in a more relaxed position than its Japanese counterpart. Many Yaeyaman dialects also contain vowel sounds not found in standard Japanese. In particular, a vowel sound somewhere between Japanese *i* and *u* is common, and is romanised as *ï*. Yaeyaman dialects distinguish between long and short vowels in a way similar to standard Japanese, and are represented, as in the modified Hepburn system, using a macron. Several Yaeyaman consonant sounds, notably *f/h* and *w*, vary according to village and island. Thus the Japanese *hana* (flower) becomes *hana*, *fana* and *pana* depending on the local Yaeyaman dialect. When notating song texts I have transcribed the lyrics as heard, noting the village from where the pronunciation is taken.

Titles of songs or dance pieces are capitalised and italicised, and Japanese terms not in general English use are italicised. Terms that are used more than once, and those that have a Japanese character equivalent, are listed in the glossary of Japanese terms (Appendix 1). Place names appear in their standard Japanese reading. Dialect versions of place names are shown in the glossary of place names (Appendix 2). Personal names are given in standard Japanese order, surname first. The Japanese character writings for names are shown in the glossary of Japanese names (Appendix 3). People in Yaeyama are often referred to by their personal name, and I have followed this convention on occasion, especially when several people with the same family name appear in the text. Thus, I refer to Ōhama Anpan as Anpan, as he is commonly known in Yaeyama.

Many Yaeyaman and Okinawan bands use romanised forms of their band names on CDs and other material, in which case I have followed this usage, including the use of capitalisation. Hence, I use BEGIN for the Yaeyaman band as it appears on album covers, rather than a transliteration of the Japanese form (Bigin). Similarly, I use Nēnēs rather than Nēnēzu for the Okinawan mainland group of that name. Where possible confusion may arise, I have given alternative forms on the first appearance of the name in the text.

All translations are by the author, unless otherwise stated. I have opted for a literal rather than a poetic translation in order to try to show the original structure of the song texts. The common use of synonyms in Yaeyaman verse, especially the use of couplets of identical meaning, has been especially difficult to translate, and on occasion I have resorted to repeating the same translation for two adjacent lines of text. As far as possible I have translated directly from dialect rather than from Japanese translations of the dialect song texts.

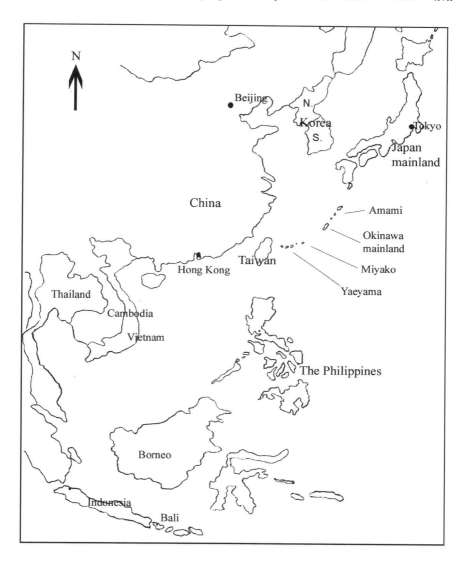

Figure 0.1   Map of East Asia

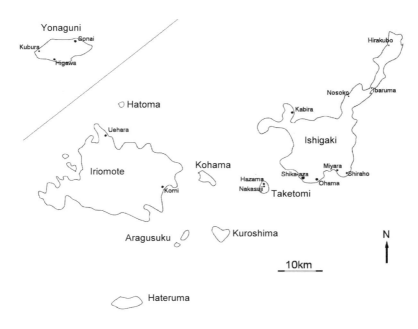

Figure 0.2   Map of Yaeyama

A Note on Transcriptions

All transcriptions are my own, except where indicated. On many of my field recordings of unaccompanied genres the pitch at which a song was sung changed during the course of a song, either going up with the singers' excitement or, especially in the longer songs, down as the singers began to tire. In the accompanied *fushiuta* genre also, although the *sanshin* accompaniment ensures a constant pitch over the course of a song, singers commonly vary the pitch at which they sing a song according to their mood or energy level on a particular day. For this reason, and for ease of comparison, I have chosen to notate most songs in the same key (usually equivalent to *f-major* or *c-major*, according to *sanshin* tuning).

島ぬ宝

Chapter 1
Island Treasures (*Sïma nu Takara*)

Introduction

Travelling down the Japanese archipelago from Hokkaido in the north, it is possible to traverse the island chain as far as the main island of Okinawa without ever losing sight of land. Going from one island to the next by boat never involved more than a day's journey overseas that are relatively easily navigated. Further south from the Okinawan mainland,[1] to the 'Sakishima' island groups of Miyako and Yaeyama, involves crossing a stretch of ocean that is both large, and renowned for its unpredictable weather. The very name by which these islands are known, *Sakishima* (which translates roughly as the islands 'far ahead'), implies their separation from the central culture, originally of the Okinawan mainland, and later of Japan itself. This separation has led to the development of distinctive cultural forms in the islands, as well as an acute sense of local identity that has been maintained despite the strong influences of Okinawa and Japan over the centuries. Furthermore, the fact that Yaeyama is made up of a group of separate islands has meant that even within the region there are distinct local identities, based on individual islands or villages within islands, each of which proudly maintains its own traditional cultural patterns. Along with these local identities, the islands' geographical and cultural position at the very 'edge' of Japan has meant that Yaeyama has featured prominently in much cultural discourse surrounding the nature of the Japanese nation since the early 20th century. Yaeyaman culture, including music, has come to have meanings far beyond its place of origin, as it has been performed and positioned within Japanese and Okinawan cultural frameworks.

---

[1]   Okinawa is modern Japan's southernmost prefecture, made up of around 50 inhabited islands, as well as many more that are not populated. I use the term 'Okinawan mainland' to refer to the prefecture's largest island, on which the prefectural capital city of Naha is situated. 'Okinawa city' refers to a smaller city on the Okinawan mainland. I have used 'Okinawa' to refer to Okinawa prefecture as a whole. The islands have also been known as 'Ryūkyū' at various stages of their history, in particular during the period of the Ryūkyū kingdom before the creation of Okinawa prefecture in 1879, and during the period of American administration between 1945 and 1972. I use this term here only in relation to the first of these.

Between the summer of 2001 and the autumn of 2002 I carried out an extended fieldwork trip to Yaeyama, studying practical performance of traditional styles and observing the performance of traditional and more modern musical genres in a variety of situations. During that time I was particularly struck by the way local musical styles were used in connection with the construction of Yaeyama's various local and national cultural identities. Two related examples made a particular impact, and contribute to the title of this chapter, 'Island Treasures (*Sīma nu Takara*)'. I first encountered the phrase as part of a lyric composed by Ōhama Anpan (1913–2001) in the mid-20th century to a well-known traditional Yaeyaman song melody *Tubarāma*. In this verse Ōhama, one of the most influential Yaeyaman traditional musicians of the 20th century, sang how 'our ancestors expressed their lives through song. As island treasures, let us preserve those songs in the present' (*mukasī pitu ya kurashi yu uta ni kake, sīma nu takara de nama ni nukushōri*; in Arashiro 2001: 70). Ōhama's expression of a Yaeyaman identity as 'island treasures' (*sīma nu takara*) in this verse is one based largely within a discourse of tradition that plays an important part in much music-making in the islands. Traditional musical genres continue to be performed throughout Yaeyama as part of everyday life, and these are implicitly bound up with the construction and maintenance of local identities. As Ōhama's verse shows, tradition itself is also something that continues to be actively imagined and discussed in song lyrics, print and everyday speech.

A counterpart to this backward-looking construction of local identity came in the early summer of 2002 with the release of the pop song *Shimanchu nu takara* (treasures of the island people) by the Yaeyaman band BEGIN (see discography). Despite the similarity of the title with Ōhama's expression of Yaeyaman identity, BEGIN's song seemed to position Yaeyama in quite a different way. First, the lyrics expressed an explicitly ambivalent attitude to the past, representative of the relationship many young Yaeyamans have towards their traditional culture in a rapidly globalising world. In one verse, for example, the singer expresses how 'doesn't even understand the words' (*kotoba no imi sae wakaranai*) to traditional songs such as *Tubarāma*, that are sung in local Yaeyaman languages. Despite this disconnection from tradition, the song concludes that modern Yaeyamans continue to have a strong and unique cultural identity – the 'treasures of the island people' (*shimanchu nu takara*) of the title.

The context behind the composition and marketing of BEGIN's *Shimanchu nu takara* also reveals much about the various cultural issues that the song addresses. The song was written to commemorate the 30th anniversary in 2002 of the return of Okinawa prefecture to Japanese rule, and came at the height of a 'boom' of interest in Okinawan music and culture throughout the nation. While Ōhama's verse is relatively unknown outside the Yaeyaman islands, the considerable success of *Shimanchu nu takara* throughout Japan shows how issues of regional identity and tradition are being played out not only at a local level, but also have a national resonance. At one extreme, within weeks of its release in 2002, I witnessed the song being performed as part of a ritual harvest festival event in Yaeyama's largest island of Ishigaki, showing its relevance to an immediately local Yaeyaman audience. By the end of the year, the band had been invited to perform *Shimanchu nu takara* as part of the NHK *Kōhaku uta gassen* programme, the most prestigious event in Japan's pop music calendar that is broadcast across the nation on New Year's Eve, indicating that the song also had strong cultural meanings at a much wider cultural level.

These two very different takes on the idea of cultural inheritance by Ōhama and BEGIN are basically concerned with the same issue – what does it mean to be Yaeyaman, and how can this sense of being Yaeyaman be expressed musically in the present? This book starts with these two very different ideas of island (people's) treasures – in Yaeyama, Okinawa and Japan – and attempts to analyse some of the cultural meanings behind music-making in modern Yaeyama and Okinawa. I draw upon fieldwork carried out since 2000 in Yaeyama itself, as well as the Okinawan and Japanese mainlands, and I analyse the meanings of Yaeyaman music largely from a contemporary perspective. I also draw on the large volume of written works by scholars and writers from Yaeyama and the rest of Japan to link Yaeyama's modern musical meanings to cultural debates that took place throughout the nation from the early 20th century. The majority of the book is concerned with what we might see as 'traditional' genres, and I consider historical aspects of the formation of these genres, with particular reference to the meanings of musical histories to contemporary musicians and audiences. I also consider the methods by which traditions are created and contested in the context of Yaeyama's position at the very edge of modern Japan, and as part of a globalising world.

As one of the few regions in Japan where traditional music thrives as a meaningful part of everyday life, Yaeyama and Okinawa are culturally important within Japan in a number of ways. In terms of the number of active learners, Okinawan music is one of the most popular 'traditional Japanese' music genres in Tokyo and other large Japanese cities as much as it is in Okinawa itself. The creation in 2004 of a nationally sponsored theatre for traditional performing arts in Okinawa, the only such theatre for a traditional Japanese genre outside Tokyo and Osaka, also speaks of the importance of Okinawan music on a national level. Yaeyaman music has had a presence in this Okinawan music scene far out of proportion to its geographic or demographic size. Traditional music thrives, as do attempts such as BEGIN's to forge new musical styles using traditional elements to various degrees. Yet behind this musical activity are always questions of cultural identity – what is Yaeyama's place in Japan and in Okinawa? How can the old ways of life and music-making be adapted to Yaeyama in the 21st century. And why does Yaeyama continue to have such a disproportionately large impact on mainland Japanese cultural life?

Why Yaeyama?

I first became aware of Okinawan music in the mid-1990s, while living and working in Shikoku, the smallest of Japan's four main islands. An acquaintance invited me to see a concert by the Nēnēs, a four piece female vocal group from the Okinawan mainland who were making waves throughout Japan with their mixture of traditional Okinawan, reggae, Hawaiian, pop, and many other musical styles. I had delved into various Japanese musical traditions, particularly the Tozan-ryū *shakuhachi* style in which I was taking lessons, but nothing had prepared me for the sound of the Nēnēs. Compared to the studied austerity and deliberate simplicity of much of the Japanese music with which I had been involved, the Nēnēs, with their combination of new and old, East and West, energy and soulfulness, were eye- and ear-opening. What was more, compared to my fellow *shakuhachi* students who were mostly at least one generation older than me, the Nēnēs seemed to appeal to audiences of all ages. Japanese music could sound and feel like this? Or was it Japanese music? Despite my – at that stage – rudimentary Japanese abilities, I could hear that much of the language used in the songs was very different from the Japanese that I was studying, and the musical aspects too, from the scales somehow reminiscent of the Balinese gamelan to the offbeat rhythms of the fast dance numbers, were unlike anything that I had heard in mainland Japan. I resolved to find out more. On a short visit to Osaka, I embarked on a search for recordings of Okinawan music in a large CD store. Scanning the Japanese traditional music rack, I went past the recordings of *shakuhachi*, *Tsugaru-shamisen*, *wadaiko*, but there was nothing from Okinawa. A store clerk eventually led me over to the 'World Music' section in a different part of the store where, in the subsection marked 'Asia', there were numerous CDs of Okinawan music.[2] This geographical dislocation, translated onto the shelves of a CD store, again raised the question of exactly what country the music came from.

Delving a little deeper into Okinawan music, I began to listen to a series of recordings of more traditional styles made in the 1970s on the Japanese Victor label. Singers such as Yamazato Yūkichi, Noborikawa Seijin, Kuniyoshi Genji and, in particular, Kadekaru Rinshō stood out for their soulful delivery and sense of playfulness. Another highlight in these CDs was the liner notes, especially those by the journalist Takenaka Rō, who had been the impetus behind the 1970s recordings, and who portrayed performers such as Kadekaru as a kind of cross

---

[2]   Large Japanese CD retailers are divided on their classification of Okinawan music, with some stores filing the genre together with traditional Japanese music, and some under world music. With a shift to Internet shopping, the situation has changed somewhat. On the Japanese Amazon.co.jp site, for example, traditional Okinawan music is filed in both the Japanese traditional music and world music sections. In 2009 the Japanese iTunes site had no category for traditional Japanese music – Okinawan music was mostly filed under world music, while traditional mainland Japanese music was distributed among a variety of genres – one (mainland Japanese) folk-song collection was filed under 'singer-songwriter'.

between a Mississippi bluesman and the last in a line of lyrical improvisers whose lineage could be traced back to ancient Japanese traditions. This image of Okinawan music as a 'living tradition', where real emotions were expressed through song, was an attractive one.

A period of six months in 2000 living in Osaka, home since the early 20th century to a large population of Okinawan migrant workers and their descendants, gave me the opportunity to take lessons in singing and *sanshin*, the three-stringed plucked lute that is the representative instrument throughout Okinawa. I was fortunate to be introduced to a teacher of the Nomura lineage of classical Okinawan music, a genre that I continue to perform and study today. I also delved into the active Okinawan music scene in Osaka, with the many folk-song bars in the Taishō ward, and frequent performances by musicians flown in from Okinawa. I began to hear frequent tales about the long history of oppression that this Okinawan community had suffered in the Japanese mainland since the early 20th century, and I started to get some sense of the power of Okinawan music to express this minority identity in the context of the mainland Japanese community. It was also while living in Osaka that I happened to see the recently-released hit film *Nabi no koi*[3] by the Japanese director Nakae Yūji, featuring a host of Okinawan musicians such as Kadekaru, Yamazato, and with a star performance from Noborikawa Seijin. The image of Okinawa portrayed here was one of blue skies, sandy beaches and, above all, amiable characters with quirky personalities who obviously knew something about life that was being forgotten in my urban surroundings. It was another enticing image.

Another aspect of the nation-wide interest in Okinawan music at this time was that many performers seemed to come from the Yaeyaman region in the very south-west of the prefecture. As well as Yamazato Yūkichi's role in *Nabi no koi*, Yaeyaman performers such as Daiku Tetsuhiro, Ara Yukito, Ōshima Yasukatsu and many more were playing a leading role in developing new concepts of Yaeyaman music throughout Japan. A little more research revealed that these new developments were only the tip of a rich Yaeyaman musical culture that included ritual genres and unaccompanied work songs, and that had long fascinated Japanese musicologists and ethnologists. I decided to focus on this region in order to try and find out why traditional music continued to be relevant in Yaeyama, and why Yaeyaman musicians had been so musically productive in the recent Okinawan music boom.

By the time I moved to Yaeyama in the summer of 2001 to carry out the fieldwork that forms the basis of this book, I had amassed a sizeable collection of recordings of Yaeyaman music and, through studying from recordings and notations, had taught myself to sing a number of Yaeyaman songs while accompanying myself on the *sanshin*. One of the first things that struck me was how much traditional music continued to exist as part of daily (or at least yearly) life in Yaeyama. Summer is festival time in Yaeyama, and traditional music, both

---

[3]   The English subtitle is *Nabbie's love.*

unaccompanied ritual song and song accompanied by the *sanshin* can be heard almost every day. Like many outsiders, I was captivated by the use of traditional music in Yaeyaman festivals, which continue almost unabated from early summer to autumn each year. The obvious depth of meaning in these songs and dances, performed ostensibly for the gods or departed ancestors, was intensely moving, and is one of the reasons I have continued returning to Yaeyama. The use of music, and especially traditional music, in social ritual too – from marriages to funerals, high school reunions to retirement-home outings – was a consistent feature of my Yaeyaman experience, and on countless occasions gave me an 'in' to meeting people that I would otherwise not have had.

Also while living in Ishigaki in 2001 I experienced another media-related cultural phenomenon brought about by the daily television drama series *Churasan*, broadcast by the national NHK station, and set partly in Yaeyama. As with *Nabi no koi*, this national Japanese drama series focused very much on the slow pace of life in Okinawa and the importance of human relationships that were being sidelined by the fast pace of Japanese city life. I often met young mainland Japanese dissatisfied with this urban life who had packed up and decided to move to Yaeyama, often supporting themselves with jobs as helpers and cleaners in the island's many hotels. In many cases the migrants that I met were enamoured with the *Churasan* dream, sometimes aping the Okinawan intonation of the Japanese language that the characters in the show used and, particularly those in my immediate social circle, learning traditional Yaeyaman music. The population of Ishigaki has seen a huge increase[4] since the late 1990s, largely as a direct result of cultural representations of Yaeyama such as those in *Churasan*. With a long history in Japan of migration away from the countryside into the big cities, this population growth is extremely rare anywhere else in the country. What is it that makes Yaeyama so attractive to Japanese mainlanders? In this book I hope to investigate some possible reasons – especially the role that music plays in Yaeyama's cultural image.

Another thing that surprised me was that although I had listened to a lot of music on CD and, to some extent, live in Osaka, the performers who were popular in the Japanese mainland weren't necessarily the same performers who were popular in Yaeyama. Many of the big names on the Japanese scene were, of course, known in Yaeyama, but were somewhat looked down upon for being insufficiently skilled, or for not being sufficiently respectful to tradition. I found myself listening with new ears to music that I had genuinely enjoyed before moving to Yaeyama, trying to appreciate how performers and performances that were so moving in Osaka could be seen as so commonplace in Yaeyama itself. Conversely, I tried to understand why the music of some performers who were little known outside Yaeyama was considered to be culturally important within the islands. While

---

[4]   The population of Ishigaki in April 2009 was 48,316 compared with 43,302 in 2000 (www.city.ishigaki.okinawa.jp/jinkou/jnkou-all.htm, accessed 21 February 2011). Many more Japanese mainlanders are believed to be living in Ishigaki while maintaining their mainland Japanese addresses.

Yaeyaman music had one perfectly valid set of cultural meanings in Osaka, it also had another, different, existence and set of meanings within Yaeyama.

Since this initial period of fieldwork in Yaeyama itself, I have continued my association with Yaeyaman music in other contexts. From 2004 to 2007 I lived in the Okinawan mainland capital Naha, carrying out fieldwork in other areas of Okinawan music while continuing my studies in Yaeyaman performance. From 2007 I have been based in Tokyo, and have seen yet another side of the Yaeyaman music world through the large number of performers based in the Japanese capital. Throughout all these experiences, my image and understanding of Yaeyaman music has continued to change, incorporating the different viewpoints and cultural contexts in which I have had the good fortune to be placed. For such a geographically small region, Yaeyaman music has had a huge cultural influence throughout Okinawa and Japan. In this book I present some of my experiences with Yaeyaman music in Yaeyama, Okinawa and the Japanese mainland, and attempt to analyse some of the reasons why this region at the very edge of Japan continues to be so musically and culturally important.

Situating Yaeyama and its Music

'Yaeyaman music' encompasses a variety of genres that are performed in a number of different cultural contexts and geographical locations with various cultural meanings. As Stuart Hall has written, 'we are all complexly constructed through different categories, of different antagonisms, and these may have the effect of locating us socially in multiple positions of marginality and subordination, but which do not yet operate on us in exactly the same way' (1991: 57). Some of Yaeyama's many musical genres never make it out of the geographical confines of the region, while others are taken up enthusiastically outside Yaeyama, although often with quite different meanings than they have within. Other genres that we might call Yaeyaman have been created largely or entirely outside Yaeyama, both by Yaeyaman diasporic communities and cultural outsiders. All of these are used, to some extent, to 'evoke and organise collective memories and present experiences of place' (Stokes 1994: 3). How, then, to make sense of these different musics and music-making contexts, all of which may be labelled to some extent as 'Yaeyaman'?

One of the ways that music has been used in the imagination of place at a local level, and one which is exemplified by Ōhama Anpan's '*sïma nu takara*' ideal of preserving the ways of the past, is through local discourses of authenticity and tradition. Connell and Gibson have described the idea of 'spatial fixity, where continuity is valued over change, stability preferred to cycles of fashion, and which links music to particular places and establishes those links as traditions and genuine aspects of local cultures' (2003: 19). One of the ways in which 'spatial fixity' has been achieved in a Yaeyaman context, as in Japan in general, is through the establishment of formal organisations and lineages for the dissemination of traditional music. Hughes has described in detail (2008: 212–24) the role of 'preservation societies' (*hozonkai*) in the 20th century Japanese folk-song world, and noted their role in the construction of regional identities in opposition to the nation (ibid.: 223). The role of formalised lineages in Japan, and in particular the *iemoto* system, where a particular lineage is controlled by a single 'headmaster'[5] (*iemoto*) to whom all major artistic decisions are deferred, have been described in several studies (for an overview, see Kanō 2002; also Keister 2004; Ortolani 1969). Preservation societies and more formal lineage organisations have both been a feature of the modern Yaeyaman traditional music world, and I examine some issues surrounding these groups at a local level in Chapter 5. Despite an image of staticness and resistance to change, ideas of spatial fixity have often been hotly debated in Yaeyama, and the negotiation of modern concepts and meanings of tradition have been far from passive. In Chapter 6 I examine some of the debates that have taken place surrounding the conflict between group identity and personal style in the performance of traditional music, and in Chapter 7 I consider some of the cultural consequences of reinterpreting traditional styles in a pop music context.

The use of language has also been an important aspect of musical constructions of place. The British folk-singer Ewan MacColl's often-quoted insistence that singers at his British folk clubs should only sing in the language or dialect they spoke or had grown up with (e.g. Brocken 2003: 35; Sweers 2005: 37) is one example. Sweeney-Turner (1998) has also described the selective use of Scots within Scottish song as a way of actively negotiating issues of place-based identity. The use of largely extinct regional dialects in the British folk revival has been described by Brocken as a way of 'insulat[ing] the listener from the present while also supplying a cloying romantic regret for the passing of a bygone era' (2003: 115), a statement that has resonances for Yaeyaman music in modern Japan, as we will see in Chapter 7. I frequently heard comments about the diversity of linguistic and musical styles between individual villages within Yaeyama. Daiku Tetsuhiro, a prominent Yaeyaman musician since the early 1970s, has said, 'Yaeyama is like a union of states. The language is different [in each village] and the songs are also completely different' (DeMusik Inter 1998a: 91). The way in which music is used in the negotiation of this village identity, and the way in which identities conflict with each other within a range of musical contexts, is a subject that arises several times in the course of this book.

Daiku's comment about Yaeyama as a 'union of states' (*gasshūkoku*) is representative of the cultural diversity within Yaeyama itself. Even within single villages, the organisation of society is far from homogeneous. The process by which people may enter or participate in certain groups depends both on personal circumstance and personal choice. One informant in Yonaguni island, whose family has lived on the island for some seven generations, told me that he was

---

    [5]   The commonly used term 'headmaster' is gender neutral, and *iemoto* can be male or female.

the first family member who had been permitted to take part in a ritual stick dance popular with young men – a genre that traditionally is only performed by families whose roots in the island stretch back into unrecorded history. Even in the relatively small Yaeyaman community, issues of pedigree, class, gender and political persuasion continue to play an important part in the transmission of traditional music. While personal choice is, of course, important in expressive culture (Slobin 1993: 55), in Yaeyama there are still groups that people are more or less obliged to identify with, whether or not they want to – for example family/village groups – and those in which they are unable to participate, however much they might want to – for example those of other families/villages (cf. descriptions of intra-communal categories in towns in mainland Japan, e.g. Robertson 1991: 93–101; Schnell 1999: 66–70). In Chapter 4 I present some examples of the way in which ritual music genres, in particular, are used as a context for the creation and maintenance of these very specific group identities.

The presence of the term *shima* (island) and its Yaeyaman dialect equivalent *sïma* seen in the two songs at the beginning of this chapter bring us also to developments since the 1980s in the academic study of island cultures. Recent years have seen the establishment of journals such as *Island Studies* (2006) and *Shima* (2007; see *Shima* Editorial Board 2007 for an overview of the development of island studies). In the context of island-based music-making, Dawe (2004a) provides a broad selection of essays, several of which I reference in this book. Islands, due to their geographical isolation, are often associated with a heightened sense of cultural identity. Suwa has noted the dual meaning of the word *shima* within Japanese society both in the geographical sense, and also as a 'socio-cultural space such as a territory, domain or a sphere of influence' (2007: 9). Despite the unique geographical characteristics of islands, many studies have also recognised the importance of islands as points of cultural *contact*, rather than isolation. Dawe, for instance, notes that islands 'are not isolates bio-geographically, nor in terms of their societies and cultures, even if they make tempting and convenient units for study' (2004b: 8). Like any island culture, Yaeyama has had a long history of cultural and political relations with neighbouring regions, and the 'island identity' of modern Yaeyama must be assessed in the context of those relationships.

Anthony Giddens has written that 'In conditions of modernity, place becomes increasingly *phantasmagoric*: that is to say, locales are thoroughly penetrated by and shaped in terms of social influences quite distant from them. What structures the locale is not simply that which is present on the scene; the "visible form" of the locale conceals the distanciated relations which determine its nature' (1990: 18–19). Likewise, there is a growing literature concerning the increasingly 'phantasmagoric' nature of local musical styles, which often exist simultaneously in the contexts of both regional and national identities. In a study of gamelan traditions within Java, Sutton describes the intersection between distinct regional traditions as a kind of 'musical and artistic "heteroglossia"' (1991: 237), while at the same time maintaining strong regional identities founded on local performance styles. Likewise, Harnish (2005) explores the use of music by minority Balinese musicians in the construction of place-based identities within the larger Islamic majority culture in Lombok island. Harnish describes how distinct musical traditions within the minority Balinese society articulate the various and often complementary historical and geographical identities that this group holds: particular musical genres are connected to specifically Balinese identities while others locate the minority group within the context of the majority Lombok society. In a study of Peruvian traditional musicians, Turino has described how, 'given the mobility of twentieth-century Peruvian life, bounded rural ethnographies are no longer practical; much of what influences rural indigenous musicians and musical style is ultimately traceable – through medium-sized highland cities-to Lima itself as the hub of the national society' (1993: 6). The production of 'local' meaning is, thus, dependent on the perception of region in a national context. Cohen has also written of the conflicting interests of local musicians in Liverpool, 'embedded in webs of kinship and collective memory' (1994: 133), with those of the national and international press and media interested in cashing in on an image of 'locality'. As another example of the multiple cultural levels on which a single genre may be constructed, the *xibeifeng* ('northwest wind') genre in 1980s China, while ostensibly connected with folk traditions of the northern Shaanxi province, was able to negotiate discourses of Chinese regionality and nationalism through the use of pop and disco elements, while also serving as a response to the 'outside' influence of Hong Kong and Taiwanese pop genres (Baranovitch 2003: 18–26; Dujunco 2002).

The cultural position of Okinawan music in modern Japan, too, is part of a larger discourse concerning regionality and national identity, and has been actively promoted by government organisations, scholars, and the national tourist and media industries. In Chapter 3 I investigate the way in which early 20th-century Japanese representations of Okinawa influenced the way music was viewed and created within the region itself in these years. From the early 20th century, Okinawa became one of the focus points for a growing folklore movement throughout Japan, led by Japanese scholars such as Yanagita Kunio and Yanagi Muneyoshi, who saw Okinawa as a region where ancient Japanese customs were preserved, while also being representative of the cultural diversity of the Japanese nation. These mainland Japanese representations of Okinawa may be partly understood in the context of Japanese cultural imaginations of its colonial regions at the time – Atkins (2010: 150–68) has described the multiple cultural meanings of pre-WWII Japanese representations of the Korean song *Arirang*, for example, and also outlined the effects that Japanese interest in Korean traditional culture had on native Korean ideas of the song. Yet much of the cultural discourse surrounding Okinawa in the pre-WWII period is concerned with Okinawa's cultural *similarity* to Japan and, in contrast to Korea, such theories were also enthusiastically endorsed by many Okinawan scholars.

Since the early 1990s images of Okinawa have been heavily promoted by the Japanese media and tourist industries, and the way in which particular images of Okinawa have been disseminated at a national level can partly be understood using recent ideas of 'place branding' (e.g. Dinnie 2008; Govers and Go 2009). As with many examples from around the globe, the Okinawan brand identity relies partly on a 'discourse founded on heritage' (Howard 2006b: xii; also Govers and Go 2009: 49), and traditional music has been one of the major aspects of this brand image. Okinawa's cultural position since the early 20th century as a treasure trove of 'Japanese' traditions has facilitated this facet of its national image. At the same time, another of Okinawa's images in modern Japan has been based on a discourse of cultural (and sometimes ethnic) difference. A 2004 book in which mainland Japanese residents of Okinawa explain their fascination with the prefecture includes many references to Okinawa as, for example, a 'foreign country where you can speak Japanese' (Kyūjin Okinawa 2004: 89) or as the 'least Japanese place in Japan' (ibid.: 30). Several recent studies in English and Japanese have examined the ways in which Okinawa's political position is maintained within the Japanese nation in the context of its historical cultural separation (Hein and Selden 2003; Hook and Siddle 2003; Oguma 1998; Tomiyama 1990). These studies come as part of a general movement towards an expansion of the view of cultural diversity in Japan as a whole, with a reassessment of older *Nihonjin-ron* theories of Japanese cultural uniformity (see e.g. Denoon and McCormack 1996; Sugimoto 1997; Sugimoto and Mouer 1989). This 'discourse of difference' has, paradoxically, also been important for the cultural acceptance of traditional Okinawan music within Japan. I have described elsewhere how Okinawan music has been used by Japanese pop musicians since the late 1980s as a way of being 'traditional' without the cultural baggage that would be associated with using Japanese mainland genres (Gillan 2009). This kind of portrayal of Okinawa as an exotic 'other' in a domestic context has been a prominent aspect of the prefecture's recent image in Japan.

Of course, regional aspects of many Japanese performing musical genres continue to be important both at local and national level – the Tsugaru *shamisen* tradition of northern Japan (e.g. Johnson 2006; Peluse 2005) has come to be performed professionally by musicians from around (mainland) Japan yet continue to maintain a discourse of locality in their place of origin. Likewise, the various *biwa* traditions of the western island of Kyūshū (e.g. de Ferranti 2008, 2009) or the Pacific island of Ogasawara (Johnson 2004) have maintained specifically local meanings while becoming known in other parts of Japan. To some extent, Okinawan music can be seen as just another musical genre of a Japanese region. In a study of the Tsugaru *shamisen*, for example, Johnson has written that, 'on different levels within Japan, Ryūkyūans and Ainu alike, just like many people from Tsugaru and elsewhere, might be considered a type of other within Japan' (2006: 80). There are certainly many similarities between Okinawa and regions like Tsugaru, geographical dislocation from the big cities of Tokyo and Kansai being one. Yet the cultural dislocation of Okinawa from mainland Japanese society seems to go beyond that of other Japanese 'regions' such as Tsugaru. To give one musical example, *Hōgaku Jānaru*,[6] the leading monthly publication devoted to traditional Japanese music, has frequent articles on *Tsugaru shamisen* – indicating the genre's acceptance as a 'Japanese' music genre – while the near non-existence of articles on Okinawan music indicates that it is not really seen as part of the mainstream of traditional Japanese music.

Another aspect of the Okinawan brand image that became prominent in the early 2000s was as the so-called 'healing islands' (*iyashi no shima*), a reference to the imagined power of Okinawa to resolve the stresses of modern city life. Part of this image comes from the tendency, in common with islands around the world (e.g. Dawe 2004b: 9; Howard 2004), for Okinawa to be seen as a 'tropical paradise' – the blue seas and skies and pristine white sandy beaches of countless tourist images are an all-pervading modern image of the prefecture. It may also derive from the statistical longevity of the Okinawan population made popular through books such as *The Okinawa Program* (Willcox et al. 2002).[7] The 'healing islands' image has also been produced very much through Okinawa-themed television and film productions such as *Nabi no koi* and *Churasan* that I mentioned above (e.g. Ko 2006; Tanaka 2002), and which have often incorporated performances by Okinawan musicians.

Okinawa's modern brand image also draws on its existence as the location for the largest contingent of American forces on Japanese soil. The islands were under direct American administration following the end of WWII in 1945 and, despite a reversion to Japanese government in 1972, still maintain a disproportionately high number of American bases. In 2008, there were 40,416 members of the American forces (and their families) stationed on the islands, accounting for some 63 per cent of the forces in Japan as a whole (Okinawa Prefecture figures[8]). The American presence has had a noticeable effect on Okinawa's musical output. Several of Japan's first 1970s hard rock bands, such as Murasaki, Condition Green and others, were Okinawan bands that had grown up performing in the American bases, and owed their language skills and authentic sound largely to this cultural background. The rock scene continues to thrive in Okinawa, with bands such as Mongol 800 and Orange Range being the latest to find fame in mainland Japan. Another legacy of WWII, when Okinawa was the only part of Japan which directly experienced fighting, is the prefecture's modern cultural image, along with Hiroshima and Nagasaki, as a symbol of peace (see e.g. Yonetani 2003). Images of the WWII invasion of Okinawa have been used countless times in songs by Japanese musicians such as Terashima Naohiko's *Satōkibi-batake* in 1967, The Boom's *Shimauta* in 1992, or Southern All Stars' *Heiwa no Ryūka*

---

[6]   *Hōgaku Journal.*

[7]   The Okinawan music producer Bisekatsu joked to me that the Okinawan diet, in particular the consumption of pork, has been used as a reason both for the Okinawan population's status as the shortest-lived in Japan (in the mid-20th century) and as the longest-lived (in the late 20th century).

[8]   www.pref.okinawa.jp/kititaisaku/1sho.pdf, accessed 21 February 2011.

in 1996 (see Gillan 2009). The fact that Yaeyama currently has no American military presence has meant that this issue has not been frequently addressed by Yaeyaman musicians, although I give some indirect examples in Chapter 7. Nevertheless, the cultural image of Okinawa both in connection with the American military and modern Japanese peace movement continues to be important.

Fieldwork Issues

This book is based on an extended period of fieldwork carried out in Yaeyama between July 2001 and September 2002, as well as several shorter trips in subsequent years. It also draws on fieldwork carried out in Yaeyaman communities in the Okinawan and Japanese mainlands between 2001 and 2011. The initial period of slightly over a year in Yaeyama was invaluable in many ways. I was able to experience Yaeyaman music-making in the context of the yearly ritual calendar and attend rehearsals and preparations for ritual events. I made sound and video recordings of performances from around Yaeyama, often as part of other social or ritual events that would have been difficult to replicate outside their original contexts. I was also able to form personal connections with informants that would have been impossible in a one-off interview situation. In common with many studies of this kind, my fieldwork approach also took a participant-observation approach – I took formal lessons in the *sanshin*-accompanied *fushiuta* genre, and actively participated in numerous study groups and workshops on a more informal basis. I believe this approach had many advantages, and opened up doors that would not otherwise have been accessible. John Baily has described in detail the benefits of learning to perform as a method for, among other things, understanding 'the music from the inside', understanding teaching and learning techniques, and providing the researcher with 'an understandable role and status in the community' (2001: 94–5), all of which were also relevant aspects of my fieldwork experience. My experience of learning, and in particular performing, also brought up a number of issues, two of which are perhaps relevant to musicological research in Japan in general, and which I consider here.

An issue faced by many ethnomusicologists in a participant observation situation is how to handle the desire to learn from a variety of different performers while respecting cultural norms which dictate that one should remain true to, and follow the performance style of, a single teacher (see e.g. Keister 2004: 33–6; Neuman 1980; Stokes 1992: 15). I had experienced this kind of relationship in a Japanese context through learning *shakuhachi* in mainland Japan for several years prior to the fieldwork for this research, but I was unsure to what extent this kind of strict teacher–student relationship existed in a Yaeyaman context. My experience of Yaeyaman music up to that point had been mainly through commercial recordings, which appeared to allow for a certain amount of individual interpretation of songs, and I assumed (naively) that the teacher–student relationship was perhaps not as rigid as in the mainland Japanese case. While this turned out to be true to an extent –

until quite recently performers would often learn from a variety of teachers – the trend in Yaeyama is definitely towards a strong link with one teacher, to whom one remains faithful throughout one's performing life.

While living in mainland Japan I had listened a lot to the commercial recordings of one particular *fushiuta* singer, Yamazato Yūkichi, who is often regarded, at least outside Yaeyama itself, as the leading Yaeyaman performer of his generation. While in Okinawa on my way to Yaeyama at the beginning of my initial fieldwork period, I was introduced to Yamazato, who has based his career in the Okinawan mainland. He offered to teach me whenever I was in Okinawa, and also to introduce me to his student Asato Isamu who lived in Yaeyama, and whose commercial recordings I was also familiar with. I jumped at the chance to be taught by these performers who had long recording careers and who were well-known throughout Japan. After several months in Ishigaki, however, it became apparent that Yamazato and Asato, although well known as performers in Ishigaki, did not play a major role in the large *fushiuta* lineages that are influential in controlling the teaching of the genre. Because of the distance of these two performers from these big lineage organisations, and because of my association with them, I was finding it difficult to become involved in the activities of the more mainstream traditional musical society in Ishigaki. After much deliberation, I eventually decided to end my affiliation with Yamazato in favour of a prominent teacher in one of the main Yaeyaman *fushiuta* lineages, Ōsoko Chōyō, who, while perhaps less well-known as a recording artist at a national level, is very well respected within Yaeyama as a teacher, and for his mastery of the 'correct' versions of the Yaeyaman *fushiuta* repertory.

While participant observation creates many opportunities that could not be otherwise obtained, several researchers have described how being an active participant can also have the effect of closing doors to other groups in that society through personal or ideological disputes. Beatty, for example, has written how 'as soon as one has settled in, one is associated with or adopted by a particular section of the community; as one becomes an insider to this section, one becomes an outsider to the rest' (Beatty 1999: 79; see also Shore 1999: 37–9). In a similar way, forming a musical alliance with a particular teacher or lineage inevitably involves affiliating oneself with a particular group of performers, thus cutting off other avenues for research. Possibly as a result of the complex social positions that arise through being affiliated to a single teacher or lineage, it became evident early on that the majority of musical scholars in Yaeyama (and Japan as a whole) are not active performers. Several Okinawan and Japanese scholars in fact specifically warned me that performing would be detrimental to my academic studies, for much the same reasons as Beatty describes. I deal with particular examples of the factionalisation of lineages in Chapter 5, and recognise that my analysis of several of these events is necessarily skewed by my personal involvement as a learner and performer in one particular lineage. Despite this, my status as an insider, at least to one faction of the traditional music world, gave me access to a lot of information which came up in the course of casual conversation, and which would probably not have been offered had I not been an active performer within a particular lineage.

A second issue that arose as a result of actively performing Yaeyaman music was the way that it affected my 'role and status in the community' (Baily 2001: 95). As one aspect of my research, I was keen to find out about the folk-song bars operating in Ishigaki, which cater to both tourist and local Yaeyaman audiences (see Chapter 5). My initial contact, Asato Isamu, ran a folk-song bar in downtown Ishigaki and told me that I could visit as often as I liked if I would sing a few songs for the customers. This seemed like a good opportunity to practice my repertory and get an inside view of how these clubs operated, and I began calling in whenever I had the chance. After word got out of my arrival in town, the story of a Westerner singing traditional music in a folk-song bar began to be taken up by the local media, and I was quite quickly being featured in Okinawan newspapers and television programmes singing in Asato's bar. A positive result of this was that it acted as a kind of publicity machine, making it much easier to form contacts with people who already had an idea of who I was. Another result was that I soon began to be bombarded with invitations to perform at all kinds of local events – I gave solo performances at a number of charity concerts and social events, all of which gave me opportunities to meet other performers and make research contacts.

As time went on, my repertory of songs increased, and I was being requested to play more and more in Asato's bar. Around four months after my arrival in Ishigaki, Asato announced that he was going on tour in the Japanese mainland and asked whether I would consider performing full-time at the bar while he was away. I was flattered that he considered me up to the challenge and agreed, somehow managing to perform three 40-minute sets a night for 10 days. While this experience was undoubtedly beneficial for my technique, and forced me to memorise a large number of song lyrics, I began to realise that I was spending most of my time performing or practising, leaving little time to do anything else. In addition, rather than being part of a musical community from which I could learn, I was rapidly becoming the centre of the event itself – there was perhaps too much participation and not enough observation! Another aspect was that, with the existing disdain of performing among much of the academic community, my continued association with a folk-song bar was maybe not one to emphasise too strongly. While I continue to visit Asato's folk-song bar on occasion, I made a conscious decision to limit my contact with such establishments after the first few months in Ishigaki. The media attention that I initially received through being an active performer was certainly beneficial in making my presence known, but I also felt a need to control the image that was being presented of me, and to limit my presence in musical events that I was trying to 'observe'. It was fun while it lasted though.

In addition to interviews and participant observation, my research has utilised the substantial popular and academic literature in Japanese on Yaeyaman and Okinawan music. Ishigaki, an island of some 50,000 inhabitants, is a highly literate society, and supports several sizeable bookshops containing hundreds of works on aspects of local Yaeyaman history, folklore, agriculture, religion, cooking, music and many other subjects. The volume of writing on Yaeyama in particular only became apparent to me after carrying out research in other parts of the region such as Miyako or Amami where, despite similar-sized populations to that in Yaeyama, the number of popular and scholarly written works is far fewer. Perhaps because of the strong historical connection between Yaeyama and the ruling court in Shuri, there has been a well-educated elite class in Yaeyama from the times of the Ryūkyū kingdom, and the written word has long been an important part of Yaeyaman culture. Many of the publications on Yaeyaman music and culture have been written by Yaeyamans largely for a local Yaeyaman readership – examples include many locally-published lyric collections outlining the backgrounds to various songs. Local newspapers, too, have been of great importance for providing a context through which the social and literal meanings of various song traditions have been actively constructed and debated, and I give examples of some of the public discourse that has been carried out in the local press over the course of this book. In addition, there are a large number of books written by mainland Japanese writers and scholars primarily for a non-Yaeyaman readership. Particularly since the early 1990s, there have been a large number of publications giving details of, and interviews with, Yaeyaman and Okinawan musicians. I quote from many of these over the course of this book, partly as for the insight they give into the activities of performers themselves, and partly as a way of understanding how Yaeyaman and Okinawan music has been presented to Japanese audiences.

Chapter 2

Islands of Song and Dance:
Yaeyama and its Music

Yaeyama is just like the island of Zeus from Homer's *Ulysses*. The music there has the power to lure passing travellers and capture them eternally. Those nameless poets sang such classic masterpieces as *Basï nu turï*. Yaeyama really is the land of song.

(Iha 2000: 362)

Yaeyama has long been known as a region where music plays an important part of everyday life, as the quote above from a 1912 newspaper article by the mainland Okinawan scholar Iha Fuyū indicates. Numerous more recent printed and Internet sources refer to Yaeyama using catchphrases such as the 'islands of song and dance' (*shi no kuni, uta no shima, odori no sato*), a sign of the continued importance of music as part of everyday life. In this chapter I give an overview of the history of the Yaeyaman islands, and the way in which historical events have affected the traditional music of the islands. I then present some of the musical and lyrical aspects of Yaeyaman traditional musical forms as they are performed today.

Yaeyama consists of 31 islands situated in Okinawa prefecture at the south-west tip of the Japanese archipelago. The westernmost island, Yonaguni, lies within sight of Taiwan on a clear day, while Yaeyama also contains Japan's southernmost island, Hateruma. Eleven of the 31 islands are inhabited, with the majority of the population living on Ishigaki Island. The average yearly temperature is 24 degrees Celsius with an annual rainfall of around 2,700 mm,[1] and the islands experience frequent typhoons in the summer and autumn months. Yaeyaman islands are divided geographically into two groups: those, such as Ishigaki and Iriomote, with mountains and therefore rivers were known as *takashima* (high islands) or *tangunjima* (rice paddy country islands), and the plentiful supply of water allowed for the cultivation of rice, while also harbouring malaria-carrying mosquitoes; while the low-lying coral islands, including Taketomi and Kuroshima, are known as *hikujima* (low islands) or *nungunjima* (vegetable country islands), and although free from malaria, were historically poorer due to an inability to grow rice. The islands are currently divided into three administrative zones, covered by Ishigaki-shi (encompassing Ishigaki Island), with a population (in 2009) of

---

[1]   Japan Meteorological Association figures. www.jma-net.go.jp/ishigaki/old/topix/tenkou2010.pdf, accessed 14 February 2011.

48,316; Taketomi-chō (comprising Iriomote, Hateruma, Kuroshima, Kohama, Taketomi, Aragusuku and Yubu islands), population 4,063; and Yonaguni-chō (Yonaguni Island), population 1,667.[2] Smaller islands, such as Hatoma and Kohama, contain only one main village, while the larger islands contain several – Yonaguni has three, Ishigaki upwards of 10. Each village is made up of two or more sub-divisions (*buraku*[3]) based on affiliation to a certain shrine (*utaki*) or ancestral house (*tunimutu*). In Hazama village (Taketomi) for example, the village is divided into East (*Higashi*) Hazama and West (*Nishi*) Hazama, while in Kohama the two areas are usually known as *Kita buraku* (North sub-division) and *Minami buraku* (South sub-division).

Yaeyama had little documented contact with the outside world prior to 1390, when it became a tribute state of the Ryūkyū court along with the Miyako islands to the north-east of Yaeyama. This arrangement does not seem to have led to any practical tax demands from the Ryūkyū court, and Yaeyama continued to exist as a collection of villages controlled by local chieftains. Despite the absence of direct taxation, the 15th century saw continued incursions by Ryūkyū, including increased efforts to exercise political control. One early Okinawan history, the *Kyūyō*, records a 1486 envoy sent from Okinawa with the intention of increasing agriculture, 'correcting' the local customs/manners, and establishing a legal system in the islands (Kishaba 1975: 108). A particularly irksome aspect of this envoy for the Yaeyamans seems to have been an increased meddling in traditional Yaeyaman religious practices. The political situation came to a head in the late 15th century when Oyake Akahachi, a local chieftain, formed a plan to invade the Miyako islands. His proposed invasion was foiled by a counter-attack from the Miyako chieftain, Nakasone Toyomioya, who subsequently managed to take political control of Yaeyaman (Kerr 2000: 121). Nakasone subsequently submitted to Ryūkyū, and Yaeyama came under the direct political control of the Ryūkyūan court in Shuri. Akahachi, despite having been defeated, has entered the Yaeyaman consciousness as a symbol of Yaeyaman courage under oppression, and the story of his uprising continues to be related in modern-day Yaeyaman cultural discourse.

The early days of the Ryūkyū kingdom saw taxes collected only on a sporadic basis, when the government was in time of need. This relaxed attitude to taxation was to change dramatically after 1609, when Ryūkyū was subjugated by the Satsuma fiefdom of Japan under the Shimazu clan. Almost immediately, the Satsuma authorities began a survey of Ryūkyū as a whole in order to establish a system of taxation (Kerr 2000: 159). A study of Yaeyama was made in 1611, and each village was graded according to its production potential, following which the

---

[2]   Population figures published by, respectively, Ishigaki-city, Taketomi-town and Yonaguni-town offices.

[3]   The word *buraku* has come to be used in the Japanese mainland with negative connotations of a 'ghetto', home to descendents of a social outcast class during Japan's feudal era. The word has no such social meanings in Okinawa, and is used simply to define particular village sub-divisions.

Satsuma government drew up a detailed list of tax obligations for each village. In 1637 the tax system was further revised into a 'poll tax' (*nintōzei*[4]) system under which Yaeyamans began to be individually responsible for fulfilling tax duties. Tax was payable by men and women from the ages of 15 to 50, calculated according to the 'rank' of the village – how much it could practically produce – and, from 1711, by the age of a particular person. There were some tax exemptions, such as those for government officials and their families, and also their mistresses from the local Yaeyaman peasantry (liaisons between government officials and local girls are a favourite topic in Yaeyaman folk songs of this period), but the tax burden on ordinary Yaeyamans seems to have been severe. The poll tax system still holds a prominent place in the cultural memory of the Yaeyaman islands: the centennial anniversary of the abolition of the tax saw of a series of symposia in the islands, and a historical book on the subject (Yaeyama nintōzei haishi hyakunen kinen jigyō kisei-kai 2003).

Together with the poll tax, another aspect of Yaeyaman history that continues to be re-imagined in contemporary life are the so-called 'island-splitting' (*shimabagari*) measures of the Ryūkyū government from the 18th century. In an attempt to combat the effects of malaria, and also due to a massive tsunami which wiped out much of the population on the eastern coast of Ishigaki in 1771,[5] the Ryūkyū government undertook a series of programmes to relocate large numbers of people both within Yaeyama and from outside, by the creation of new villages. In 1713 over 300 people were moved from Hateruma island to Ishigaki, where Susabu (present-day Shiraho) village was created. In 1732 Nosoko, Tōzato and Takana villages were created by moving over 400 people from Kuroshima island, while over 400 people were moved from Hateruma island in 1734 to create Haimi village in Iriomote. As late as 1863, 553 people were moved from Tonoshiro village to Nagura village. Examples of families, friends and lovers being split up in these forced relocations were common, and it is a subject which arises frequently in the songs of the period such as *Tsïndara bushi*, *Sakiyama bushi*, *Kubayama kuitsï bushi* and *Funakuya bushi* that are still popular today.

---

[4]   Also pronounced 'Jintōzei' (lit. 'head tax'). A popular (but probably false) belief, possibly attributable to Kishaba (1975: 128), has it that the amount of tax payable was defined by the amount of rice or grain which could be bundled into a diameter the same as the taxpayer's head.

[5]   The tsunami, named after the (Japanese) Meiwa period in which it occurred, killed an estimated 9,393 people, approximately one-third of the population of Ishigaki at the time (Yaeyama nintōzei haishi hyakunen kinen jigyō kisei-kai 2003: x).

Tsïndara Bushi

Tubarāma tu ban tu ya	My sweetheart and I
Yarabi kara nu asïbitōra	We were playmates from childhood
(tsïndara, tsïndara yo)	(how sad, how sad)
Kanushama tu kuri tu ya	My lover and I
Kuyusa kara nu mutsïritōra	We were best friends since we were small
sïma tu tumi de umōdara	I thought we'd always be together
Fun tu tumi de umōdara	in this island, in our village
ukïna kara uishi un	But an order came from Okinawa
Miomai kara usasï nu	From the king
sïma bagari de ufarare	I was ordered to relocate to a different
Fun bagari de ufarare	island, a different village,
Ubatan ga dukï nari	On my own,
Nusuku ni bagirare	I moved to Nosoko village

(Translated from Ōhama 2004a: 46)

The effect of these forced relocations is still present in the collective memory of modern Yaeyamans, partly embodied in the continued similarities between the dialects and cultural traditions of villages with a relocation connection, as well as in the lyrics of these songs. Residents of Miyara village in Ishigaki feel a strong attachment to Kohama island, from where they relocated after Miyara was destroyed in the 1771 tidal wave. The Yaeyaman dialect used in Miyara is very close to that of Kohama, and the defining festival, and rite of passage of boys into adulthood, the *Akamata-kuromata* festival (see Chapter 4), is performed in both Miyara and Kohama.

As a consequence of the *nintōzei* tax system, Yaeyaman society was divided quite sharply into two classes: the peasants (*buzā*) who paid taxes, and the upper class (*yukarupitu*) who administered the islands. The upper class included both indigenous Yaeyamans who worked in the offices of the Shuri government in Yaeyama, and officials who were sent on fixed-term appointments. This class division system had a profound effect on music-making in Yaeyama, and many songs in the traditional repertory tell of the relationships between these two social classes (for an example, see *Shūritsï yunta* below). The class system in Japan was officially abolished in the early Meiji period, but the Yaeyaman *nintōzei* tax system survived until 1903, and the division of society into the two-tier system of peasants and aristocrats effectively continued until after WWII.

Song Classification Systems

Traditional music-making in modern Yaeyama is largely based around a repertory that was established during the years of the *nintōzei* system, and the division of traditional music into sub-genres reflects the social structure of Yaeyama prior to the 20th century. Genres connected with the old peasant class, most of which are performed unaccompanied, or with rudimentary stick drum (*taiko/tēku*) and gong (*kane*) accompaniment (in the case of ritual songs), are often described using the blanket term *koyō* (lit. 'old songs'). The origins of the term are unclear but it was in use by the third decade of the 20th century when the Yaeyaman linguist Miyara Tōsō used it in the title of his 1928 book *Yaeyama koyō*. The term presumably entered Yaeyama from the early 20th century Japanese folk-song movement – it crops up occasionally in early writings on mainland Japanese folk music such as Kurita Hiro's 1903 *Koyō-shū* (see Hirano et al. 1989: 43), and is sometimes used by modern Japanese folk-song scholars to refer to 'old' versions of 'modernised' Japanese folk songs (see e.g. Machida et al. 1975: 9). In common with its contemporary use in other regions of Japan, the term *koyō* in Yaeyama has connotations of unaccompanied songs that have not been adapted for staged performance. One of the most important sub-genres of the *koyō* group is a large repertory of work songs, known as *yunta* or *jiraba*, that were sung in chorus by peasants carrying out communal labour, and which often describe the reality of daily life under the *nintōzei* system. There are also a similarly large number of ritual songs (*ayō*) that continue to be an important part of agricultural and household ceremonies in the islands. The *koyō* genre also contains a number of less-frequently-performed songs, such as the recitative sub-genre *yungutu*, an often-humorous style of solo singing/rhythmic intonation that is still sometimes performed at social gatherings. There are also a number of recitative chants known by the general term *kanfutsi*[6] that are usually performed by female ritual specialists.

In addition to the *koyō* genre of the peasant class is another genre of songs that are connected with the ruling upper class. This genre, known variously as *fushiuta* (lit. 'melodic' song), *min'yō* (folk song) or, more recently, *koten min'yō* ('classical' folk song), is always accompanied by the three-stringed lute (*sanshin*), with the optional addition of the 13-string zither (*koto/kutu*), transverse bamboo flute (*fue/pī*) and *taiko*. The use of instruments, particularly the *sanshin*, was a marker both of financial status – until recently the *sanshin* was prohibitively expensive for most – and social status – the leisure time needed to learn an instrument was only available to the upper classes. In contrast to the peasant *koyō* styles, which usually had a social function as part of daily agricultural or ritual life, *fushiuta* were created predominantly as art music for the entertainment and self-edification of the more leisured class. *Fushiuta* have been notated using the Okinawan *kunkunshi* notation system (see below) since the late 19th century,

---

[6]   Probably analogous to the Japanese 'kami' (god), and 'kuchi' (mouth).

and their performance has been increasingly controlled by formal lineage organisations, which I discuss in Chapter 5.

Yaeyaman musical in general is sometimes described using the blanket term *min'yō* (lit. folk song), a translation of the German *folkslied* that began to be used in the Japanese language towards the end of the 19th century (Hughes 2008: 8–15). Studies of Yaeyaman songs by Japanese scholars (e.g. Koizumi 1989 [1958]; Nippon Hōsō Kyōkai 1990a) usually include all Yaeyaman traditional songs, including work songs, ritual songs, *fushiuta* and other sub-genres under this heading. Like the English term 'folk song', the Japanese word *min'yō* has been defined in a fairly fluid way, and its meanings have been socially contested within Yaeyama itself. Several aspects of Yaeyaman music, especially the *sanshin*-accompanied *fushiuta* genre, put it outside the normal Japanese definition of the term – the use of musical notation for *fushiuta* from at least the late 19th century, for example, is a phenomenon not found in even in Japanese *min'yō* until the early 20th century (Hughes 2008: 180). In addition, the performance of *fushiuta* mostly by members of the ruling upper class is at odds with the usual 'peasant' connotations of the term in Japan. Partly in an attempt to emphasise the cultural distinction of the genre in Yaeyama, the term *min'yō* has often been amended to '*koten min'yō*' (classical folk song) since the early 1970s when referring to *fushiuta*.

Another term used to describe Okinawan music in general, dating from around the 1970s, is *shimauta* (lit. island songs). The term was adopted from the Amami islands of Kagoshima prefecture, directly north of Okinawa, where it refers to 'local' *sanshin*-accompanied songs (the term '*shima*' in Okinawan and Amami dialects means 'village' or 'hometown' as well as 'island'). Through the influence of Okinawan broadcasters such as Uehara Naohiko and musicians such as China Sadao, the use of this term has become quite widespread in the Okinawan mainland, especially in the context of recorded music and music-making connected with the tourist industry. Since the success of the mainland Japanese band The Boom's song *Shimauta* in the early 1990s, the term has continued to spread in some circles (for an overview of the use of the term in Okinawa see Takahashi 2002). Within Yaeyama itself, the term has made relatively little impact – I never heard the term used among either *fushiuta* or *koyō* performers. I saw it used occasionally in the context of tourist brochures and posters advertising traditional music performances. Yaeyaman musicians based in Okinawa, and those who perform regularly in the Japanese mainland, have adopted the term to some extent. Daiku Tetsuhiro, who has had a long career performing in the Okinawan mainland, regularly uses the term to describe Yaeyaman songs. Another informant, the veteran singer Yamazato Yūkichi, uses the term in the introduction to his published notations (1989 and 1991), though I never heard him use it in everyday speech.

Work Songs

The *yunta/jiraba* repertory is extensive (most villages maintain a repertory of around 30 songs), and the singing style is unusual both in a Japanese and Okinawan context, due to the 'call-and-response' antiphonal singing style by two groups (usually male and female) with interspersed *hayashi-kotoba* – meaningless lyrics used to punctuate the main melody. Yaeyamans are justly proud of their work song repertory, both for the musical and lyrical quality of the songs, and for the sheer size of the repertory, which is far larger than in other parts of Okinawa, and is sometimes linked to the particular harsh *nintōzei* tax obligations of Yaeyamans in the past.

The terms *yunta* and *jiraba*, as well as being used to describe the work song repertory in general, are used in the title of most its songs. Thus, the song title *Asadōya yunta* could be translated as 'The *yunta* about the girl from the *Asato* household', or *Yubi ga yū jiraba* as 'The *jiraba* about the events of last night'. The literal meaning of the terms is unclear. Kishaba (1970: introduction) sees '*jiraba*' as a corruption of the mainland Japanese term *shirabe*, usually meaning investigation, but historically used with the meaning of melody/piece (e.g. in the *koto* piece *Rokudan no shirabe*). Miyara Tōsō (1980: 9) writes that it is an abbreviation of the place name *Jirabaka*. Possible derivations for *yunta* include *yui-uta* (work-group song), *Yo-uta* ('world' song; see Miyara 1980: 9), or *yumi-uta* (recited song, see Kishaba 1967: 2). There seems to be no intrinsic difference between the songs described as *yunta* and those described as *jiraba*. I was told by various informants both that *yunta* tended to be faster than *jiraba*, and that *jiraba* tended to be faster than *yunta*, but there was no general consensus either way. Variant versions of the same song are described as *yunta* in one village, and as *jiraba* in a neighbouring village. In Tonoshiro, for example, the majority of the work song repertory is known as *yunta*, whereas in Kohama the corresponding songs are mostly known as *jiraba*.

The use until the mid-20th century of *yunta* and *jiraba* to accompany agricultural work means that they are often described in Japanese as 'work songs' (*rōdōka/shigoto-uta*). While many Japanese folk songs with titles such as *Herding song* (*ushioi uta*), or *Planting song* (*taue uta*) have an obvious connection with a particular kind of labour, or at least to a certain activity, most *yunta/jiraba* were sung to accompany a range of agricultural activities, and some Japanese scholars (Kaneshiro 1997: 123; Kojima 1994: 20) place them outside the normal Japanese idea of 'work songs'.[7]

---

[7] Kaneshiro suggests that the difference in cultural structure between the Japanese mainland and Yaeyama, with the former having a strongly feudalistic society in which people had a strong connection to one 'profession', and the latter having a less organised society in which all jobs, from agricultural work to house building were carried out by the 'group', led to the predominance of job specific work songs in one and an almost total absence of these in the other (see Kaneshiro 1997: 127–9). Hughes (1985: 78–83) points

Example 2.1   Shūritsï yunta. Tonoshiro version as performed by Tonoshiro Kayō no kai

Musical and Lyrical Aspects

In this section I consider some of the musical and lyrical aspects of *yunta* and *jiraba* through an analysis of *Shūritsï yunta* (Example 2.1). This is one of the better known work songs in the *koyō* repertory and is found in various forms in many Yaeyaman villages, as well as in a *fushiuta* version. The song is also well-known in the Okinawan mainland, where it was adapted by the actor/playwright Makishi Kōchū in the mid-1960s into a musical drama of the same name.

---

out that in Japan, there is often no clear distinction between work songs per se, i.e. which accompany and give rhythm to the work, coordinating group action, and songs with origins outside the workplace, but which have been adopted as songs sung in a 'work song' context.

Shūritsï yunta – Funku ('main section')

1) *Shūritsï nu (yo) hatsï nu fā*   The first born son of the Shuri official
[hi ya sā]   [*hayashi* sung by opposite group]
Myōmaitsï nu (yo) tumi nu fā   The beloved son of our governor
2) *Pituryā fā nu (yo) maresō yo*   He was born as the only son
Tanugyā fā nu (yo) sudesō yo   Raised as an only child
3) *Ama nu kïmu (yo) dagasan*   He was so full of confidence
Dugyanu iru (yo) dagasan   He had such a personality
4) *Piturya tuzï (yo) mutumuna*   He wasn't content with just one wife
Tanugya tuzï (yo) nizïmuna   He wasn't happy with a single partner
5) *Nisumi nāga (yo) wataryōri*   He travelled to Nisumi village
Uhatsï nāga (yo) utsïryōri   He travelled to Uhachi village
6) *Miyarabi ba (yo) tumesāri*   Searching for girls
Mamuyanī ba (yo) tumesāri   Looking for girlfriends
7) *Ikikara nu (yo) ifuka yanzan*   Only a few days after he left
Mumuka yanzan (yo) naranuke   Within a hundred days
8) *Shūri kara (yo) guyushiba*   An order came from Shuri
Myōmai kara (yo) guyushiba   A command came from the king
9) *Kïn ya nēnu (yo) nayu du sï*   'Where are the official *kimonos*?'
Ishō ya nēnu (yo) ikya du sï   'What about the official costumes?'
10) *Yu nu mitsï ba (yo) muduri iki*   So he set off back home
Yui nu pē fumi (yo) kairi iki   He retraced his steps
11) *Manga kara (yo) irï make*   Too ashamed to enter by the front door
Mashōmen kara (yo) irï make   Unable to go through the entrance
12) *Suba yā nkai nu (yo) iribashi*   He crept in through a side door
Kuyado nkai nu iribashi   He went in through the outhouse

Shūritsï yunta – Tōsï (second section)

13) *Idararara kadararara pazïkirā*   14) 'You dirty contemptible rogue
[eiyāsuri] (yanza yō nu haitōya)   *hayashi*
15) *zïma nu kïmu dukya nu iru kumakïda*   16) How can you show your face here?'
17) *naseru fā nu dageru fā nu kutu umui*   18) I came back to see our child
19) *kïnkishi nu sudi nu kïnu naranāri*   20) I don't have a *kimono*
21) *ura tuzï nu mamuyanē nu seru kïn ya*   22) 'What about the *kimono* your girlfriend made?'

23) *Tatihada du sayagashi du yayuriba*   24) It's lying unfinished on the loom
25) *Un kara du nara yunkan hari pēri*   26) Then she went into her room
27) *Yafungai panpizïn kiri akē*   28) opened up the *kimono* chest
29) *Tsïkï nu kata pusï nu kata idashōri*   30) and took out a *kimono* with patterns of moon and stars

31) *Kïn kisashi sudi nukashi fā nu bune*   32) Let me have this *kimono*, mother of my child

33) *Kïn kisashi nu sudi nukï nu amarin ya*   34) As well as the *kimono*
35) *Ura tumu ni sana tumu ni mutsashōri*   36) let me accompany you and hold
                                                    your parasol
37) *Shūri idē nu myōmai idē nu umui nu*   38) When you appear before the king
39) *Mutu nu sū nu fā nu bunē nu takinēnude*   40) There is no-one who compares to
                                                    your real wife

(Translated from Ishigaki 1992: 33–40)

Like most *yunta/jiraba*, *Shūritsï yunta* is a narrative song, telling the tale of the son of a Shuri government official (*yakunin*), who gets into trouble by messing around with the local Yaeyaman peasant women. The song has a strong moral conclusion, warning that only a man's real wife will look out for him in times of need.[8] The theme of the interaction between Shuri officials and local Yaeyaman girls, who were excused from payment of taxes through becoming concubines of an official, is a common one in the *yunta* and *jiraba* repertory, and can also be seen in many other songs. *Asadōya yunta* and *Nzatōra yunta*, for example, both weigh up the relative merits for a young peasant woman of marrying a local man or becoming the mistress of a government official (both of these songs conclude that the stability offered by a local man is preferable to the temporary luxuries of a *yakunin* relationship). The common occurrence of this theme indicates the extent to which the political control of Yaeyama by Shuri had an effect on the daily lives of Yaeyamans before the 20th century.

With the exception of the very first line (*shūritsï nu*), *Shūritsï yunta* is made up of lines of 5 + 4 mora. Verse two, for example, has *pï* + *tu* + *ryā* + *fa* + *nu* = 5; *ma* + *re* + *sō* + *yo* = 4.[9] This combination of 5 + 4 mora (5 + 5 + 4 is another combination) is by far the most common form for *yunta* and *jiraba*. Another characteristic of the genre is that verses are made up of couplets where the meaning of the first line of a verse is the same as that the second line – the meaning of the phrases *Shūritsï nu hatsï nu fā* (the first born son of the Shuri official) and *myōmaitsï nu (yo) tumi nu fā* (the beloved son of our governor) are equivalent, as are the couplets in subsequent verses.[10]

An aspect of Yaeyaman work songs that has provoked interest among Japanese scholars is their antiphonal singing style, usually (though not always) by separate groups of men and women. The main lyrics of each verse are sung by each group in turn, and the other group 'replies' with phrases made up of meaningless

---

[8]   He gets off rather lightly by present standards – Okinawa has the highest divorce rate in modern Japan.

[9]   Unlike in much mainland Japanese poetry, long vowels (such as *ryā* and *sō* in this example) count as only one mora in most Yaeyaman and Okinawan song forms.

[10]   This lyrical technique bears some resemblance to the 'incremental repetition' commonly found in Scottish and English ballads (Gummere 1907: 90–98), and can be seen as a method of maintaining interest and continuity in long narrative songs.

syllables (*hayashi*) such as '*yuisa*' (shown in the first verse of *Shūritsï yunta* only in square brackets. In performance these are sung in every verse). Another kind of '*hayashi*', such as the '*yo*' in the middle of each line (shown in round brackets) is sung by the singer of that line. This use of meaningless syllables interspersed into the lyrics of the song is found in almost all *koyō*. Some Japanese scholars make a distinction between *hayashi (-kotoba)*, which are sung by the main singer or backup singers, and *kake-goe*, which are sung by a second singer or group of singers, although in practice the use of these terms varies greatly. In Yaeyama both types are usually referred to, if at all, as *hayashi*.

Like many *yunta* and *jiraba*, *Shūritsï yunta* is divided into two sections with different melodies: a slower first section, known in Tonoshiro as the *funku* (main section) followed by a faster second section (from verse 13) known as the *tōsï*.[11] The narrative first part of the song tells the story, in the third person, of the escapades of the Shuri official's son, while the second part takes a humorous approach by acting out the scolding he receives from his wife after his infidelities. In rare cases, such as the song *Uni nu yā* (as sung in Miyara and Shiraho), there is a third section in between the first and second sections, known (in Miyara) as *nakan'gui* (middle voice). Other songs, such as *Asadōya yunta*, *Mayā yunta* or *Matsun'gane yunta* consist of only one melody, repeated throughout the song.

The second section of Example 2.1 shows the first two verses of the *tōsï* section of *Shūritsï yunta*, with verse 13 in bars 1–6, and verse 14 from bar 6 to 11. These two verses are melodically identical except for the first four beats which start alternately on a low f# (verse 1, 3, etc.) and a high d (verse 2, 4, etc.), an alteration technique usually known as *utinan-susanan*.[12] Although formal musical theories in Yaeyama are few, and rarely discussed in musical circles, the *utinan-susanan* technique is fairly widely known and discussed by singers of *yunta* and *jiraba*. The literal meaning of these terms is unclear, but is believed to be related to the Japanese words 'set up' (*tateru*) and 'receive' (*ukeru*).[13] The principle usually describes the practice, when singing *koyō* in alternation (in two groups), of varying the first few notes of a musical line in successive verses between a high and low pitch. The variation of this initial pitch can range from a 3rd to as much as an octave (discounting the difference in pitch between male and female singers who sing an octave apart). While the *utinan-susanan* variation in modern performances of *Shūritsï yunta* is limited to these two melodic variants,

---

[11] The slower first part is known as *funku* (main section) in Tonoshiro, and in other villages by names such as *nagami* (long), *fun'gui (hon'goe* – main part – lit. main voice). The second, faster section is called *tōsï* in Tonoshiro, and in other villages is known as *hayami* (fast), *uran'gui* ('behind' voice), *ni-agi*, or *hayashi*. See Ōshiro (1987) for a full description of these terms.

[12] I also heard *tatenan-utenan* (in Ishigaki village*)*, *tachinan-utinan* (in Hirae) and *sakinā-utinā* (in Kohama).

[13] In Kohama it is believed to be 'before' (*saki*) and 'after' (*ato*) (see also Kaneshiro 1987).

the technique was probably freer and more complex in the past. Arasaki Zenji describes one definition of *utinan-susanan*: 'the fact that you sing in alternation goes without saying, but the real attraction of the singing style is that the first verse, the second and third verses are all varied, and expression is produced by singing from above and from below' (1992: 57). This way of singing is difficult to achieve when large groups are singing, but I heard verification of this type of *utinan-susanan* variation from several singers who experienced singing before or shortly after WWII.

The precise way in which *yunta/jiraba* functioned in a work context has been little documented. Sakihara outlines the practice of singing certain songs at certain times of day while doing agricultural work, in order to regulate and encourage the speed at which people worked (1979: 122–3). In most villages there seems to have been some sort of loose order in which songs were sung during the day: songs were chosen according to their tempo, and the ability to create momentum in work patterns. Urahara (1970: 13) gives a rough outline of a repertory in one (unnamed) village in Ishigaki in the early 20th century: 'In the early morning was *Urafuni yunta*, followed by faster songs throughout the morning; around mid-day *Basï yunta*; in the evening the '*ufu-yunta*' [lit. 'big' *yunta*], very slow and melismatic songs such as *Kunnōra nu bunarema, Arozatē yunta*'. Informants in Tonoshiro agreed with this rough outline, although there seems to have been considerable freedom for people to change the song order from day-to-day (Nakashima, pers. comm. October 2001). Another common aspect seems to have been that towards the end of the day, when the energy of the group was low, there were songs of a comic or sexual nature to hold people's attention.

Munguru kubasā yunta

1) *Mun'guru kubasā ya nayusharu munu yaryādu*	A straw hat is such a thing,
Miyarabi yumuchï ba kakushōru	it covers up a girl's face
2) *Uri ga budu du namaburi munu yaryādu*	Her husband, the fool
Mun'guru kubasā du dinki ba shōru	is jealous of the hat
3) *Shinta nu ottā ya nayusharu munu yaryādu*	The pig in the sty (connected to the
Miyarabi pisantā ba ugamyōri	outside toilet) is such a creature he sniffs at a young woman's private parts
4) *Uri ga budu du namaburi munu yaryādu*	Her husband, the fool
Shinta nu ottā du dinki ba shōru	is jealous of the pig

(Translated from Ishigaki 1992: 165)

With the mechanisation of agriculture from the mid-20th century, the old communal work practices died out, removing the most important context for the performance of *yunta* and *jiraba*. The repertory is still performed at a village level by preservation societies (*hozonkai*) that were formed after WWII (see Chapter 5). They have also been arranged for performance with *sanshin* accompaniment and, since the early 1990s, have been recorded in pop/rock arrangements by professional performers such as Daiku Tetsuhiro (see Chapter 7).

Fushiuta

The *sanshin*-accompanied song genre *fushiuta* was developed by Yaeyama's government officials, probably between the 18th and 19th centuries. The term *fushiuta* (*fushi* and its variant form *bushi* literally means melody, *uta* means song) derives from the fact that all songs in the genre have the word *bushi* in the title: *Akanma bushi*, for example, could be translated as 'Red Horse Melody'. *Fushiuta* were developed as a kind of art music by the more leisured ruling class, and although many are adaptations of the *yunta* repertory, they do not have the work song connections of *yunta* and *jiraba*. Whereas *koyō* are typified by a group-centred singing style, *fushiuta* are often characterised by solo or small group singing (Kaneshiro 1997: 138–9).

Lyrically, *fushiuta* comprise a mixture of songs in the Yaeyaman 5-4 (also 5-5-4) mora structure that we saw in *yunta* and *jiraba*, as well as songs in the mainland Okinawan *ryūka* (8-8-8-6) form that show the influence of the Shuri officials. In addition, there are a number of songs such as *Kuroshima kuduki*,[14] which show a direct Japanese influence through the 7-5 mora structure that is thought to have been introduced into Okinawa by the 18th century (see Tanabe 1976). *Kuduki* are not officially classed as *fushiuta* (they do not take the suffix '*bushi*') but are included in Yaeyaman *fushiuta kunkunshi* notations.

Whereas *yunta/jiraba* often make fun of the *yakunin*, describing their amorous adventures or comparing them to various animals, *fushiuta*, perhaps not surprisingly given their historical background, contain a large number of songs praising the *yakunin* and the Shuri king. For example, *Tsuru-kami bushi*:

1) *Kabira-mura uinaka*	In Kabira village
Miruku yū ba taborare	We have had a good harvest
2) *Kabira-shū nu ukagin*	It's because of the *yakunin*
Mizashi-shū nu mibukïn	Thanks to the *mizashi-shū* (rank of official)

(Translated from Ōhama 2004a: 20)

Songs of this type, rather than being derived from work songs, often show a strong ritual connection, and probably grew out of the *hōnō geinō* (offertory performing arts) tradition at festivals in the summer and autumn (see Chapter 4).

---

[14]   Also *kuduchi*, both words derived from the Japanese *kudoki*.

There are also a large number of *fushiuta* in mainland Okinawan *ryūka* form which praise the land (island, village) of the inhabitants. (The genre is often known in Japanese as *tochi sanka* – land praise songs.) Variations on the same theme can be found throughout Yaeyama, although the melodies to which the lyrics are set are often completely different from village to village. A well-known example is Kohama island's *Kumōma bushi*:

Kumōma bushi

Kumōma tiru sïma ya (8)	The island of Kohama
Kafu nu sïma yariba (8)	is a rich island
Ufu-daki ba kusadi (8)	Ufudaki mountain behind
Shiru pama mainashi (7¹)	A white beach in front
Ufu-daki ni nubuti (8)	Climbing up Ufudaki
Ushikudashi miriba (8)	and looking down
Ini awa nu nauri (8)	The rice and barley is ripening
Miruku yugafu (6)	The gods have favoured us
Ini awa nu iru ya (8)	The colour of the rice and barley
Hatachi guru myarabi (8)	Is like a 20-year-old woman
Iru shigata uchati (8)	The grains are so beautiful
Uhatsï agiru (6)	we'll offer them to the gods

Note: ¹ This verse has an extra mora in the final line – 8-8-8-7 instead of the usual 8-8-8-6. Verses 2 and 3 have the normal *ryūka* mora count of 8-8-8-6.

(Translated from Ōhama 2004b: 6)

Exact equivalents of these lyrics, with only the local landmarks changed, exist from Shiraho and Tōzato villages, and there are also close variants such as *Hanjō bushi* (Sakieda village) and *Yugafu bushi* (Aragusuku). The *ryūka* form of these songs, and their similarity to songs in the Okinawan mainland, suggest the influence of Shuri officials, and again, their lyrical connection with the harvest hints at a ritual *hōnō geinō* connection. The fact that quite different melodies are used for songs in different villages also suggests that the lyrics and melody arrived in each island separately, or that the *yakunin* supplied lyrics to an extant melody, possibly as a way of building morale and stamping his own authority in a village (Morita Son'ei, pers. comm. April 2002. Morita told me that the *yakunin* 'composed' original melodies for these compositions).[15]

---

[15]   In Hirae village in Ishigaki I encountered a work song known as *Kohama yunta*, using the lyrics of *Kumōma bushi* (*Kohama tïru sïma ya* ...) and the melody of the Shiraho song *mājan'gā*. This is a very rare example of a *yunta* in *ryūka* form, one that is almost

A feature of *fushiuta*, compared to the *yunta/jiraba* songs from which many of them developed, is that the number of verses sung is greatly reduced. Whereas *yunta/jiraba* typically contain from 20 to 30 verses, usually in narrative form, the *fushiuta* versions of these songs usually take only a small number of these verses, often slowing the tempo down dramatically, and stressing the musical aspects of the melody line over narrative content. In extreme cases the original meaning of a song is all but lost in this process. *Kuigushiku bushi*, for example, which is considered to be the pinnacle of the *fushiuta* repertory in terms of difficulty of performance, is believed to have been an adaptation of a work song from Aragusuku island (although the work song version is no longer extant). The slow tempo of the *fushiuta* means that, although six verses of the song are commonly published in lyric collections, only the first verse of the song is ever performed:

Kuigushiku bushi

Kuigushiku Imarani   Imarani of Kuigusuku
Uri (yo) utudu nu Yubusani   And her sister Yubusani

(Translated from Ōhama 2004a: 41)

The highly refined melody of this one verse takes some four minutes to perform, and is indeed one of the musical highlights of the *fushiuta* repertory. However, the original narrative content of the song, relating the tale of two beautiful sisters and how they ignore the advances of the local men in favour of the *yakunin*, is lost.

Two songs, *Tubarāma* and *Yonaguni shonkane* (*Sunkani*), which appear in all Yaeyaman *kunkunshi*, are often regarded as being separate from the rest of the *fushiuta* repertory on the basis of both their lyrical content and social meaning. In contrast to the majority of *fushiuta*, in which a fixed set of lyrics to a particular melody, *Tubarāma* and *Sunkani*, known as the 'Yaeyaman lyrical songs' (*Yaeyama jojōka*), have traditionally been a context to sing largely improvised lyrics over a basic melodic pattern. I deal with *Tubarāma* in depth in Chapter 6.

The *Sanshin*

Another defining characteristic of *fushiuta* is that the singing is always accompanied by the three-stringed plucked lute known most commonly as the *sanshin*. The instrument currently enjoys a position of cultural distinction throughout the prefecture as a symbol of Okinawan cultural identity. A well-known saying makes the point that, while the literary Chinese commonly display a poetry scroll in the main room of their houses, and the samurai-influenced Japanese display a

---

certainly derived from a *fushiuta*, rather than the more common work song to *fushiuta* transmission.

sword, music-loving Okinawans still commonly display a *sanshin* as the focal point of their living rooms[16] and, while it would be an exaggeration to say that all Okinawans have direct experience of, or even interest in, the *sanshin*, it is nevertheless a 'popular' instrument in a way that is rarely seen for traditional instruments in other parts of Japan. The instrument has been known in Yaeyama by a variety of names – in Yonaguni dialect it is called *santi*, while in the song *Yagujāma bushi* from Komi village it is referred to as *samishin*. Many Yaeyamans (and mainland Okinawans) use the Japanese word *shamisen* when speaking in standard Japanese, although younger generations mostly use the word *sanshin*. The word *jamisen/jabisen*, commonly used in the Japanese mainland to describe the Okinawan *sanshin*, is almost never used in Okinawa. I use the term *sanshin* to refer to the Okinawan instrument here.

The *sanshin* is related to the Chinese *sanxian*, also a three-stringed plucked lute with a snakeskin resonator, but the exact origins of the Okinawan instrument are unclear. It is assumed that the *sanxian* was introduced to the Okinawan mainland some time after the late 14th century, probably from Fujian province, although it doesn't begin to be documented until around the mid-16th century (Kaneshiro 2006: 101–4; Yano 1993: 76–80). The earliest reference comes from the Chinese envoy Chin Kan, who led a mission to invest the new Ryūkyūan king[17] in 1534, and reported the playing of 'stringed instruments', probably including a version of the *sanshin*.[18] The first named reference to the instrument comes in the diary of an official of the Shimazu clan in southern Kyūshū, who described members of a Ryūkyū envoy to Satsuma in 1575 playing an instrument described as a *shahisen*.[19] This instrument was almost certainly a version of the *sanshin*, and we can assume that the instrument was a feature of the Ryūkyū court by this time. The *sanshin* has continued to be associated particularly with the royal household in Ryūkyū – in 1710 the king created the official post of *sanshin* manufacturer within the court, and the instrument became the primary instrument of the ruling class. Its introduction to Yaeyama was presumably also at the hands of Ryūkyū government

---

[16]   Gibo Eijirō (1999: 15) attributes part of this quote to the Okinawan musicologist Yamauchi Seihin. The idea also appears in Matayoshi Shinzō (1985) and Ōta Ken'ichi (1999). The specific reference to the *samurai* spirit in Japan can be seen in Ōshiro Tatsuhiro (1985). The idea seems to be bound up equally with the image of Okinawa in modern-day Japan as a symbol of peace, and with the image of the *sanshin* as a symbol of Okinawan cultural identity.

[17]   These 'investiture' (*sappō*) missions to formally crown a new Ryūkyūan king were sent from China on 23 occasions between 1404 and 1866.

[18]   While the Okinawan and Chinese instruments are obviously related organologically, there are relatively few examples of common musical practices. Wang (1998) examines some examples of the importation of repertory from China to Ryukyu, and Kaneshiro (2006) and Gillan (2008b) have identified common composition techniques, but this is a subject that needs further investigation.

[19]   Written in the *hiragana* script: しゃひせん.

officials sent to govern the islands, although again no detailed records exist of its history there. Yaeyaman *fushiuta* appeared in the earliest mainland Okinawa *kunkunshi* notations and lyric collections[20] of the late 18th century, indicating that the *sanshin* was fairly well established in Yaeyama by this stage. The frequent departure and arrival of Shuri government officials (*yakunin*) in Yaeyama meant that there was ample opportunity at this early stage for the *sanshin* to be introduced to the islands, and for Yaeyaman songs to be taken back in *sanshin* arrangements by the *yakunin*.

It was also around the late 16th century[21] that the *sanshin* is thought to have been transmitted to the Japanese mainland, where it developed into the modern Japanese *shamisen* (for information in English on the Japanese *shamisen*, see e.g. Johnson 2010; Tokita 1999; a comprehensive history in Japanese can be found in Tanabe 1963). The Japanese instrument, at around 100cm, is considerably longer than the modern Okinawan *sanshin*, and uses a cat- or dog-skin membrane rather than the python of the *sanshin*. Another development found on mainland Japanese instruments is the distinctive *sawari* sound caused by the lowest string being allowed to vibrate against the fingerboard. *Sawari* is not a feature of the Okinawan *sanshin*, and the innovation was presumably made after the instrument's arrival in Japan to imitate the sound of the *biwa* that the *shamisen* largely replaced in Japanese narrative musical styles (e.g. Johnson 2010: 36–8; Tokita 1999: 79).

The need to import the python skin for the membrane of the *sanshin* from the Asian mainland, together with the use of expensive ebony and the high level of skill needed to produce the instrument, meant that until the mid-20th century the *sanshin* was primarily connected with the wealthy elite. Nevertheless, there is some evidence of similar instruments also being performed by members of the peasant class in Yaeyama. In 1857, for example, a Shuri official published a list of 418 amendments to the governance and regulation of the islands, including the following:

> #345 Men and women occasionally gather on the beaches in front of Ishigaki's four villages and indulge in singing and playing the *sanshin*. This disturbs the peace of the officials who live there, and also the activities of the government offices. This activity shall therefore be banned.

> #346 The peasants of Ishigaki (the four main villages) are accustomed to walking and singing near residential districts, and also to gathering together and playing the *sanshin* and singing. This is undesirable and from now on should be strictly banned. (Ishigaki-shi Sōmu bu shishi henshūshitsu 1990: 108)

---

[20]   The *Yakabi kunkunshi* compiled by Yakabi Chōki (1716–74) contains the song *Agi kunnūra bushi*. The *Ryūkyū Hyakkō* lyric collection (1795) contains the songs *Ishi nu byōbu bushi*, *Kui nu pana bushi* and *Kumōma bushi*.

[21]   The Eiroku era (1558–70) is often quoted but there is no direct evidence for an exact date (Tokita 1999: 70).

From this source we can see that the *sanshin* had come to be played by peasants as well as by the aristocracy in Yaeyama at least by the mid-19th century. Other references to peasants playing the instrument can be found in song lyrics such as the work song *Yamabarē yunta*:

7) *Sanshin de sō ya*	For the neck of the *sanshin*
Kuba nu ude ba sanshin deshī	use a branch of the kuba tree
8) *Tsuru de shīso*	For strings
Uma nu zūba tsuru deshī	use the hairs of a horse's tail
9) *Nma deshīso*	For the bridge
Magayagi ba nma deshi	use a curved branch

(Translated from Arakawa Kōminkan Bunkabu 1986)

The (now abandoned) village of Yamabarē on the northern coast of Ishigaki was populated entirely by peasants, and the playing of the *sanshin* mentioned in this song very likely refers to peasant use of the instrument. As the song suggests, this less-wealthy class had no access to imported snakeskin or ebony, but they would improvise construction of the instrument using locally available materials. This practice seems to have been widespread until the mid-20th century. Many informants in Yaeyama and the Okinawan mainland described making a so-called *shibubari (shibubai) sanshin*, with a membrane of home-made paper strengthened with the sap (*shibu*) of a plantain (see also Noborikawa 2002: 30–35). One singer from Taketomi described making a *sanshin* body out of a coconut shell in the mid-20th century, with a membrane made from a pig's bladder (Takamine Hōyū, April 2002). A common innovation after WWII, known as a *kankara sanshin*, used a body made from a tin can (originally introduced by the American army during and after the war) and strings of telephone cable or parachute cord, an obvious extension of this practice of fashioning instruments from readily available materials.

While the *sanshin* in the early 21st century enjoys high social status throughout Okinawa prefecture as a symbol of an Okinawan cultural identity, the instrument had a more ambivalent image until the mid-20th century, and *sanshin* players were often seen as socially undesirable. A common term to describe *sanshin* players was '*piratsïkā*' – lazy.[22] Opposition to the *sanshin* seems to have been particularly strong within peasant society – as many older informants told me, the instrument requires a significant amount of practice in order to build up technique, time which could be better spent working in the fields. The Shiraho singer Yamazato Yūkichi (b. 1925) told me (May 2002) how his youth revolved around the song gatherings[23] that took place in his village in the evenings, which often impacted on his ability to work in the fields the next day. Many performers,

---

[22]   Lit. 'scythe holder' – rather than someone who uses the scythe to cut grass.
[23]   Yamazato referred to them in Japanese as '*nodo jiman*' (lit. throat pride).

especially those born before WWII, have described opposition to their desire to learn traditional music. The well-known musician Ōhama Tsurō, from a peasant farming background in Tonoshiro, had to fight to get accepted into *sanshin* playing circles (see e.g. Makino 1988: 142). Even younger performers have expressed similar negative attitudes towards the *sanshin* in Yaeyama. Ara Yukito (born 1967) describes how 'In Yaeyama *sanshin* players can't find wives. They say that being a performer ruins your character' (in Fujita 1998: 35). Nishidomari Shigeaki (born 1969) has described (ibid.: 42) how he was rarely allowed near the instrument in his childhood due to its low social status, despite the fact that his father was a *sanshin* player at Yonaguni ritual events. Another informant in Yonaguni told me how the playing of the *sanshin* was banned in his extended family due to the misdemeanours of an ancestor who had ruined his economic and social standing by becoming obsessed with the instrument.

Construction

The soul of a *sanshin*'s sound lies in the wood used for the neck (*sao, sō*), although it also depends to some extent on the material used for the resonating skin (*kawa*), and the tension with which the skin is stretched over the body (*chīga*) of the *sanshin*. The wood most favoured for the neck is the ebony (*kokutan, kuroki* or *kuruchi* in Okinawan) indigenous to Okinawa, and Yaeyaman *kuruchi* is particularly favoured throughout Okinawa. Unlike the neck of the mainland Japanese *shamisen*, which is often made up of three or more interlocking pieces, the neck of the *sanshin* almost always consists of a single piece of timber. With resources of these indigenous woods becoming scarce, prices for these top level *sanshin* are high (around US$4,000 in 2010) and most makers make do with varieties of ebony imported from the Philippines, Vietnam and other South-east Asian countries. At the cheaper end of the scale, *sanshin* are made from a variety of timbers such as mulberry, coated in black lacquer to resemble the traditional ebony instruments. These instruments usually start from around 20,000 yen ($200), and are often made overseas in China where labour costs are considerably lower than in Okinawa. In 2010 the *sanshin* market was estimated at 1.2 billion yen (13.5 million US$), or 40,000 instruments, of which 75 per cent were instruments made overseas especially for the Okinawan market.[24]

The body (*chīga*) of the *sanshin* traditionally consists of two pieces of python skin (front and back) stretched over a wooden frame (see Figure 2.1). The Washington Convention limits the import of this skin into Japan (from South-east Asia) and, with the additional tendency for the skin to split after a few years, many cheaper *sanshin* use a synthetic skin, usually printed to resemble snakeskin.

---

[24] *Okinawa Times*, 13 April 2010.

Figure 2.1   *Sanshin* and *tsume*

The synthetic membrane produces an acceptable sound, although most performers prefer the sound of real snakeskin. The three strings (*tsïru, chiru* or *gen* in Japanese) are known, from the lowest to highest, as *ūzïru* (male string), *nakazïru* (middle string) and *mïzïru* (female string). These strings were originally made from silk but more recently are almost always synthetic. The strings are tied at the bottom of the instrument to a small loop (*chirudumi*) and pass over a small bamboo bridge (*nma/uma*) up the neck, over a nut (*utaguchi*) usually made of bone, and onto the pegs (*mudi*), which are also usually carved from ebony. The curved head (*chira*) of the instrument is said to be one its most important aesthetic features, and *sanshin* lovers will often comment on the exquisite balance of form obtained by a good maker. The *chira* is also thought to add to the acoustic qualities of a *sanshin* and to give a weight balance over the whole instrument. While the standard length of *sanshin* is fixed at about 76–80cm, there is quite a variety in the intricate details of contour and shape into which the instrument is carved, particularly the curvature of the *chira* and the thickness of the neck. *Sanshin* collectors can discuss the intricacies of the various shapes (*kata, gata*) at great length, and a mainland Okinawan association, the Sanshin Preservation and Education Group (*Sanshin gakki hozon ikusei-kai*) is dedicated to researching aspects of the construction of *sanshin*.

The strings of the *sanshin* are plucked with a plectrum (*tsimi, chimi, tsume*) placed lightly on the index finger of the right hand and supported with the thumb and middle finger. The plectrum is usually made from water buffalo horn or plastic, and varies from around 4 to 9cm in length. In less formal contexts it is often replaced by a guitar pick or the player's natural index finger nail.

There are a number of standard tunings for the *sanshin*, most of which are analogous to the tunings of the mainland Japanese *shamisen* (see e.g. Johnson 2010: 85). The basic tuning (*honchōshi*) consists of (from bass to treble) intervals of a 4th and a 5th. The exact pitches depend on a particular singer's vocal range but, in practice, range from around A-d-a to d-g-d'. The *niagi* (cf. *niagari* in the

Japanese *shamisen* tradition) tuning raises the middle string to produce intervals of a 5th and a 4th (e.g. c-g-c'), while the *san-sagi* tuning lowers the highest string (from the *honchōshi* tuning) to produce intervals of a 4th and a 4th (e.g. c-f-b♭). The *ichiagi* tuning (also *tō nu tsindami* – Chinese tuning) raises the lowest string (from *honchōshi*) by an interval between a minor and major 3rd, producing intervals between strings of a 2nd and a 5th. The exact tuning of this first interval can vary, depending on the performer, between a major 2nd and slightly more than a minor 2nd, producing quite different musical results (Wang (1998: 85–99) provides an interesting analysis of the different scales produced by different performers using the *ichiagi* tuning).

Kunkunshi Notation

As with *sanshin*-accompanied song traditions around Okinawa, *fushiuta* are usually notated using the *kunkunshi*[25] system. Although *kunkunshi* is never used while performing on stage, all of my *fushiuta* teachers used it in lessons and emphasised the need to sing and play *sanshin* according to the notation. *Kunkunshi* have existed in Okinawa since the mid-18th century, when the notation system was created as an adaptation of the Chinese *gongche* notation, possibly by the Okinawan court musician Yakabi Chōki (1716–75) (see Garfias 1993/1994 for a history and critique of the *kunkunshi* notation system). Unlike the Chinese *gongche* system which represents musical pitches, *kunkunshi* is a tablature system, referring to left-hand finger positions on the *sanshin*. Early versions were rhythmically vague and gave no indication of vocal melody. The mainland Okinawan Nomura-ryū *kunkunshi* of 1869 made the improvement of enclosing each beat of the music into a separate box, allowing rhythm to be notated, and editions from the late 1930s began to show the vocal melody using the *sanshin* finger positions of equivalent pitch. While Yaeyaman songs appeared in late 18th century Okinawan notations and lyric collections such as the *Yakabi Kunkunshi* and the *Ryūka Hyakkō*, the *kunkunshi* notation system does not seem to have been in use in Yaeyama until considerably later. Kishaba (1967: 74) mentions the existence of a *kunkunshi* for the *fushiuta Basï nu turï bushi* dated 1842, but the manuscript is not in evidence today, and the first verifiable Yaeyaman *kunkunshi* manuscripts began to appear only in the late 19th century. The cultural distinction afforded by these written notations was the focus for the creation of several formal lineages in Ishigaki island, and I examine their history in detail in Chapter 5.

Example 2.2 shows an example of a modern Yaeyaman *kunkunshi* for the song *Tsuki ya pama bushi*, a song students usually study early in the learning process.

---

[25] The notation system is most commonly referred to in Yaeyama using the (mainland) Okinawan dialect reading *kunkunshi* or *kunkunshī*. In mainland Okinawa, older generations sometimes refer to it as '*kururunshī*' and in Yaeyama I heard many older informants call it '*kunkunsī*' using the Yaeyaman dialect pronunciation.

Example 2.2   *Kunkunshi* (section) for the song *Tsuki ya pama bushi*

Notes: a) Ōhama Anpan's 2004 (1976) version showing vocal pitches (in Ōhama 2004b: 11. Used with permission).

b) Staff transcription of the first two columns.

The notation is read from top to bottom starting at top right, and there are three vertical columns for (from left to right) *sanshin* finger position (divided into boxes representing rhythmic beats), lyrics and vocal pitch. Each finger position on the *sanshin* is represented by a Chinese character. For example, the first note 合 (ai) signifies that the lowest pitched string (*ūzīru*) should be plucked without fretting[26] with the left hand, while the second note 老 (*rō*) signifies the same string fretted with the middle finger. As with other tablature systems, the exact pitches produced thus depend on the tuning of the *sanshin*, and different pitches are produced for a given character in *honchōshi*, *niagi*, etc. Each box represents one rhythmic beat, with the 'downbeat' coming in the middle of the box, and the 'offbeat' coming on the line between boxes. Further rhythmic intricacy is achieved by placing symbols between the centre of the box and the dividing line, as can be seen with the second note (老). Vocal pitches are notated using the same system in the right-hand column. In this way, modern *kunkunshi* can be used to notate songs with quite a high degree of melodic and rhythmic accuracy. This accuracy is a relatively recent phenomenon – vocal pitches were not included in Yaeyaman *kunkunshi* until 1952, for example – and one way in which the various *fushiuta* organisations have established credentials and veracity as legitimate carriers of tradition is through the production of increasingly intricately notated *kunkunshi* collections. I examine the development of *kunkunshi* in more detail in Chapter 5.

Scales

An aspect of Yaeyaman and Okinawan music that sets it apart from traditional music in the rest of Japan is its distinctive scales or modes.[27] As in other parts of the world, Okinawan scales present a minefield of conflicting theories and terminologies that continue to be contested by scholars and largely ignored by the performers themselves. I make no attempt to provide a single unified theory for Yaeyaman scales here, but give an overview of some of the ways that scales have been theorised by Japanese musicologists.

One of the most characteristic scales used across Okinawa, usually known as the *ryūkyū* or *okinawa* scale, can be seen in the *fushiuta Yunaha bushi*.

---

[26] Pushing the string down to the fingerboard with the left hand. The *sanshin* has no frets.

[27] The distinction between scale (*onkai*) and mode (*senpō*) is often ignored: see Hughes (2001: 818); for a discussion of mode and scale in Japanese shamisen music see Tokita (1996).

Example 2.3 *Yunaha bushi*

Source: Transcribed from Ōhama (2004a: 33).

The scale used in this song (*f, a, b♭, c, e, f'*, or do, mi, fa, sol, ti, do) can be found in traditional music from Okinoerabu in the north of the Ryūkyū archipelago all the way down to Yaeyama in the south, but not in that of the Japanese mainland. Many scholars, following a theory developed in the mid-20th century by the Japanese ethnomusicologist Koizumi Fumio (1989[1958]: 99–251), have seen the *ryūkyū* scale in the context of Koizumi's 'tetrachord' theory (e.g. Nippon Hōsō Kyōkai 1990a: 9–10), in which the vast majority of Japanese music is seen to be unified by its dependence not on octave-based scales but on a modal system composed of intervals of a 4th (tetrachord). Stable 'nuclear tones' (*kakuon*) making up a tetrachord are connected by a less-stable infix (*chūkan-on*), which varies according to region or musical style within Japan. Koizumi identified four main tetrachords used in Japanese music, which are usually combined as pairs of 'disjunct[28] tetrachords' to form what are commonly known as the *miyako bushi* scale (Example 2.4a), the *ritsu* scale (b), the *min'yō* scale (c) and the *ryūkyū/okinawa* scale (d).

Example 2.4 Koizumi's four scale types: a) *miyako-bushi* scale; b) *ritsu* scale;
c) *min'yō* scale; d) *ryūkyū* scale

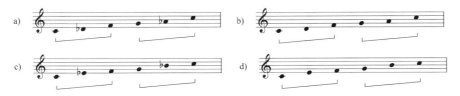

These scales differ only in the position of the infix, which varies from a semitone above the lower note of the tetrachord in the case of the *miyako bushi* scale, to a major 3rd in the case of the *ryūkyū* scale. Under this theory, the scale in *Yunaha bushi* can be seen as two disjunct *ryūkyū* tetrachords, from f to b-flat, and c' to f' respectively, making up a *ryūkyū* scale. Examples of this kind of scale can be found in *fushiuta* and most *koyō* genres, although it is by no means the predominant scale in Yaeyaman music.

---

[28]   I.e. the two tetrachords are separated by a major 2nd.

A more common scale used in Yaeyaman music can be seen in the song *Asadoya yunta*.

Example 2.5 *Asadōya yunta.* Tonoshiro *kayō no kai*, 2002

Source: Field recording by the author.

This 'anhemitonic[29] pentatonic' scale (*f, g, a, c, d, f′* or do, re, mi, sol, la, do), appears often in Yaeyaman songs, as well as (less frequently) in the Okinawan mainland, and throughout mainland Japan. One interpretation of this song would be to identify two *ritsu* tetrachords with nuclear tones c-f and g-*c′* intersected by the infixes *d* and *a*. Many scholars, in an attempt to emphasise the relative strength of the *f* and *c*, with *g* having a more subsidiary position, describe an 'altered' *ritsu* scale (*ritsu onkai no henshu*), often also described as the *ryo* scale (or mode[30]) for this kind of melodic movement (e.g. Fukui 2006: 110; Kaneshiro 1990; Kojima 2008: 52). The *ryo* scale is seen to be based on stable intervals of a 5th (f-c′ in the *Asadōya yunta* example), rather than the 4ths of Koizumi's model, a fact that has implications for Koizumi's tetrachord model (see below).

Many Yaeyaman songs also use a combination of *ritsu* and *ryūkyū* tetrachords in a single song. For example *Kuigusuku bushi* (Example 2.6).

---

[29]   A five-note scale containing no semitone intervals. One of the most commons scales found throughout the world.

[30]   Kaneshiro and Kojima use the term *ryo-onkai* (*ryo* scale) while Fukui uses *ryo-sen* (*ryo* mode).

Example 2.6 *Kuigusuku bushi*

Source: Transcribed from Ōhama (2004a: 39).

This song can be seen to consist of nuclear tones between c-f and g-c' In the first line of this example, the infix between c and f is d, indicating a *ritsu* tetrachord. From the end of the first line the infix changes to e – indicating a *ryūkyū* tetrachord.[31] The infix of the upper tetrachord between g and c in line 2 can also be seen to be unstable, sometimes being sung slightly nearer bb (e.g. the second note of bar 8), and sometimes nearer to b♭ (the fourth note of bar 8). This kind of microtonal 'shading' (Hughes 2008: 36) is also common in the Japanese mainland with, for example, an 'unstable' infix in a *ritsu* tetrachord 'shading' into a *miyakobushi* infix in the course of a single performance. This kind of 'shading' has no particular consequences for Koizumi's theory, as the pitches of the infix are assumed to be inherently unstable and the pitches of the nuclear tones do not move in these examples.

In some Yaeyaman examples, however, minute variations in pitch between performer of variant form cause shifts in the resultant scale that are troubling to the tetrachord model. From the late 1960s several Japanese scholars such as Kakinoki Gorō (1969) and Kojima Tomiko (1974, 1976) began to develop theories of Okinawan scales that didn't depend on Koizumi's tetrachord model. Kojima (1976: 258), for example, noted that in some cases[32] infixes under Koizumi's tetrachord theory were shading to become nuclear tones and vice versa, breaking down the idea of their inherent stability or instability (i.e. their 'status' as nuclear tones or infixes). In what is probably the most comprehensive musicological analysis of Okinawan scales to date, Kaneshiro (1990) developed these ideas further, noting that in many cases variant forms of songs appear to switch between *ritsu/ryo* scale and *ryūkyū* scales in neighbouring villages or versions.

This kind of pitch shifting is very hard to explain using Koizumi's tetrachord model. Kaneshiro concludes that, like the *ryo* scale, this kind of *ryūkyū* scale is based not on tetrachords, but on a pentachordal structure (see Example 2.7).

---

[31]   This use of a high infix in ascending passages and a low infix in descending passages is also a feature of mainland Japanese genres (alternating between *min'yō* and *miyakobushi* infixes in ascending or descending passages for example).

[32]   Kojima gives the example of *Miruku bushi*.

Under this system, the kind of movement between *ryo* and *ryūkyū* scales is relatively easy to explain.

Example 2.7 Summary of movement between *ryo* and *ryūkyū* scale

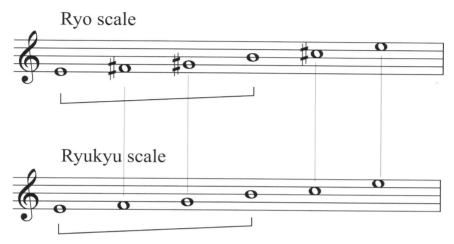

Source: Adapted from Kaneshiro (1990: 112).

A fixed pentachord between the notes e–b exists in both the *ryo* and *ryūkyū* scales in this example. The intermediate pitches are unstable allowing for movement from f to f♯, g to g♯ etc. Kaneshiro notes that both of these scales have the same combination of small (minor or major 2nd) and large (minor or major 3rd) intervals (the pattern is small-small-large-small-large between adjacent notes in Example 2.7). A characteristic of songs using the pentatonic *ryūkyū* scale is that, unlike the tetrachordal *ryūkyū* scale [do mi fa sol si do] which often begins and ends on do or fa, the pentachordal scale [equivalent to mi fa sol si do mi] very often has mi as *finalis* (as in *Yunaha bushi* in Example 2.3), a situation that would be unusual in the tetrachord model. Kaneshiro does not discount the tetrachordal model of the *ryūkyū* scale completely, but concludes that it has two distinct types: one based on a tetrachordal nucleic structure (do mi fa sol si do), in which the nuclear tones are do-fa, sol-do, while the other is 'based on a pentachordal nucleic structure (mi fa sol si do mi), in which the nuclear notes are mi, sol and si (1990: 114–16; also English summary on p. 8).[33]

---

[33] Also see Tōkawa (1990: 23–7) for a specific criticism of, and alternative to Koizumi's theory. For an in-depth analysis of the use of scales in female *eisā* in the Okinawan mainland see Y. Kobayashi (1986); also see Nippon Hōsō Kyōkai (1990a: 10);

A consequence of this new model of Okinawan scales has been the possibility that the *ryūkyū* scale need not necessarily be positioned within a 'Japanese' cultural framework. Despite the fact that, in some cases at least, the *ryūkyū* scale can be fitted into the 'Japanese' scale family based on 4ths, there are obvious similarities with scales in other parts of Asia, particularly Indonesia. Koizumi's positioning of the *ryūkyū* scale in his tetrachord system might be seen as an attempt to position Okinawan music in a Japanese cultural sphere. In fact, his writings show a more ambiguous stance. On one hand, he wrote that 'the possibility that the *ryūkyū* scale developed from the basic (*kihon*) Japanese *min'yō* scale ... cannot be ruled out' (Koizumi 1989[1958]: 178). Yet he also caused a minor sensation among music scholars in 1983 (shortly before his death) when he suggested that the *ryūkyū* scale was 'older' even than the *ritsu* scale found across Japan, noting the existence of scales similar to the *ryūkyū* scale in culturally isolated regions of countries such as Burma, Nepal, Vietnam, Bhutan, India, and to some extent in Micronesia, Indonesia and Bali (Okinawa is roughly in the geographical centre of these countries) (Koizumi 1983). Kaneshiro has also cited the existence of a pentachordal *ryūkyū* scale as evidence for 'non-Japanese' roots of that scale, noting in particular that the highest concentration of the scale is found in Yaeyama, while a tetrachord-based *ryūkyū* scale becomes more and more common in parts of Okinawa nearer to the Japanese mainland (1990: 116).

While the majority of traditional performers have little understanding of, or interest in, these academic ideas of musical scales, the use of scales as a way of constructing musical images of place has nevertheless been a feature of the music of several new compositions since the early 20th century. In Chapter 3 I give an example of the use of the *miyakobushi* scale in early 20th century music as a way of imaging Japanese cultural connections. In Chapter 7 I present some examples of more modern discourse surrounding the use of traditional scales in new Yaeyaman music.

K. Kobayashi (1986: 99); for a brief analysis of Yaeyaman scales see Kojima (1974); see also Narusaka (1979), who emphasizes the tetrachord nature of the *ryūkyū* scale.

Chapter 3

The Southern Islands –
Yaeyama and Okinawa in the
Japanese Cultural Imagination

The 'traditional' Yaeyaman repertory that I outlined in the previous chapter derives largely from the Ryūkyū kingdom period prior to Okinawa's incorporation into the modern Japanese nation in 1879. The creation of Okinawa prefecture had obvious consequences for music-making in Yaeyama, and the early 20th century saw a flurry of interest from performers and scholars, both from Yaeyama itself as well as Okinawa and Japan, aimed at negotiating cultural issues of Yaeyama's position within Japan. At a practical level, the implementation of a Japanese education system influenced factors such as the language used in songs and the way music is seen in society. At an ideological level, too, the 'discovery' of musical connections between Yaeyama and mainland Japan was one way in which Yaeyama's cultural place in the nation was culturally imagined. In this chapter, I examine some of the discourses surrounding Okinawan and Yaeyaman music in the context of Japan as a whole, and consider some of the cultural meanings that Okinawa's regional 'minority' culture has had in the production of ideas of modern Yaeyaman identities.

A number of studies have considered the way in which minority or regional cultures are reinterpreted in the context of the nations to which they belong. In 1973 Clifford Geertz described what he termed an 'integrative revolution' involving the 'aggregation of independently defined, specifically outlined traditional primordial groups into larger, more diffuse units whose implicit frame of reference is not the local scene but the "nation"' (1973: 306–7). Drawing particularly on Geertz's work, Tuohy has described in detail the incorporation of minority musics into the cultural life of the Chinese nation as a 'mutually transformative process of making music national and of realizing the nation musically' (2001: 108), as a part of what she calls 'musical nationalism' in 20th century China. Tuohy draws on a wide range of musical discourses, such as the inclusion of regional or minority repertories into national folk-song anthologies, and the representation of minority musics in the national broadcast media, outlining the ways in which 'a Chinese national identity is a flexible one created within situated social-musical interaction' (2001: 119). Rees (2000) and Harris (2008) have also described similar examples of the incorporation of Chinese ethnic minority musics into a national context. While the Chinese situation is obviously different to that of Japan – in particular the specific acknowledgement of the existence of 'ethnic minorities' contrasts with the more ambiguous ethnic status of Okinawans – the processes of 'nationalization' of regional traditions bear some resemblances.

The nature of Okinawa's 'assimilation' into the Japanese nation, and the extent to which Okinawan cultural identities were 'suppressed' in favour of dominant Japanese ones, is contested. Christy (1993) has argued that a pre-existing Okinawan ethnic identity was 'subsumed under Japan' (1993: 609) after 'annexation' in the late 19th century, and suggests that the assimilation process should be seen as one of 'colonization'. Siddle, conversely, questions the very 'existence of a self-conscious Ryūkyūan *minzoku* [ethnicity]' (1998: 133) prior to assimilation. While it may be tempting to distinguish between mainland Japanese views of Okinawa, perhaps with colonialist intentions, and views of Okinawan culture held by Okinawans themselves, perhaps in the face of Japanese hegemony, the reality is that from the very early 20th century there was vigorous and enthusiastic interchange between Japanese, Okinawan and Yaeyaman scholars, artists and educators. One of the prominent features of the reimagining of Yaeyaman music within the context of Japan has been that, far from being a one-way, or top-down process, these imaginings have taken place on a variety of geographical levels, which have often interacted with each other.

Early examples of the representation of Okinawan culture in mainland Japan were not always flattering. An often-cited incident at the Osaka Industrial Exposition in 1903, in which 'natives' of Ryūkyū were displayed in a so-called 'Human race hall' (*jinruikan*) alongside Ainu, Korean, Taiwanese aboriginal and other Asian ethnic groups as examples of Japan's 'less-developed' neighbours, prompted an Okinawan newspaper article deploring both the cultural condescension involved, and also pointing out that Okinawa, as a fully-fledged 'prefecture' (*ken*) of Japan, should not be treated as a mere colony (e.g. Christy 1993; Siddle 2003: 138; Tomiyama 1990: 8). The very strong reaction from Okinawa to the *jinruikan* and its implicit suggestion that Okinawans were a different ethnic group from mainland Japanese, can be taken as indicative of a movement within Okinawa at the time, at least among much of the Okinawan elite, to emphasise the prefecture's position as a legitimate part of Japan. The urge to assimilate into mainstream Japanese society had many implications for traditional music throughout the prefecture. Some sections of Okinawan society, as in mainland Japan, were in favour of the complete abolishment of what were seen as 'backward' cultural practices. Ueunten (2008: 173), for example, quotes an early 20th century Okinawan graduate of the University of Southern California, who lamented the fact that 'Okinawan emigrants in the past were less cultured than other Japanese'. Likewise, in Chapter 5, I outline a strong resistance to traditional music in the school system which lasted at least until the 1960s, an attitude that was largely connected to a feeling of the inferiority of traditional culture.

Despite early negative images of Okinawa such as these, and perhaps because of them, many early 20th century representations of Okinawan culture in a Japanese context emphasise the cultural connections between the two regions. Concepts of the shared cultural and ethnic origins of Okinawa and mainland Japan, often referred to in Japanese as the *Nichiryū dōsoron* (Japan-Ryūkyū shared ancestor theory) had existed in Okinawa since at least 1650, when they had been posited in the *Chūzan seikan*, an official history of the islands. These ideas were revisited and extensively theorised in the early 20th century writings of the Okinawan scholar Iha Fuyū (1876–1947). Iha had studied in the Japanese mainland for 10 years from 1896 where, under the influence of Japanese academic society, he had become increasingly aware of his Okinawan identity, leading him to carry out research on the Okinawan language at Tokyo University from 1903 (see Siddle 1998: 125). His groundbreaking work translating the *Omoro sōshi*, an ancient Okinawan poetry collection, and writings on a range of Okinawan cultural issues, meant that he is commonly referred to as the 'father of Okinawan studies' (*Okinawa-gaku no chichi*).

Iha subsequently came to be influential on a number of mainland Japanese scholars such as Yanagita Kunio (1875–1962) and Yanagi Muneyoshi (1889–1961). Yanagita, in particular, the 'father of Japanese folklore studies' (*Nihon minzokugaku no chichi*), was influential in promoting conceptions of folk music in Japan, and made an extended trip to Okinawa (including Yaeyama) between 1920 and 1921. These scholars developed a theory that has come to be called the *Nantō-ron* (Southern Island theory), depicting the Ryūkyū archipelago as 'a treasure trove of unchanging religious beliefs and practices, which were fundamental to the figure of an enduring Japanese daily life' (Harootunian 1998: 155; for an analysis of the *Nantō-ron*, see Hara 2007; Tanaka 2009). Through these writings many parts of Japanese academic society came to see Okinawa, rather than an undeveloped colony, as a region where aspects of ancient *Japanese* culture survived as part of the living customs of the islands. An early example can be found in a 1926 essay by Iha, who wrote that 'not only is the language of ancient Japanese poetry collections preserved in the Ryūkyū islands, but the ancient [Japanese] ways of life are also preserved there' (Iha 1975: 98). Similarly, Yanagi Muneyoshi wrote in 1939 that:

> The biggest surprise was that these islands in the very south have preserved the old Japanese ways so correctly. Wherever one travels in Japan, one can't find anywhere that preserves the essential characteristics of the Japanese like Ryūkyū. This is true linguistically and in its customs, but one can encounter the very oldest features of Japan in a variety of other facets [of Okinawan life]. (Yanagi 1981: 139)

In a similar way, Okinawan music was sometimes seen as a repository for extinct Japanese musical traditions. The Japanese musicologist Tanabe Hisao begins his account of a 1922 research trip to Okinawa with the following passage:

In Ryūkyū, one can find Japanese music from the old Ashikaga to Genroku[1] periods, which has been preserved to the present day. For example, *Yatsuhashi-ryū koto* pieces, *Ashikaga kouta*, old *kyōgen*, original forms of *noh*, *okuni kabuki*, *wakashū kabuki*, most of which have disappeared from the Japanese mainland and are no longer transmitted. Information about these genres is hard to obtain and they remain poorly understood. However, all of these are preserved in Ryūkyū in their original forms [*furui katachi*]. Most of them were probably originally imported many years ago from the Japanese mainland. (Tanabe 1968: 254)

Thus, for these and other early 20th century Japanese scholars the interest of Okinawa lay at least partly in its existence as a way of understanding fundamental aspects of 'Japanese' history and culture. The *Nantō-ron* has continued to be one of the dominant discourses surrounding Okinawan culture in Japan throughout the 20th century and beyond. Writers such as Yanagita, in addition to pointing out the presence of ancient Japanese traditions 'preserved' in Okinawa, also began seeing Okinawa as the possible 'roots' of Japanese culture. Yanagita had published these ideas as early as 1925, and his seminal 1961 book *Kaijō no michi* (Pathways over the Seas), towards the end of his career, outlined aspects of Japanese culture that he suggested had followed the sea route up from the south-west through the Okinawan islands into mainland Japan (Yanagita 1998). The novelist Shimao Toshio's 'Yaponesia' theory, too, portrays the Ryūkyū islands as part of a cultural zone stretching the length of the Japanese nation, while stressing the cultural diversity of individual regions within that zone (see Gabriel 1999: 160–214). The idea of Okinawa representing 'forgotten' aspects of Japanese culture can also be seen in the artist Okamoto Tarō's 1961 (1996) book *Okinawa Bunkaron – Wasurerareta Nihon* (Theory of Okinawan Culture – Forgotten Japan), as well as in many publications by the folklorist Tanigawa Ken'ichi (e.g. 2000).

The Yaeyaman Canon

The interest in Okinawan culture as a window into Japanese traditions led to a need, both inside and outside the region, to identify a specifically Yaeyaman musical canon. Bohlman has noted how the formation of canons is often carried out by 'multiple agents' (1992: 203), and attempts to formulate a canon of Yaeyaman music in the early 20th century show well how ideas surrounding Yaeyaman music were developed simultaneously in Yaeyaman, Okinawan and Japanese cultural contexts. At a local Yaeyaman level, one of the key figures in establishing a Yaeyaman canon was an Ishigaki school teacher called Kishaba Eijun (1885–1972) who, in parallel with Iha and Yanagita, has come to be known

---

[1]   The Ashikaga (or Muromachi) period ran from 1336 to 1573; the Genroku period from 1688 to 1733.

affectionately within Yaeyama as the 'father of Yaeyama studies' (*Yaeyama kenkyū no chichi*). Kishaba published on a range of subjects including music, folk customs and history, and in particular his 1924 *Yaeyama-jima Min'yō-shi* (Yaeyama Folk Song Collection), containing Japanese translations and lengthy explanations into the background behind the songs,[2] remains the standard reference work on Yaeyaman *fushiuta* lyrics.

Kishaba's folk-song research can be directly linked to a general interest in indigenous folk song throughout Japan in the early years of the 20th century, both among private individuals and at a more official level. In the first decade of the 20th century the Japanese ministry of education had implemented an extensive survey of songs throughout the nation, leading to the publication of *Riyōshū* ('*Folk Song' Collection*) in 1914. Presumably as part of the preparation for this collection, the Yaeyaman education office had been approached directly by the ministry of education in Tokyo in 1906 with a request to supply an informant knowledgeable about Yaeyaman music (Kumada 2007: 45; Nishimura 1987: 10). The job was assigned to the 21-year-old Kishaba, who had just begun a career as an elementary school teacher. Perhaps because of a lack of experience and musical training, Kishaba's initial research attempts seem to have been somewhat fruitless, and no songs from Okinawa or Yaeyama finally appeared in the education ministry's 1914 song collection. Nevertheless, he was spurred on by the 1907 visit to Yaeyama of Iha Fuyū, who encouraged him to continue his local research. Iha seems to have been particularly enamoured with the songs of Yaeyama from early on, portraying a romantic image of the islands as a repository for ancient Okinawan culture in a similar way to Okinawa itself was compared in relation to Japan (the quote at the beginning of Chapter 2 is an example). Iha's biggest influence on Kishaba in particular, and on the formation of a Yaeyaman musical canon in general, was his suggestion, on his second visit to Yaeyama in 1912, that Kishaba investigate the composers and dates of composition of Yaeyama songs. Iha had become enamoured early on with the work song *Basï yunta*, and its *fushiuta* version *Basï nu turï bushi*, as examples of 'folk literature', and had introduced the song to his Tokyo colleagues, who in turn encouraged him to find out more about the song's background (Kishaba 1967: 65). At least part of Iha's fascination with the song presumably came from its lyrical content – in its *yunta* form it describes an eagle nurturing her newborn chicks who, on the morning of New Year's day, 'fly away to Yamato, fly away to Japan' (*ufu-Yamatu nu sïman maitsïke, yasurari nu fun maitsïke*. Iha 2000: 346). The desire to assimilate with the Japanese mainland, and to show a historical basis for Okinawa's position in the Japanese nation among many Okinawans at this time, was perhaps well captured in this verse.

Iha's suggestion was to have a profound effect on Kishaba's approach to his study of Yaeyaman songs. Taking Iha's advice, Kishaba set out on foot around Ishigaki, asking the elders of each villages directly whether they knew who had

---

[2]   The book was reprinted in a revised edition in 1967.

composed certain songs. His recollections regarding *Basï yunta* are indicative of his approach:

> I started out in my birthplace of Tonoshiro and from there went to Ōkawa, Ishigaki and Arakawa asking the village elders and local learned people about the song. However, they told me that they had learned the lyrics and the melody, but knew nothing of the composer or when the song was composed. They all said that if they were to ask their teachers about the origins of a song, they would be scolded, and so I refrained from asking. I continued my research, but with waning enthusiasm and with little idea about the way forward. Iha Fuyū was being urged to find an answer to this question, and in turn he sent me telegrams encouraging me to resolve the issue quickly. One Sunday I set out on a study trip to Arakawa. The results of the expedition were unsatisfactory, and with a heavy heart I set out for home. On the way I met an old man called Murayama Shinji. When I asked him about *Bashi nu turï* he informed me that the composer was a member of the Nakama house of Ōkawa, so I immediately hurried there and was warmly greeted by an old man named Kana. My conversation with Kana is still branded on my memory. I will never forget that day, April 2nd 1912. (Kishaba 1967: 65–6)

The 79-year-old Kana explained to Kishaba how the song had been composed by Nakama Sakai, a female ritual specialist (*tsukasa*) in Ōkawa, who had seen crested eagles nesting in the mulberry trees at the shrine and improvised the song praying for them to raise their chicks and fly off towards 'the sun'. No family record survived for Nakama Sakai, but from the date of her death, 1813, in which year she was reported to have been 101 years old, Kishaba established a composition date of 1762. Iha Fuyū was delighted at the work of his Yaeyaman protégé, writing in an article in the *Okinawa Times* in 1912, 'how little could Nakama Sakai, poet of the Southern Islands, have imagined that one day she would find success throughout Japan' (Iha 2000: 351). Kishaba continued his attempts to ascertain historical composers and dates for Yaeyaman songs for much of the rest of his life. By the time of the publication of the revised edition of his *Yaeyama Min'yō-shi*, a collection of the complete *fushiuta* canon, in 1967, he had assigned composers and composition dates to all but a few songs in the repertory. Whatever the accuracy of Kishaba's investigations, his way of thinking has had an immeasurable effect on the place Yaeyaman songs hold within Yaeyama society, and the results of his investigations into composers and dates are still frequently quoted in recent publications by Yaeyaman and Okinawan writers (e.g. Nakasone 1993; Nakasone 1998a).

From this account of the formation of a Yaeyaman musical canon, it is evident that the process was led as much by events happening in Tokyo and Okinawa as by those in Yaeyama itself. While the details of Kishaba's comment that Iha was being urged (by his Tokyo colleagues?) to find an answer to the question of composers of particular songs is unclear, we can see that Yaeyaman conceptions of folk music were being influenced by Tokyo academic circles at least as early as 1912. The presence and active participation of the three 'father' figures, Kishaba, Iha and Yanagita, in the development of Yaeyaman music in the early 20th century is indicative both of the way in which the conception of local music in Yaeyama was driven by events taking place in Okinawa and the Japanese mainland, but also of the role Yaeyama played in the early 20th century formation of ideas of Japanese folklore and Okinawan identity.

Folk versus Classical

One of the ways in which Yaeyama can be seen to play an active part in emerging Japanese ideas of 'folk culture' is the through the various uses of the term *min'yō* (folk song) to describe Yaeyaman songs. The use of this word is relatively early even in a Japanese context – Iha Fuyū uses it in his 1909 essay *Min'yō ni arawareta Yaeyama no Kaitaku* (The Re-settlement of Yaeyama seen through its *Min'yō*; in Iha Fuyū 2000: 323–34), reflecting his close links to the emerging folk movement in the Japanese mainland. The first book-length publication to use the word *min'yō* in its title to describe Yaeyama songs was Kishaba Ten'yo's 1920 lyric collection *Yaeyama Min'yōshū*, and the term appears in several subsequent publications from the 1920s, including Kishaba Eijun's 1924 *Yaeyama Min'yōshi*, the result of his initial investigations into song composers and backgrounds. Despite the frequent interactions between Yaeyama, Okinawa and Tokyo in these years, Kishaba's approach to the study of Yaeyaman music, and his interest in authenticating aristocratic lineages for songs, contrasts with the approach taken by the majority of outsiders, who were more interested in the 'communal' aspects of folk songs (Kumada 2007). While the initial impetus for Kishaba's research seems to have come through strong encouragement from Iha Fuyū, Iha himself later came to question the importance of this approach. In 1938 he wrote, for example, 'that the tradition has been handed down probably means that there was an original composer ... but as the original form has long since been forgotten – the song has become a product of society – it is unprofitable to debate the "correct" forms of these songs' (Iha 2000: 269). Kumada (2007) has suggested that Iha's change of ideology was influenced by developments of the concept of *min'yō* by Yanagita Kunio, who in 1927 wrote that 'Japanese *min'yō* are a product of society and communal space' (1998: 464). From the Yaeyaman side, conversely, the need to show that songs had verifiable origins could possibly have been more of a concern – the songs could be made respectable by connecting them to composers of the ruling class. One Yaeyaman scholar suggested to me that Kishaba had a motive to present Yaeyaman songs in as favourable a light as possible so that they would stand up in front of any mainland Japanese traditions (Ōta, pers. comm. January 2002). The distinction between 'folk song' (*min'yō*) and 'classical' (*koten*) traditions is one that pervades traditional music in Okinawa to the present, and one that was also born in the early years of the 20th century, influenced by analogous concepts in the Japanese mainland.

The portrayal of the rural and 'folk' aspects of Yaeyaman music were, from early on, one of its biggest selling points in the Japanese mainland. An example can be seen in 1928, when a Yaeyaman music and dance troupe, under Kishaba Eijun's supervision, was invited by Yanagita Kunio to perform in Tokyo at the third annual meeting of the *Kyōdo buyō to min'yō no kai* (local dance and *min'yō* organisation). This was one of the first major performances of any Okinawan music or dance genre in the Japanese capital,[3] and had many significant cultural repercussions throughout the prefecture. From the Tokyo side, with an intention to keep the performance as 'authentic' as possible, a somewhat arbitrary request was made that the dancers should be 'amateur' and 'female', wearing 'ordinary' costumes with no additional make-up (Miki 1989: 53; also Kumada 2007). After Kishaba had managed to assemble a suitable cast – no easy task as it was relatively uncommon for Yaeyaman women to perform staged dances in the early 20th century – the troupe set sail for Japan. During a stopover in Naha they ran into further problems when commanded to perform a dress rehearsal in front of the prefectural authorities and assorted mainland Okinawan musicians and dancers (who were presumably disgruntled not to have been invited themselves). Kishaba describes how the Naha performance was harshly criticised by the assembled mainland Okinawans as being, among other things, 'unpolished' (*gijutsu ga amari ni mo mijuku*), with shabby costumes, insufficient make-up, and unworthy of representing Ryūkyūan culture (Kishaba 1977: 231–2). This incident shows well the conflicting desires of the Tokyo folklorists such as Yanagita, who wished to portray Okinawa (Yaeyama) in its 'folk' guise, and an influential element of Okinawan society wishing to stress the refined and artistic aspects of 'classical' Ryūkyūan culture. As Kumada notes, Kishaba seems to have been fully aware of the image he was being asked to present, writing a repost to his critics some months after the Tokyo tour that the performance presented 'an ancient, earthy and rough folk performing art, rich in local colour' and that the refined Ryūkyūan classical performance might be better off on the stage of the Kabuki-za, rather than the more downmarket Nihon Seinen-kan where the Yaeyaman performance took place[4] (Kishaba 1977(II): 233; Kumada 2007: 53).

---

[3]   Okinawan music had of course been performed as part of diplomatic missions sent from the Ryūkyū court throughout the Edo period, although not in front of the general public. There are also a few examples from the late Meiji era, including the Okinawan classical music performer Kin Ryōjin's 1910 performance at the Tokyo School of Music.

[4]   The *Nihon Seinenkan* (Japan Youth Hall) was established in 1920 by the Nihon Seinen-dan (Japan Youth Organization), and was a common venue for performances of 'folk' culture. The first large-scale mainland Okinawan (Ryūkyū classical music) performance also took place in the Nihon Seinen-kan in 1936, at the invitation of the Yanagita's student Orikuchi Shinobu.

In Okinawa itself, a distinction came to be made in the early decades of the 20th century between the *koten* (classical) music of the old Shuri court and the songs of the common people, which came to be called *min'yō*. *Min'yō* in the Okinawan mainland comprise a variety of genres, including songs of the various *shibai* dramatic genres, courting songs from the *mōashibi* tradition, and new songs disseminated through recordings in the 20th century. In the popular Okinawan musical imagination, there is a strong distinction today between the refined, artistic and emotionally restrained *koten* (classical) tradition, and a more lively and emotional *min'yō* (folk) tradition that allows for individual variation and interpretation. One result of this distinction, for example, has been the overwhelming support and recognition of both local and national governments for the *koten* genres, while mainland Okinawan '*min'yō*' performers have been largely ignored. In Yaeyama too, the respectable ring of the '*koten*' term as used in mainland Okinawan music has led, since the 1970s, to the widespread introduction of a new term '*koten min'yō*' (classical *min'yō*) to describe Yaeyaman *fushiuta*. The first use of the term seems to be in the Yaeyaman music educator Itosu Chōryō's 1974 *Yaeyama Koten Min'yō, Koyō Zenshū* (Yaeyaman Classical *Min'yō* and *Koyō* Collection), in which he wrote:

> In mainland Okinawa the genre of new folk songs known as '*Okinawa Min'yō*' is very popular. This *min'yō* is often broadcast on television and radio. The term '*min'yō*' has come to refer primarily to this form of popular song. In order to distinguish (*Yaeyama min'yō*) from these [new] songs I have used the term *Koten Min'yō*. (Itosu 1990 [1974]: 4)

Itosu thus emphasised the verifiable 'classical' lineage of *fushiuta*, while at the same time maintaining their position, developed in the early 20th century, as 'folk songs'.

Despite an important distinction within Okinawa between ideas of 'folk' and 'classical' repertories, there is a tendency among mainland Japanese scholars, even in the 21st century, to 'file' all Okinawan music, from the highly sophisticated art music of the old Shuri court to work and ritual songs, under a general heading of '*min'yō*'. Most of the recently published textbook-style introductions to Japanese music, for example, either ignore Okinawa completely (e.g. Tanaka 2003), or present Okinawan music as a branch of Japanese 'folk music' (Fukui 2006). Another example is the dance drama *kumiodori* of the old Ryūkyū court which, despite being designated by the Japanese government in 1972 as an Intangible Cultural Heritage (along with other 'classical' genres such as *noh* and *bunraku*), was publicised on the National Theatre's website[5] in 2008 as a *minzoku geinō* (folk performing art).

---

[5]   www.ntj.jac.go.jp/kokuritsu, accessed 15 February 2011.

Utakake, Sexuality and East Asian Roots

Another example of the use of Okinawan music as a way of imagining concepts of Japanese history can be seen in the cultural representation of the so-called *mō-ashibi* tradition. The *mō-ashibi* (or *Yū-asïbi* in Yaeyama) was a cultural practice prevalent in the Okinawan countryside until around the time of WWII, in which young unmarried men and women would gather in a secluded spot outside the village limits (*mō* = an open space, a hill) to sing, dance and party, often with the motive of finding sexual/marriage partners (see e.g. Maeda et al. 1972: 382–3; Uchida 1989: 5). A key aspect of the *mō-ashibi* was the practice of antiphonal singing between men and women, with partially improvised lyrics, often of an erotic nature. The *mō-ashibi* has been a prominent theme for mainland Japanese writers and scholars of Okinawan music. In a book aimed at the popular (Japanese) market, for example, the music journalist Fujita Tadashi describes the *mō-ashibi* as 'one of the foundations (*kiten*) of Okinawan folk song' (2000: 45). The music writer Matsumura Hiroshi likewise devotes a chapter of his 2002 Okinawan music guide to the *mō-ashibi* and related traditions (2002: 81–119).

The practice of antiphonal singing, the lyrics of which form a kind of musical conversation, is a characteristic of many of the traditional folk music styles of the Ryūkyū islands. One of the earliest references to similar traditions comes in the *Nantō zatsuwa* (Assorted Stories from the Southern Islands), an 1828 document recording the customs of the Amami islands in the north of Ryūkyū. This document records a custom described as *kakeuta*, in which:

> Men and women divide into two groups, and sit facing each other separated by a short distance. They sing without *shamisen* accompaniment, but clap and slap their hands on their thighs in time to the singing … The songs are improvised on the spot, and the singer who can make up verses without faltering is considered to be talented, while those singers who get tongue-tied are considered to have lost. (Nagoya 1984: 92–3)

While this document makes no mention of sexual practices associated with *kakeuta*, the connection between this antiphonal singing style and the pursuit of sexual/marriage partners seems to have been prevalent throughout the Ryūkyū islands. An investigation carried out in 1894 by an official of the Japanese ministry of home affairs reported that 'in the villages, marriages are often decided as a result of the *mō-ashibi*, and most parents of these couples openly accept the situation' (quoted in Iha 1975, vol. 7: 49).

Part of the attraction of the survival of the *mō-ashibi* in Okinawa until very recent times has been that it provides a 'living connection' to what are seen as being ancient Japanese traditions, in particular an ancient Japanese singing tradition known as *utagaki*.[6] Various authors have commented on the similarity

---

[6]   Also *kagai*.

between lyrics from the Okinawan and Amami *utakake* tradition, and those found in ancient Japanese poetry collections such as the *Kojiki*, *Manyōshū* or *Kokin waka shū* (see e.g. Ogawa 1988: 224–30; Shigeno 1960; Tanigawa 2000: 68; Tsuchihashi 1984; Uchida 1989: 13; Yamashiro 1988). Tanigawa Ken'ichi, in particular, has written extensively on the connection between the *mō-ashibi* and ancient Japanese literature, and he provides a lengthy literary transcription of a musical conversation typical at an Okinawan *mō-ashibi* (Tanigawa 2000: 62–7). The Japanese literary scholar Tatsumi Masaaki's 2001 book, *Man'yōshū ni aitai* (Meeting the *Man'yōshū*), also draws a direct connection between the M*an'yōshū* and extant Amami *utakake* singing traditions.

The cultural connections between the Ryūkyū islands and ancient Japanese traditions have also been expanded to include similar practices in much of East Asia that have been described in English by Yang (1994, 1998) as 'Erotic Musical activity' (or EMA). Several Japanese researchers have carried out fieldwork on extant Chinese *utagaki*-like singing traditions, and many have focused on the connection with ancient Japanese customs and living Okinawan traditions. Suzuki (1988) makes a connection between the singing traditions of the Yunnan region and ancient Japanese tradition, describing *utagaki* as the 'foundation of [Japanese literary] culture' (15–24). Uchida (1989: 13–15) also draws similar comparisons between Japanese *utagaki* and song traditions throughout East Asia, describing Okinawa as the 'last place in Japan where the tradition has survived' (ibid.: 13). In some cases, attempts have been made to emphasise cultural links between Japan, the Ryūkyū islands, and mainland Asia. In December 2007, for example, I attended a symposium at Kokugakuin University in Tokyo, titled *Utagaki samitto* (summit), that aimed to show the shared *utagaki* traditions of East Asian countries, with performances from Akita in northern Japan, Amami in the north of the Ryūkyū islands, and the Dong[7] ethnic group from the Chinese Guizhou province.

The fascination with the *mō-ashibi* in many recent popular writings on Okinawan music can be traced partly to the activities of a Japanese journalist Takenaka Rō (1930–1991) who, as well as writing extensively on Okinawan music in the 1970s (e.g. 1975, 2002), was active in releasing recordings of Okinawan musicians onto the mainland Japanese market, and bringing Okinawan musicians to perform in mainland Japan. Takenaka's introduction to Okinawan music came in 1969, while researching a series of LPs for the URC label entitled *Nihon kinkashū* (Japanese 'banned song' collection). The series (three records were released early in 1970) featured performances from mainland Japanese working-class performing arts,[8] with the third disc devoted to the mainland Okinawan musician Kadekaru Rinshō, and the Yaeyamans Yamazato Yūkichi and Daiku Tetsuhiro. Takenaka seems to have fallen in love with Okinawan music from early on, and he was particularly drawn to an earthiness and eroticism that had all

---

[7] 侗

[8] The Edo Kappore performer Sakuragawa Pinsuke and the Kyushu performer Hakata Tankai.

but disappeared from mainland Japanese *min'yō*. Regarding this initial encounter, he wrote in 1972 that:

> On my first trip [to Okinawa] I was attracted by the eroticism inherent in the Ryūkyū *uta-sanshin* tradition, and on the subsequent six trips I have devoted myself to collecting *shunka* [erotic songs] and *nasake-uta* [love songs]. (2002: 313)

At least part of the reason for Takenaka's attraction to Okinawan music seems to have come, like so many Japanese scholars, from the perceived preservation of ancient Japanese *utagaki* traditions in the *mō-ashibi* repertory. He makes specific comparisons, for example, between 20th century Okinawan musicians and musical practices and ancient Japanese poetry collections such as the *Man'yōshū*[9] (e.g. 1975: 103). Takenaka was very much attracted to a romantic image of the erotic aspects of the *mō-ashibi*, which he famously described in 1972 in the Japanese magazine *Erotica* (albeit at the tail end of the flower-power movement) as a 'free love party' (2002: 276). Indeed, Takenaka envisioned his series of Ryūkyū festivals in Tokyo and Kyoto in the mid-1970s as a kind of 'modern-day *mō-ashibi*' (1975: 103–45).

This celebration of the sexual nature of the *mō-ashibi* and Okinawan folk song was not well received by all parts of Okinawan society. In a reaction similar to that faced by Yanagita Kunio's 1928 attempts to present the 'folk' elements of Okinawan culture, many Okinawans felt that an overemphasis on the bawdy elements in Okinawan music was detrimental to the prefecture's image. Takenaka describes, for example, being accused by left-wing elements of Okinawan society of 'discrimination for blackening Okinawa's name with images of sexual anarchy' (2002: 313). Takenaka himself was very much aware that:

> These [songs] are discriminated against and held in contempt in Okinawa as a vulgar part of the repertory. Of course the singers [of such songs] are seen in a similar way, and it's the classical [court music] musicians who control the traditional music world and are socially respected. (1975: 103)

Nevertheless, his depiction of what he saw partly as the living carriers of ancient Japan's musical culture to mainland Japan, with an overt emphasis on the sexual nature of the music and the connection to the *mō-ashibi* tradition, was hugely influential in creating both an image of, and a market for, Okinawan music in Japan. The unease on the Okinawan side at the appropriation of images of the *mō-ashibi* as a representation of Japan's primitive past is understandable, especially in the context of earlier 20th century portrayals of Okinawans as 'backward', such as that at the Osaka exposition in 1905. The desire to 'catch up' with Japan, and

---

[9]   He refers specifically to a section known as the *sōmon*, which contains songs connected with the *utagaki* tradition.

'consequent hypersensitivity to any perceived backwardness' (Siddle 2003: 138) have been strong forces against the practice and cultural memory of the *mō-ashibi* within Okinawa for much of the 20th century.

Language

Languages and dialects have been one of the most important foci around which ideas of nationhood and regionality have been constructed in countries around the world (e.g. Geertz 1973: 241–3). In an influential book *The Hegemony of Homogeneity* (2001), an analysis of the so-called *Nihinjinron* (theory of Japanese-ness), the anthropologist Harumi Befu has argued that the (standard) Japanese language has been one way in which discourses of Japanese cultural unity have been played out – that the ability to speak Japanese is a prerequisite for claiming Japanese identity. Since the early 20th century, guided by a need to integrate into the Japanese political and cultural system, local Okinawan languages and dialects began to be largely abandoned in favour of the national Japanese standard modes of speech, and one of the ways in which this change in language use was encouraged and legitimised was through the creation of a local Yaeyaman song repertory in standard Japanese. Similar movements can of course be found around the world – Tuohy has described how, in 20th-century China, 'vocal music proved to be a vehicle for the dissemination of national standard speech' (2001: 117). In this section I look at how Yaeyaman music-making has been influenced by the spread of standard Japanese in Yaeyaman life, and give some examples of Japanese being actively promoted through the use of music.

The difference between standard Japanese and Okinawan languages[10] has been likened to that between French and Italian (e.g. Lebra 1966: 8), in that while the two are obviously of the same origin, they are largely mutually unintelligible. Even within Yaeyama, the dialects of certain islands are largely unintelligible to those from other islands – the Yonaguni and Hateruma dialects, in particular, are considerably different from Ishigaki dialects. In a study of Okinawan life in the mid-1960s Lebra wrote that 'generally, old people and children speak only

---

[10] Okinawan languages are generally known when speaking in standard Japanese as 'dialects' (*hōgen*) of Japanese. Although I heard the term '*Okinawa-go*' (Okinawan *language*) used on occasion, it is a somewhat politically sensitive term, and would often be qualified by a statement to the effect that Okinawan is actually a part of the 'Japanese' language. In Yaeyama the Okinawan expression '*Uchināguchi*' (Okinawan) normally refers to the dialect(s) of Okinawan based in Shuri and Naha in the Okinawan mainland. Local dialects are described using terms such as '*kutuba*' (cf. Japanese *kotoba* – word) or '*muni*'. In Yonaguni, for example, the local dialect is known as '*Dunan kutuba*' (Yonaguni speech). The Taketomi dialect is known in Taketomi as '*Tēdun muni*' (Taketomi speech). In other villages I heard expressions such as '*sïma muni*' and '*sïma kutuba*' (local speech – *sïma*, normally meaning 'island', can also mean village/home town).

Okinawan, and country people, especially women, appear to be more articulate in the native tongue ... the use of Okinawan may be expected to decline rapidly in the next two decades' (1966: 9), a prediction that has certainly been fulfilled. Although there are Yaeyaman villages and islands such as Miyara or Yonaguni where dialect is still spoken to some extent in everyday life by young people, there is a general division in most areas of modern Yaeyama between people born during the Taishō period (1912–1926) who use local dialects as a first/preferred language when speaking to people of the same age, and those born in the Shōwa period (1926–1989) and after, who speak predominantly standard Japanese. Despite efforts to teach local dialects in schools, or through the recent phenomenon of 'dialect competitions' (*sïma muni taikai*), the children I encountered in the early 21st century spoke almost no Yaeyaman language, and often had great difficulty understanding the speech of their (great) grandparents. One informant in his seventies told me that he spoke dialect with friends of the same age, not because he finds it easier than Japanese, but merely so that he doesn't forget it. When he speaks to younger people, however, they can't always understand him perfectly, so he finds it easier to speak in standard Japanese. Another comment I frequently heard was that young people have trouble mastering the complex patterns of polite speech that exist in Yaeyaman dialects (as they do in standard Japanese) and, rather than being scolded for appearing impolite in a language in which they were only partly fluent, many preferred to stick to standard Japanese, in which they were more confident of using the correct forms.

The move away from the use of local dialects, and the widespread adoption of standard Japanese in the early 20th century were largely connected with the national school system. The first schools in Yaeyama, established towards the end of the 19th century under the central Japanese education system, naturally used standard Japanese as the official language of instruction, but local dialects continued to be used in most aspects of everyday life until the early 1930s. While Taishō Japan was seen as a period of democracy with a relatively liberal attitude to local customs, the early Shōwa period saw a rapid move towards militarisation of the country accompanied by the active promotion of a national identity. In an effort to promote this national identity, a move to establish the use of standard Japanese seems to have been rigorously implemented and embraced by many levels of Yaeyaman and Okinawan society. From 1931 the local Okinawan prefectural government adopted slogans such as 'local dialect must be eradicated without fail' (*hōgen wa kanarazu bokumetsu seraru beki*) and 'standard Japanese from the time of the baby's first bath' (*ubuyu no toki kara hyōjungo*), and a drive was implemented to use only standard Japanese both in educational institutions and in general society (Morita 1999: 182). By 1939, as part of a general movement towards the promotion of a feeling of national unity as Japanese nationals, the use of standard Japanese began to be emphasised further. By 1940 the use of standard Japanese was an official policy throughout Okinawa prefecture – all public meetings and political speeches had to be performed in standard Japanese, children were expected to speak standard Japanese inside and outside school, and fines were introduced for teachers who used the Yaeyaman language in the classroom. One of the principal methods used in the eradication of local languages in schools was the 'dialect board' (*hōgen fuda*), a wooden board worn around their neck to shame students who had transgressed the 'standard Japanese' rule (for an in-depth study of the *hōgen fuda* in Okinawa see Kondō 2008). The strict educational environment in schools in Yaeyama had noticeable results – according to one Yaeyaman journalist, within a year of the implementation of the '*ubuyu no toki kara hyōjun'go*' slogan the majority of households in Yaeyama were using standard Japanese to communicate at home (Tōbaru 1970: 57).

While it is tempting to see the suppression of Okinawan languages in favour of standard Japanese as a colonial-style imposition of power by the Japanese mainland, the movement seems to have been pushed particularly hard at a prefectural government level also. The so-called *hōgen ronsō* (dialect controversy) in 1940 is indicative of the political climate in Okinawa at the time, and reveals again the complex discourses taking place between Okinawan and Japanese spheres of influence. The controversy centred around the Japanese mainland folk crafts scholar Yanagi Muneyoshi and members of his Folk Crafts Association, who had visited Okinawa in late 1939, and publicly criticised many aspects of a rapidly modernising prefecture in early 1940, including the prefectural government's attempts to eradicate local languages in favour of standard Japanese (see Oguma 1998: 392–407). As we saw earlier, Yanagi and other Tokyo scholars had been interested in Okinawa as a site for the preservation of diversity within 'Japanese' culture, and they were particularly worried about the detrimental effects that rapid abolishment of Okinawan languages in favour of the standard speech of Tokyo would have. The prefectural government countered that the ability to use standard Japanese was essential for the acceptance of Okinawans into Japanese society, and objected to Yanagi's attempts to hold back progress in Okinawa in favour of a group of Tokyo scholars. In a similar way to the 1903 Osaka incident, the Okinawan government objected particularly to a kind of 'ethnic' objectification by Yanagi that attempted to prevent them from being full members of the modern Japanese state.

The suppression of local language culture by the Okinawan government naturally extended beyond spoken language to have profound effects on folk songs sung in local dialects. Two graduates[11] of Hatoma elementary school in the pre-WWII years remember:

> At that time, as well as speaking in dialect, the singing of folk songs was punished [in school]. Now people who can play *sanshin* are respected, but at that time they were seen as a lower class. At that time you couldn't even imagine that children would play the *sanshin*. Education was centred on the emperor system – Yamato-based. (Hatoma Shōgakkō sōritsu Hyakushūnen Kinenshi Henshū Iinkai 1997)

---

[11] Yonemori Seiyu (graduated 1931) and Fuzato Zen'ichi (graduated 1941).

There are several examples of pre-WWII compositions by Yaeyaman composers that, as well as being written in standard Japanese, also actively promote its use. Miyara Chōhō's 1919 song *Hatsuon Shōka* (Pronunciation Song), composed while working as head teacher of a primary school in the Okinawan mainland, is one such example. The very real problems encountered by Okinawans at this time in speaking standard Japanese can be seen from the first verse, attempting to teach Okinawan schoolchildren to distinguish between the 'r' and 'd' consonants of standard Japanese, a distinction not present in many Okinawan dialects.

Hatsuon Shōka 発音唱歌 (Pronunciation Song)

Waga manabigo no hatsuon wa	Let's all pronounce
Da gyō to ra gyō o yoku tadashi	our 'da' and 'ra' sounds correctly
Shisō tokki ni shitasaki o	touch your tongue to the alveolar bone
Furete dashitara da ji dzu de do	And make the sound Da Ji dzu de do
Shitasaki magetara ra ri ru re ro	Curl the tip of your tongue for ra ri ru re ro
Maeba ni furetara za ji zu ze zo	Put your tongue on your front teeth for Za ji zu ze zo

(Words and music: Miyara Chōhō, 1919. In Ōyama 2003: 16)

The results of these early attempts to promote standard Japanese were by no means immediate. In another example from 1939, some 20 years later, the Ishigaki elementary school commissioned the *Hyōjungo Kōshinkyoku* (Standard Language March):

Miyo wa Shōwa da, kōa no kaze da	This is the age of Shōwa, sweeping through Asia
Bokura wa akarui Nihon no kodomo	We are cheerful Japanese children
Kyō mo niko niko hogaraka ni	Every day we smile happily
Kotoba wa hatsuratsu hyōjun'go	And enthusiastically speak the standard language

(Words: Miyara Takao; music: Itosu Chōryō.[12]
In *Kainan Jihō* newspaper, 2 July 1939)

The imperialistic overtones of these lyrics are of course indicative of the age in which they were written but, again, it is important to remember that this impetus did not come solely from Tokyo, but was largely supported within certain sections of Okinawan society.

---

[12]   Itosu Chōryō, a prominent Yaeyaman teacher of (Western) classical music in the 20th century, would play a leading role in promoting traditional music in Yaeyama (see Chapter 5).

In addition to these early musical attempts to encourage the use of standard Japanese, the early 20th century also saw a movement to reinterpret Yaeyaman folk songs in the language of Tokyo. The issue of language appeared prominently in attempts by Yaeyaman musicians at this time to present a 'traditional' Yaeyama in a 'modern' context. Miyara Chōhō's radical arrangement/re-composition of the *fushiuta Hatoma bushi* in 1921 added completely new lyrics in standard Japanese extolling the virtues of this tiny island.

Umi no ma(n)naka ni tada hitotsu	Standing alone in the middle of the sea
Nio no ukisu ka Hatoma-shima	Like the floating nest of a grebe,
	Hatoma island

(Ōyama 2003: 19)

As well as re-writing the lyrics of this song in standard Japanese, musical aspects of the composition/arrangement also suggest an attempt to position the song within a mainland Japanese context. A comparison of the piano introduction of Miyara's version with that of the traditional version (usually played on *sanshin*) shows a close resemblance (Example 3.1). The original version of the song uses two *ritsu* tetrachords – e-f#-a and b-c#-e in this transcription.[13] The shift of the notes c# and f# to c and f respectively corresponds to a drop of the infix of these two tetrachords to produce two *miyakobushi* tetrachords: e-f-a and b-c-e.

Example 3.1   Instrumental intro to *Hatoma bushi*: traditional version on *sanshin* (a) from Ōhama (1964); Miyara Chōhō's 1921 version on piano (b)

Source: From Ōyama 2003: 19.

The *miyakobushi* scale, while commonly used in a variety of mainland Japanese genres, is never found in Yaeyaman traditional music, and its use here is suggestive of an attempt to position his song, and by association Yaeyama, within a Japanese cultural framework.

---

[13]   Absolute pitch is arbitrary in the performance of Yaeyaman music. The song is more commonly performed around a major 3rd lower than shown in the transcription.

Another example of the use of standard Japanese in an attempt to position Yaeyama within a Japanese cultural framework can be seen in 1934, when the Nippon Columbia record company decided to make extensive recordings of songs from all parts of Okinawa prefecture for the commercial Japanese market (see Ishigaki-shi Sōmu bu shishi henshūshitsu 1990 for an account of the making of these recordings). A Yaeyaman group was assigned by the Okinawa Prefectural Board of Education under the musical instruction of Miyara Chōhō, and organised largely by Kishaba Eijun. The Yaeyaman musicians Ōhama Tsurō, Sakiyama Yōnō and Nakamoto Masako[14] were designated as performers. In planning the programme for recording, the record company decided that in addition to traditional songs in the Yaeyaman language, there should also be a performance in standard Japanese. In a newspaper article relating the events leading up to the recording session in Osaka (Ishigaki-shi Sōmu bu shishi henshūshitsu 1990), Kishaba described how the objective was to present folk songs in a way that could be understood by listeners from all over Japan by recomposing lyrics in standard Japanese, while retaining the Yaeyaman 'local colour' (*rōkaru karā*) in the form of the traditional melodies. The logic behind this approach seems to have been inspired, at least in part, by examples of 'local' Japanese folk songs such as *Ohara bushi* from Kagoshima prefecture, and *Sado Okesa* from Niigata prefecture, which had gained nationwide popularity after being rearranged into standard Japanese versions (ibid.: 521). The direct result of this musical ideology was the creation of the most famous, and still the most widely performed Okinawan song, *Shin-asadōya yunta* ('New' *Asadōya yunta*). Kishaba Eijun commissioned standard Japanese lyrics from the Shiraho-born poet Hoshi Katsu, and Miyara Chōhō re-arranged the melody of the work song *Asadōya yunta*, which in its original lyrics told the story of a beautiful young Taketomi girl and the advances made toward her by local government officials (Kishaba 1990: 520–21; see also Miki 1992: 130–32). This new 'popular version' (*fukyūban*) of the song was released as the B-side of a 78rpm record, with the original version of the song on the A-side. While the song is usually accompanied today by *sanshin* and other 'Okinawan' instruments, in an effort to be more 'modern' and accessible to a national audience, the original 1934 recorded version contained only piano and violin accompaniment. In contrast to the 32 or so verses in the original song, the new version had been trimmed down to just four (a fifth verse extolling the virtues of Okinawa prefecture was subsequently added), and the original 5-4 syllabic structure of the Yaeyaman lyrics was replaced by the Japanese-influenced 7-7-7-5 form.[15] The 1934 Columbia recording also contains a middle verse containing only the piano and violin accompaniment, over which the

---

[14]   The choice of performers is interesting as, with the exception of Ōhama Tsurō, they were not big names in the *fushiuta* lineages. Sakiyama and Nakamoto (who was Miyara Chōhō's sister) were both known as performers in Ishigaki drinking establishments (*sakanayā*).

[15]   Often known as the *dodoitsu* form (*keishiki*).

listener can sing – a forerunner of the 'karaoke versions' of songs widely available on modern Japanese pop recordings.[16]

Shin-Asadōya yunta (1934)

(sa) Kimi wa nonaka no	(7)	You are like the flower
Ibara no hana ka	(7)	on a bramble bush
(sā yui yui)		
kurete kaereba	(7)	When I try to return home
(yare honni)		in the evening
hiki tomeru	(5)	you snare me
(mata harinu chindara		*(hayashi)* how sad, my darling
kanushama yo)		

(Lyrics: Hoshi Katsu. Translated from Ōhama 2004b: 63)

The strategy worked, and the song became popular all over Japan,[17] and has entered the 'traditional' Okinawan canon as one of the most widely-known songs in the repertory, and one of the first songs that a performer of traditional music is taught. The song continues to be widely known throughout Japan, partly due to recent cover versions by mainland Japanese musicians such as Hosono Haruomi and Sakamoto Ryūichi (see Chapter 7).

The Columbia recordings show an attitude at the time both of the Japanese industry wanting to use Yaeyaman songs within the context of 'Japanese musical culture', and also the willingness of the Yaeyamans, under the guidance of the cultural elite of the day, to reinterpret Yaeyaman music in a Japanese context. While *Shin-asadoya yunta* is by far the best known of the standard Japanese re-workings of traditional Yaeyaman material from this period, there are numerous other examples of songs in a traditional style using standard Japanese. *Yaeyama sodachi* by the Tonoshiro singer Ōhama Tsurō in conjunction with the lyricist Hoshi Katsu, or *Urizun no uta* by the Shiraho-born Nakasone Chōichi are well known examples that have entered the canon of Yaeyama music and are regularly performed today.

Following Japan's defeat in WWII, and with Okinawa under American control from 1945 to 1972, Okinawa began to experience a rebirth of confidence in the use of local languages in traditional music. Nevertheless, the urge to suppress Okinawan language use in schools was still strong, and there was a movement to promote standard Japanese throughout the 1950s and 1960s as part of the

---

[16]   This was a common feature of Japanese pop recordings of the time.

[17]   The song was reinterpreted once again in a 1944 war song (*gunka*) entitled *Nanpō bushi* by the Japanese composer Hattori Ryōichi. The *hayashi* lyrics '*chindara kanushama yo*' (how sad my sweetheart) were reputedly reinvented by war-time Japanese soldiers as '*shindara kamisama yo*' (if you die you become a god).

reversion (to Japan) movement (Oguma 1998: 556–96). I return to the question of language in more recent Yaeyaman music in Chapter 7, when we will see that, despite these pre-WWII attempts at the promotion of standard Japanese, local Yaeyaman dialects have continued to play an important part in local music into the 21st century.

神ぬ世

Chapter 4
Music for Gods, Ancestors and People – Yaeyaman Music in a Ritual Context

For much of the year Taketomi is a sleepy island community, famous – thanks to a 1987 architectural planning law – for preserving the old-style Okinawan houses and gleaming white coral-scattered paths. The current (2010) population of 313[1] belies a much larger Taketomi diaspora in Ishigaki, Okinawa and mainland Japan, which maintains strong links to the ancestral island. Taketomi sees a steady flow of tourists throughout the year taking the 10-minute ferry ride from Ishigaki, yet the absence of the large-scale resort-style hotels found in other parts of Okinawa has largely maintained the somnambulant atmosphere in this subtropical time-slip. All of this changes for two days every year in autumn, as the population is temporarily multiplied well beyond its logistical capacity with the return of the Taketomi diaspora from around Japan, together with Tokyo film crews, folklorists, university research students and tourists, to witness the spectacle known as *Tanadui*[2] – the 'rice planting festival' that is the focal point of the Taketomi ritual calendar. Singing groups accompanied by drums and gongs parade through the villages performing ritual songs in the open area in front of important houses well into the small hours of the morning. But the main event takes place during daylight hours on a temporary stage set up facing towards one of the most important shrines of the island, as villagers offer offertory performances (*hōnō geinō*) to the gods of the shrine and the assembled spectators.

Tanadui is probably Yaeyama's best-known ritual event, and its designation by the Japanese government as an Important Intangible Folk Cultural Property (*Jūyō mukei minzoku bunkazai*) in 1977 has given it a national prominence, yet similar ritual events continue to take place throughout Yaeyama, with a variety of sacred and social functions and meanings.[3] From the unaccompanied *ayō* used in rituals to welcome the gods on their visits from the otherworld, to the *fushiuta* used to accompany dancing for the gods at agricultural festivals and for the ancestors

---

[1]   Figure published by Taketomi town tourist society, www.painusima.com/data.htm, accessed 15 February 2011.

[2]   *Tanedori* in standard Japanese.

[3]   The first Okinawan festival to be designated in this category was Tarama's Harvest festival in 1976. Other Yaeyaman designations include Yonaguni's 'festival performing arts' (1985), Iriomote's *Shichi* festival (1991) and Kohama's 'ritual performing arts' (2007).

at Buddhist festivals, the use of ritual is often cited as a primary reason for the strength of survival of traditional music making in Yaeyama (e.g. Daiku Tetsuhiro in DeMusik Inter 1998a: 90; Misumi 1976: 233; cf. Schnell 1999: 288). One of the group BEGIN's defining images of Yaeyama in their song *Shimanchu nu takara* at the beginning of Chapter 1 was the traditional music that is performed at festivals in every Yaeyaman village. While songs continue to be performed in a ritual context throughout Okinawa, the depth to which traditional music is tied to ritual events is a defining characteristic of most Yaeyaman villages. In the Okinawan mainland the presence of a court music tradition, followed by a thriving professional music and drama scene in the 20th century, has meant that the presence of village-based ritual events and in turn village-based music-making, while still important, has been somewhat eclipsed by the use of traditional music as pure entertainment. In Yaeyama, however, the absence of a major professional music scene has meant that village ritual music has continued to play a major part in people's traditional musical lives.

Many studies have shown how ostensibly religious musical traditions may serve both a ritual and secular function, often at the same time. Terence Lancashire's (1997) study of Iwami Kagura, for example, showed how this genre retains to some extent its traditional shrine performance contexts, while also serving as entertainment and as a symbol of local traditional culture through completely secular contexts in concert halls. Sociologists from Durkheim (1912/1926) onwards have noted the role of religion in regulating other aspects of society, and Yaeyaman rituals, too, play an important social function in modern Yaeyaman life. Many Yaeyaman belief systems are intrinsically linked with ancestral systems, which are in turn connected to the way that most Yaeyaman village societies are structured, and thus concepts of ritual belief and social identity are often intricately connected.

The continued importance of ritual music performance within Yaeyama has also given the islands a prominence within the Okinawan and Japanese cultural worlds – of the nine Okinawan ritual genres currently (in 2009) designated as national Important Intangible Folk Cultural Properties, four are from Yaeyama (while Yaeyama's population accounts for less than 4 per cent of the Okinawan total). With the increase of tourism since the reversion of Okinawa to Japan in 1972, festivals have been used to some extent, as in towns all over Japan, to promote tourism, and many festivals have thus taken on cultural meanings outside their original ritual ones. Some islands, such as Taketomi, have been extremely successful in promoting their culture outside Yaeyama, and have used *Tanadui* very skilfully as part of a tourism campaign. Yet these changes have often prompted discourses concerning the proper role of ritual and traditional music in the context of a diversifying Yaeyaman society.

In this chapter I examine aspects of Yaeyaman festivals and rituals, and the role they continue to play in providing a context for the performance of traditional music in Yaeyama. I begin with an outline of Yaeyaman ritual life, followed by several short accounts of traditional music in Yaeyaman festivals, performed ostensibly for the agricultural gods and the spirits of the ancestors. In the final section I consider some of the debates surrounding the role of ritual music 'for the people', as the performance of ritual music has adapted to a changing Yaeyaman society in the 20th century and beyond.

Religion in Yaeyama

Indigenous Yaeyaman beliefs show many resemblances to mainland Okinawan and ancient Japanese religious systems, with an emphasis on ancestor worship that has to some extent been incorporated into a Buddhist framework. The importance of ancestral connections can be seen from the fact that Yaeyaman towns and villages are still divided into districts based on *tunimutu*,[4] households which are regarded as being the place where the founders of a village lived. Villages were originally formed around single family groups, and *tunimutu* are still connected with particular families to whom related families maintain allegiance (e.g. Miyara 1973: 153). A more important focus for many Yaeyaman festivals are the village shrines (*utaki*[5]), and religious services based in these *utaki* are usually led by female ritual specialists known as *tsukasa* (also *tsïkasa*, *chikasa*. For an account of female ritual specialists in Okinawa see Allen 2002). *Utaki* operate separately from the *tunimutu* system, but there is still a strong connection between membership of a *tunimutu* and the *utaki* to which one is connected, and both *tunimutu* and *utaki* membership have a strong influence on membership of performance groups for festival music.

A general feature of festivals in Yaeyama is that they are performed for gods who visit the village for the duration of the festival. Consequently, an important part of most festivals is a ceremony greeting the gods at the beginning and seeing them off at the end, at which music usually plays an important part. These gods are usually divided by Japanese researchers into intangible (*mukei*) – i.e. unseen by the festival gatherers – or tangible (*yūkei*) – represented by members of the village wearing costumes and masks (Karimata 1999: 77). The indigenous gods of agriculture in Yaeyama are believed to reside in a mythical 'other world', *Nirai-Kanai*,[6] usually considered to be situated over the seas to the east. While the ancestors also reside in an 'afterworld' (*gusō*), there is disagreement over its exact location and nature. Orikuchi regards the ancestral afterworld as being essentially the same place as *Nirai-Kanai* (1995: 29), while many Yaeyaman scholars, such

---

[4] In the Okinawan mainland, *tunimutu* are known as *nīdukuru*, *nīya* or *murudukuru*. The gods (*nīgami*) worshipped in *tunimutu* are somewhat analogous to the mainland Japanese *ujigami*.

[5] Also *on*, *wan*, *wā*, *ugan*, *yama* (see e.g. Hateruma 1999: 15). The term *utaki* was encouraged by the Shuri government in the days of the Ryūkyū kingdom, but never penetrated totally into Yaeyama culture (Hateruma 1992: 44).

[6] Known also by a number of related terms such as *Nirasuku-Kanerasuku* or *Nīran*.

as Kishaba Eijun and Karimata Keiichi, make a clear distinction between the two, with *Gusō* connected to an Buddhist-influenced ancestor worship belief system, and *Nirai-kanai* to a separate agricultural belief system (see Karimata 1999: 51–2).

A distinction is also made between songs sung by festival participants to accompany the gods as they progress around the village, and the music and dances performed as part of a staged entertainment, ostensibly 'for the gods' but also naturally directed towards a human audience. The former type, often referred to as *ayō*, includes a wide range of performance situations, including processional songs (*michiyuki uta*), ring dances (*maki-odori*), and songs sung inside houses or gardens of village members, and are usually sung accompanied only by stick drums and gongs. The fact that these songs are usually performed while moving between different village or island locations means that they often have a function of constructing and reinforcing the connection between ritual belief and particular places in a village. Several studies have noted the way music is used as a way of delineating geographic spaces, and serving as a way in which communal memory of history is connected with physical sites in the present. Roseman (1998) has written of the way the Temiars of peninsular Malaysia 'map and mediate their relationships with the land and each other through song'. Cohen, likewise, has described the use of music as a way of 'sounding out the city', in many cases enabling the 'creation and performance of place through human bodies in action and motion' (1995: 445). In a study of the way in which brass bands in New Orleans are used as a way of constructing and negotiating communal conceptions of space, Sakakeeny has similarly described how the 'making of particular sounds in particular places is a way of producing locality' (2010: 24). In a ritual context, the way in which concepts of faith are physically embodied through the performance of music and dance has been examined by Sklar (2001) and Barz (2003). Likewise, many Yaeyaman ritual songs serve as a way of sonically 'performing' the spatial connections between the gods and particular locations in the village in a public way. I examine a number of examples below.

The second type of songs, often known as *hōnō geinō* (offertory performances), are usually performed on a stage set up in front of the main *utaki* (shrine) of a festival, and often consist of dances together with *sanshin*-accompanied *fushiuta*. While *hōnō geinō* are ostensibly offerings for the gods, they are of course also the focal point of a festival in terms of entertainment for the people. The richness and ubiquity of Yaeyaman *hōnō geinō* in Yaeyama (in comparison to Miyako for example) is a defining feature of the musical life of the Yaeyaman islands, and one of the reasons for the continued importance of traditional music.[7]

---

[7]   Hateruma (1999: 636) distinguishes between songs sung directly in praise of the gods (*kami-uta*), songs that describe the purpose of a festival, and songs which are incidental to the rituals making up a festival. He views the *fushiuta* used in *hōnō geinō* as being in peripheral position in the overall picture of ritual song (ibid.: 635–6). This is certainly true in as much as they (and their lyrics) do not serve a direct ritual purpose, and are therefore not necessarily 'ritual songs' as such. However festivals remain an important context for

Offertory performances in Yaeyama are particularly connected with the Buddhist-inspired deity *Miruku*[8] (Figure 4.1). This masked deity is worshipped at festivals in most Yaeyaman villages – for example at the Harvest festival (*pūrï* or *hōnensai*) in Ishigaki, Shiraho and numerous other villages, or at *Tanadui* in Taketomi. In Kohama the similar (in appearance) god *Fukurukujū* appears instead of *Miruku* at the *ketsugan* festival. While *Miruku* has origins as a Buddhist deity, in his Okinawan incarnation he has been reinvented in the context of the indigenous *Nirai-Kanai* belief system, and is seen primarily as an agricultural ritual god (see Karimata 1999: 118–19). Yet in contrast to the indigenous gods that reside in *Nirai-Kanai* in often strange and frightening forms, *Miruku*'s smiling and friendly appearance gives him a unique place among Okinawan deities.[9] Karimata (1999: 183) suggests that *Miruku*'s 'friendly' personality was crucial in promoting the cultural importance of festivals in Yaeyama in the Ryūkyū kingdom years. As the aristocracy spread belief in *Miruku*, they also encouraged the performance of the offertory song and dance performances in festivals that continue to the present. In Miyako, where there was less interaction between aristocrats and peasants, and where a *Miruku* belief was not disseminated strongly, there is no strong *hōnō geinō* tradition comparable to that in Yaeyama (Karimata 1999: 185–6). This influence of Shuri officials on the formation of a large number of festivals containing *hōnō geinō* also seems to have led to the 'staggering' of the timing of festivals around the various islands in Yaeyama. While most villages and islands perform roughly the same set of festivals throughout the year – *Pūrï, Ketsugansai, Shichi matsuri* – the festival at which the island stages its big *hōnō geinō* performances is not the same. Taketomi stages its most important *hōnō geinō* at *Tanadui*, Kuroshima at the Harvest festival, Kohama at the *Ketsugansai*, etc. During the period of rule by the Shuri court, festivals played a key role in defining and maintaining relations between the common people and the ruling elite, and the 'staggering' of *hōnō geinō* so that the biggest event in one village does not coincide with that in other villages is evidence that the festivals were organised largely for the benefit of the government officials and were timed so that they were able to travel around Yaeyama visiting as many festivals as possible throughout the year (Karimata 1999: 131).

---

the performance of these songs, and it is in this sense that I include their performance in this chapter.

[8]   Japanese *Miroku*. From Sanskrit *Maitreya* – lit. 'the benevolent one'. This god is also common in the Japanese mainland where it has been worshipped from as early as AD 584 (Kodansha 1983: 198).

[9]   This 'approachable' image has entered the Okinawan consciousness to such an extent that in the early 21st century *Miruku* appeared for a time in a television commercial for the *Ryūkyū Shinpō* newspaper.

Figure 4.1   *Miruku* at 2002 Harvest festival in Hatoma

Ritual Music in Yaeyaman Society

Yaeyaman rituals take place at a variety of societal levels, including the village/island, various sub-divisions of the village (such as *buraku*, *tunimutu* or *utaki*), and individual families. Eligibility (and in some cases obligation) to participate in a ritual or part of a ritual usually depends on membership of one or more of these groups. For example, the Harvest festival of all sub-divisions of a particular village takes place on the same two days in a particular year, yet rituals and performances usually take place separately depending on *utaki* division within each village. In most Harvest festivals, the first day of the festival[10] is held separately at each *utaki* in the village, whereas the second day (*mura-pūrï*) is generally performed in a single location by the village as a whole.

While many agricultural rituals in Yaeyama were abandoned or considerably downgraded in importance during the 20th century, ritual and spiritual belief continue to play an important part in festivals. In Taketomi, for example, although most festival participants take part almost entirely through the performance of offertory song and dance performances, the role of the festival as an interface with the world of the gods is still taken quite seriously. One informant described to me how, in September 2001, Taketomi sent a group to perform dances from *Tanadui*

---

[10]   *On* is another term for *utaki* (shrine), *pūrï* is the usual Ishigaki language term for 'harvest festival'.

in Shuri castle in the Okinawan mainland. The days before the concert saw the approach of a typhoon which threatened to cancel the outdoor performance. On the day of the performance, the skies had miraculously cleared and the event took place. On the advice of the Taketomi performers, the (mainland Okinawan) organisers of the event subsequently visited Taketomi to thank the gods for allowing the performance to go ahead (Kamei, pers. comm. November 2001). Likewise, the Kohama flute player Ishigaki Yasunobu told me, 'of course, the way we carry out festivals has changed to a certain extent. The songs people play and the clothes they wear are different now. But the basic meaning of the festival hasn't changed. We are still basically playing songs and dances for the gods (*hōnō geinō*)' (pers. comm. September 2001). Even outside festivals themselves, the ritual calendar and belief systems still determine the songs that can be performed at particular times of year. Songs such as the semi-ritual song *Funā bushi* (*Kunā bushi*) are only allowed to be performed at certain times of year (early summer in the case of *Funā bushi*). Sakieda Kiyo, a *tsukasa* in Arakawa who I interviewed in December 2001, refused to sing the song for me, saying that I would have to come back in May the following year. The attitude seems to be weakening among the younger generation, however. The head of the Arakawa *koyō* preservation group, Takemoto An'i, told me:

> The older people say that you shouldn't sing *Funā bushi* except in the early summer. Really you shouldn't sing it, but I sing it at any time. The trouble is, if you have these restrictions, then nobody will learn the song. Nowadays few people can sing it anyway. Soon there will be nobody at all. (pers. comm. September 2002)

A conflict between the use of ritual songs in their ritual context and the desire to prevent them from disappearing completely was one that I encountered often in Yaeyama. At certain times of year, the playing of music is banned altogether in certain places. Especially in the period prior to certain festivals, it is still considered taboo to play music 'for fun', i.e. outside the organised festival practice sessions. In the summer of 2001 I visited Kohama a few days before the *Akamata-Kuromata* festival (see below) was due to take place. I had travelled with a local Kuroshima-born musician, Asato Isamu, and a Kohama resident, Ishigaki Yasunobu, who was to accompany him in a concert in a large resort hotel in Kohama. Ishigaki was visibly nervous when we were in the main village in Kohama, telling us that we weren't allowed to play music there, and that the 'after-concert party' would have to take place outside the village in the tourist hotel. The secret nature of the *Akamata-Kuromata* festival meant that he did not tell us directly that this was the reason we were not allowed to play music (although everyone else present presumably understood this: Asato filled me in on the details later). A similar attitude exists before *Tanadui* in Taketomi. Although a certain amount of 'dress rehearsal' is now allowed for offertory performances on the day before the main festival starts, older members in their fifties and sixties told me that even this wasn't allowed in the past. The Hazama group that I observed in 2001 practised their performances in the car park of the Taketomi visitor centre, as it was 'outside the official village boundaries' (Ōyama Takeshi, pers. comm. November 2001).

Outside official festival periods, too, ritual beliefs have a strong impact on music-making in Yaeyaman villages. A death in a village, for example, places certain restrictions on the performance of music by other village members. When I observed the Miyara work song preservation group in September 2002, I learned that an elderly woman had died in the village on the previous day, and the leader of the group, Miyara Jitsuan, told me that he had personally been to get permission to sing, as they knew that I was coming to record them on that day. On another occasion the death of the sister of a member of the Tonoshiro *yunta hozonkai*, which I participated in every week, forced her to stop attending the practices of the group for a period of about two months. This seems to have been less a matter of personal choice, than that it 'would not be considered proper for her to sing after a close relative had passed away' (Tominaga, pers. comm. July 2002).

Songs for the Gods: Performed Ritual Beliefs in Taketomi Festivals

Taketomi's *Tanadui*, held in the middle of autumn, is probably the best-known Yaeyaman festival outside Yaeyama due to its national designation in 1977 as an Important Intangible Folk Cultural Property (*Jūyō mukei minzoku bunkazai*). The festival has often been featured by the local and national media, and a number of television companies and journalists were covering the festival when I saw it in 2001. This national interest has obviously had a beneficial effect for the Taketomi economy, encouraging tourists to visit the island throughout the year. Nevertheless, *Tanadui* maintains an important ritual and social function in the island, and I encountered an explicit discourse concerning both the tourist and ritual aspects of the festival among many informants. The festival is known particularly for its *hōnō geinō* (offertory) performances, performed on a temporary stage in the main Taketomi settlement. It also contains an important repertory of ritual songs performed throughout the night after the first day of *hōnō geinō*. In this section, I examine some of the discourses surrounding *Tanadui*, drawing on fieldwork carried out in 2001 and recent publications connected with the festival.

Taketomi, like most of the smaller Yaeyaman islands, has seen a drastic population decrease in recent years. The 1932 figure of 1,400 rose temporarily in 1947 to around 2,200 people due to an influx of returnees from Taiwan after WWII, but a lack of fresh water on the island, accompanied by a lack of jobs, has caused the population to drop to a present (2010) figure of 313, most of whom live in two villages, Hazama and Nakasuji, situated in the centre of the island. Many of the inhabitants are elderly, although there are a considerable number of younger Japanese mainlanders who have been drawn to Taketomi's traditional lifestyle. Until the mid-20th century, Taketomi islanders survived mainly on subsistence farming and small-scale livestock production. Work patterns were still dominated at this time by the traditional communal methods (*bafu*), in which the whole community would come together to perform large jobs such as house building, and *yuimāru*, the working of fields belonging to specific individuals on a 'rotation' basis. From the 1950s, cash crops such as beans, barley and sugar cane began to be grown, but until the late 1960s, trade with Ishigaki and Japan was mainly by barter (Akiyama 1997).

The return of Okinawa to Japan in 1972 meant that suddenly Japanese nationals could visit Okinawa as tourists without the need for a passport. One of the most profound effects on life in Taketomi was the sudden transferral of the main source of income from agriculture to tourism. By 1975, tourism had increased to the extent that there were 23 guesthouses operating on the island, compared with two in 1962. Akiyama (1997) identifies this period as the start of what he calls a 'preservation equals tourist development' (*hozon suru koto ga kankō kaihatsu*) mentality that has led to an explicit approach to preservation of traditional practices in order to make the island more appealing to Japanese tourists. The island itself was included in a national park designation in 1972, providing some protection from development, and the 1977 designation of *Tanadui* as a cultural asset has given the island national prominence. The villages were designated by the Japanese government as a 'National Traditional Architectural Preservation Zone' (*Dentōteki Kenzōbutsu-gun Hozon Chiku*) in 1987, so that even modern concrete houses must be clad in traditional-style wooden boards. As a result of these designations, and in contrast with some other parts of Yaeyama, Taketomi has seen little 'resort-style' development, and the tourist industry is run very much by locals. While mainland Japanese companies started buying up land in Taketomi for development in the early 1970s, this land was mostly bought back by local Taketomi syndicates, and Taketomi today is marked by an almost total lack of the 'resort'-style development to be found in many other parts of Okinawa.

The use of ritual and ritual performance as a way of maintaining and expressing a relationship with the gods is still taken quite seriously by many Taketomi islanders, and while *Tanadui* is by far the biggest and best known of Taketomi's rituals, it is only the tip of an iceberg of ritual and musical activity that takes place throughout the year.[11] One of the most important of Taketomi's rituals, from both a religious and a musical point of view, is the *Yūnkai* (lit. greeting the 'world') ritual on the eighth day of the eighth lunar month. The ritual is particularly important in the ritual calendar as the occasion when the gods visit from *Nirai-kanai* bringing good luck for the coming harvest. Although the ritual lasts only a few hours, and is attended mainly by Taketomi residents actually living on the island, it is still regarded as a key event in the Taketomi ritual year. As one Taketomi informant told me early on during my stay in Yaeyama,

---

[11]   The municipal office lists 19 ritual events throughout the year for 1988 (see Hateruma 1999: 138–9), although there are many smaller rituals that do not appear in this list – Kamei, for example lists 28 (1990: 392–4).

'You can't possibly understand *Tanadui* if you don't also see the *Yūnkai* ritual. Everything starts from there' (Ōyama, pers. comm. August 2001).

I observed the *Yūnkai* ritual in September 2001. The event had been announced across the island on the public address system the night before, and by 7 a.m. there were a handful of tourists and photographers waiting on Tomodoi beach on the west coast of the island,[12] with Kohama and Iriomote islands visible across the water. A group of six *tsukasa* from around the island arrived shortly afterwards, accompanied by the head of the Taketomi municipal office and male representatives from Nakasuji and Hazama villages. They set about arranging mats and ritual *sake* utensils on the beach in front of the '*Nīran*' stone that, according to legend, was used by the gods as an anchor when visiting the island for the first time, bringing the seeds used to feed the islanders (Kamei 1990: 402). After about 20 minutes the *tsukasa* began intoning a chant in barely audible voices (a version is transcribed in Karimata 1999: 78). Ritual *sake* and salt for purification was passed round, after which the head of the municipal office announced '*nza shōri*' (let's sing). Following a brief drum and gong introduction, the group began to sing *Tunchāma*, the principle *Yūnkai* ritual song, while beckoning to the gods with their arms.

Tunchāma

1) *Agato kara kuru funi ya*	The boat coming from over the seas
Baga wi nu tunchāma	Our masters, tunchāma
(uyaki yu ba taboraru)	(Refrain) *We receive the harvest*
2) *Uhara kara kuru funi ya*	The boat coming from the east
Nayushicharu kuru funi	What kind of boat is it?
3) *Miruku yu ba nushiōru*	It contains gifts from Miruku
Kan nu yu ba nushi ōru	It contains gifts from the gods

(Translated from Kamei 1990: 402)

The lyrics of the song, describing the arrival of the gods from *Nirai-kanai*, complement the fact that it is performed facing towards the sea next to the *Nīran* stone where the gods are believed to arrive on the island, to enact the spatial aspects of this aspect of the Taketomi belief system. The presence of the Buddhist deity *Miruku* in the verse – a relatively recent introduction to Yaeyaman ritual life – in what is ostensibly a song welcoming the gods from *Nirai-Kanai*, shows the syncretic nature of Yaeyaman religious beliefs, as well as demonstrating the importance of *Miruku* in Yaeyaman ritual life in general.

After singing the song on the beach, the gods were then led by the *tsukasa* and village representatives up into the villages of Taketomi. The procession began in Nakasuji village, continuing to *Kontu-on*, one of the island's six most sacred

---

[12]   In contrast with the majority of Okinawan villages, *Nirai-kanai* is situated to the west in Taketomi beliefs.

shrines, where a further ritual was performed, and finally to Hazama village, where the procession ended at the municipal office. Originally the procession used to walk up from the beach to Nakasuji, but the few kilometres were covered by minibus in 2001. In both Nakasuji and Hazama, the procession was met by members of each village, also singing *Tunchāma* and beckoning to the gods with their arms, while the *tsukasa* had now altered their hand movements to usher the gods on from behind. The two groups – the procession led by the *tsukasa,* and the welcoming party in the village – started singing while still out of earshot of each other, and as the procession approached the village the songs of the two groups, which were obviously out of synch (and pitch) with each other, gradually come together until the two groups were singing as one group. After a few minutes the song changed to a repetitive '*sā, sā, sā*' motif, as the villagers danced *gāri*, a lively improvised dance similar to the Okinawan *kachāshī* to drum and gong accompaniment.

In this example, we can see the use of the ritual song *Tunchāma* and the *Yūnkai* ritual itself as a way of 'sounding out the island' (cf. Cohen 1995) in the imagination of spatial aspects of traditional Taketomi ritual beliefs. The arrival of the gods from *Nirai-kanai* is described literally in the lyrics of the song, but the fact that the song is performed as the gods are accompanied up from the beach and through the main settlement of Taketomi acts as a way of musically embodying these ideas within the geographical framework of the village. While the number of actual participants in the ritual is relatively few – six *tsukasa* and a similar number of municipal employees greet the gods on Tomodoi beach – the performance of the song while advancing through the streets of the village reinforces the importance of the ritual to all islanders within earshot.

Tanadui itself takes place in mid-autumn on a schedule calculated according to the Chinese zodiacal calendar. The entire festival lasts nine days,[13] with the main musical events taking place on the seventh and eighth days and throughout the intervening night. (For a detailed outline of *Tanadui* timetable see Hateruma 1999: 133–8; Kamei 1990: 199–223; Karimata 1999: 125–31.) Songs performed at the festival are divided into two main types based on performance context: those sung as part of the *hōnō geinō* performances in the garden and on the stage in front of the *Yūmuchi* shrine, consisting mostly of *fushiuta* and Okinawan *sanshin*-accompanied songs; and those sung as part of the *Yūkui* (lit. 'praying for the world') ritual in the streets and houses of the villages from dusk on day seven until daybreak on day eight of the festival. Like *Tunchāma* at the *Yūnkai* ritual, these are sung with only drum and gong accompaniment, and the fact that they are performed at individual houses in the villages, and while walking in between, also serves a similar purpose of 'embodying' the village through song.

In 2001 the *hōnō geinō* section of the festival took place on the 23rd and 24th of November (days seven and eight of the festival), and were performed

---

[13]   The festival previously lasted 11 days, but the rituals of the 10th and 11th days are no longer carried out.

more or less continuously between 10 a.m. and 6 p.m. in front of the *Yūmuchi* shrine. The first hour, known as *niwa no geinō* (garden/yard performances) was performed in a sandy clearing in front of the shrine, while the remainder of the performances (from around 11 a.m. to 6 p.m.) took place on a stage constructed facing towards it. The arrangement of the stage in this fashion, facing directly towards the shrine rather than the audience, is another spatial emphasis that *hōnō geinō* performances are essentially performed for the gods resident in the shrine. Members of the human audience sat on the floor to one side of the stage, with elder members of the Taketomi community occupying the most prestigious area next to the stage. In addition, a special area had been roped off to one side of the stage, from which several television crews were invited to film (on payment of a gratuity).

The content of the performances at *Tanadui* varies from year to year, but some dances and plays are always featured, including the song *Miruku bushi*, performed to accompany the appearance of the masked *Miruku* deity on the stage, and a set of ritual *kyon'gin*[14] plays relating the mythical origins of Taketomi society (see Arai 2000; Hateruma 1999: 556, 574). In addition to these fixed performances, the festival usually includes a large number of *fushiuta* of Taketomi origin, such as *Shikida-bun bushi*, *Tarakuji bushi* and *Asadōya bushi*, as well as a number of *sanshin*-accompanied Taketomi songs such as *Jicchu* and *Nma nu sha* which haven't been incorporated into the Yaeyaman *fushiuta* repertory and are rarely heard outside the context of the Taketomi community. The lyrics of most of these songs have no particular ritual meaning, but describe elements of Taketomi geography and everyday life, reinforcing a sense of Taketomi history and cultural identity in the festival. These songs are performed by a small ensemble (*jikata*) consisting of around six male *sanshin* players and singers, accompanied by *fue*, *taiko* and (female) *hayashi* singers. The Taketomi *jikata*, like other aspects of *Tanadui*, have been proactive in disseminating the music of the festival outside Taketomi, and have recorded a commercial CD on the Okinawan Kokusai Boueki label (see discography), and released a *kunkunshi* of the festival repertory (S. Sakiyama 1997). There are also a number of *kumiodori* and other musical dramas with origins in the Okinawan mainland. The 2001 festival, for example, included *Fushi chūshin*, a *kumiodori* play with origins in the Okinawan mainland that is currently only transmitted in the Taketomi community. The relatively large number of mainland Okinawan songs and dances such as *Kajadifū* reflect Taketomi's historically strong connections with the Ryūkyū court, as well as the fact that these dances are still popular in Taketomi.

---

[14]   Cf. Japanese *kyōgen*.

Songs for the Ancestors

Taketomi's *Tanadui* and other ritual events connected with the agricultural cycle are ostensibly used as a way of communicating with gods from the mythical otherworld *Nirai-kanai*. Another aspect of Yaeyaman traditional beliefs can be seen through a number of ancestor rituals, many of which have a Buddhist origin. The best known of these rituals is *Sōron*, from the 13th to the 15th day of the seventh lunar month (usually between early August and September[15]), when the spirits of the ancestors are believed to return from the afterlife (*gusō*) and temporarily reside in the houses of their living descendants. The *Angamā*[16] ritual, which takes place in the evening of the three days of *Sōron* in Ishigaki, Taketomi, Kohama and Hatoma[17] islands, involves the appearance in tangible form of the spirits (*fāmā*, lit. 'children and grandchildren') of the (village) ancestors who proceed around the houses of a village performing songs and dances for the residents. In Ishigaki the *fāmā* are led by two masked characters, *Ushumai* (old man) and *Nmi* (old woman), who represent the oldest ancestral spirits. A highlight of *Angamā* in Ishigaki is the opportunity for village members to ask these two characters questions concerning the afterlife in an often comical exchange known as *montō* (question and answer).

Yaeyama's *Sōron* is obviously related to the Buddhist *bon*[18] festival found throughout Japan and, in particular, the musical aspects of the *Angamā* ritual show similarities to *Eisā* genres of the Okinawan mainland. There is evidence of Japanese Buddhist influence in the Okinawan mainland through individual travelling monks such as the priest Taichū who travelled to Ryūkyū in 1603, but the religion did not reach Yaeyama until some time after the Satsuma invasion of 1609 (see Karimata 1999: 52). One of the earliest examples was the establishment of the Tōrinji temple in Ishigaki by the Shin'gon sect in 1614. While this official branch of Buddhism was influential among the upper classes, one of the strongest Buddhist influences on the lower classes was that of the wandering monks of the *Jōdo* sect known as *ninbū*, *ninbuchā* or *chondarā*. These disseminators of 'folk-Buddhism' were known all around Okinawa until the early 20th century both for their religious connections, introducing a variety of *nenbutsu*[19] songs to the region,

---

[15]   *Sōron* usually takes place at a different time from the mainland Japanese *bon* festival, which operates according to the Western calendar.

[16]   The meaning of the word *Angamā* is unclear. Miyara Tōsō suggests that it is derived from *anegama* (sister), while Orikuchi Shinobu suggests *amogama* (mother). Although the *Angamā* performed at *Sōron* are the best known, the word is also used to describe dancers in Iriomote's *shichi* festival, at Taketomi's *Tanadui* festival, and in the past at house blessing rituals in Kuroshima.

[17]   The tradition has been discontinued in such places as Hateruma, and has been replaced by *eisā* from the Okinawan mainland in Yonaguni.

[18]   Usually known in its honorific form, '*o-bon*'.

[19]   *Nenbutsu* refers to the reciting of the name of Amida (namu amida-butsu), a practice linked to the Nichiren sect of Buddhism. *Nenbutsu* songs (*nenbutsu uta*) are derived from

and also as entertainers, especially of puppet theatre. It is from these wandering monks that the *Angamā* tradition is believed to derive.

Like Taketomi's *Tanadui*, *Angamā* is performed at a village level, in this case by members of the village youth organisation (*seinenkai*). These organisations generally include members of both sexes, aged from their late teens to mid-thirties.[20] In September 2001 I participated as part of the musical accompaniment of the Arakawa *Angamā* group, which consisted of a musical ensemble of five (four *sanshin* players/singers and one drummer[21]) and about 20 dancers. The head of the youth organisation told me that members should ideally be born in or have a family association with Arakawa, but recently a shortage of participants has prompted them to welcome members from outside (Tominaga pers. comm., September 2001). Four veteran members of the group alternated the *Ushumai* and *Nmi* roles, considered the most demanding because of the need to lead the proceedings in the local dialect, and improvise answers to questions in the *montō* exchange in a convincing and entertaining way. In contrast to *Tanadui* and other agricultural rituals, the audience for the performing arts of the *Angamā* troupe consists not of gods from *Nirai-kanai*, but of the spirits of the ancestors of individual houses, and the main performance activity in the Ishigaki island *Angamā* tradition was directed towards the Buddhist shrine (*butsudan*) in the living room (*ichibanza*) of each house. The Arakawa group performed at four or five private houses during the course of each evening, each house having made a donation to the youth organisation in advance. The visit of the *Angamā* troupe to a family house is an important occasion, and usually celebrates an important life event such as the building or renovation of a new home that must be reported to the ancestral spirits. Typically, 20 or so of the house's extended family formed the core audience inside the main living room, with up to 40 or 50 spectators standing outside the house's open windows to watch the proceedings. A performance at one house usually lasted from 30 to 50 minutes depending on the atmosphere, and the degree of audience participation.

---

this tradition and usually contain Buddhist-influenced lyrics. The basic melodic lines of many Yaeyaman *nenbutsu* songs are very similar, although the accompaniment varies considerably between villages. In Arakawa, *Nzō nenbutsu* is sung during the *Angamā* ritual with the standard *sanshin* accompaniment used by the Ishigaki *sanshin* schools. *Shichigwachi nenbutsu*, however, which is performed in the afternoon of the last day of *Sōron*, is performed with only drum and gong accompaniment. In Kohama *Nzō nenbutsu* and *Shichigwachi nenbutsu* have developed into the fast *hayabiki sanshin* style, and are performed at increasingly fast tempos as the night goes on. All of these songs are believed to have been introduced from the Okinawan mainland, and bear a strong melodic resemblance to songs such as *Chunjun nagari* used in Okinawan *eisā* dances.

[20]   Marriage is often the impetus for retirement from a youth organisation, although I encountered a number of married members in their forties who told me they had stayed on because they enjoyed taking part in the ritual.

[21]   *Fue* (bamboo flute) is also included in some villages.

The group had a repertory of 17 dances, of which seven or eight were performed at any one house. The most important, *Nzō nenbutsu bushi*, was danced at every house visited by the *Ushumai* and *Nmi* characters, and is the only song performed by the Ishigaki island *Angamā* groups that is strictly a *Sōron* ritual song:

Uya nu u-gunu wa (7) *fukaki munu* (5)	The debt to our parents is deep
Chichigu nu u-gunu wa yama takasa	The debt to our father is high as a mountain
Fafagu nu u-gunu wa umi fukasa	The debt to our mother is deep as the sea

(Translated from Ōhama 2004a: 101)

The closeness of the language used in the song to standard Japanese, and the predominantly 7-5 mora structure,[22] show the strong influence of the Japanese mainland on Okinawan *Nenbutsu* songs in general, and the lyrics also reveal the importance of *Sōron* as an ancestral festival. Like *Funā bushi* above, several informants commented that it was taboo to sing *Nzō nenbutsu bushi* 'out of season', and it is usually played only in the weeks leading up to *Sōron* (also Iramina 2002: 50). Of the remaining songs in the Arakawa repertory, *Akanma bushi* was danced by the *Ushumai* and *Nmi*, and the remainder, all from the Yaeyama *fushiuta* repertory, were danced by the *fāmā*. The lively free-dance song *Rokuchō bushi* was performed as a finale, and was usually used as an opportunity for the head of the household to join the dancers, along with the *Ushumai* and *Nmi*.

The Arakawa group also performed a *michi-uta* (road song) while walking through the streets from one house to the next. In common with Taketomi's *Tunchāma*, this song serves to announce the *Angamā* group's presence in the village and to perform their role as an incarnation of the spirits of the ancestors.

Michi-uta

Sōron ganashi nu ushumai da	The lords of the spirit world are here
Shokkoi shī na ottane	Come to burn incense
Shokkōsī oisharā	Burn incense for them
Mīshun māshun fai ōri	Eat *miso* and salt

(Transcribed/translated from field recording, September 2001)

A central feature of *Angamā* as performed in Ishigaki is the *montō* (question and answer) section of the ritual, where members of the public ask questions to the *Ushumai* and *Nmi* characters regarding various aspects of the afterlife. Questions are wide-ranging, and are often light-hearted or comical. In one example that I recorded in Arakawa in 2002, the questioner quizzed Ushumai on what kind of food people eat in the afterlife – the Ushumai explained that the toothless ancestors

---

[22]   As usual there are exceptions, as in lines 2 and 3. Subsequent verses in the 5-verse song follow the 7-5 structure more closely.

could eat only soft foods such as tofu. In the context of the *Angamā* ritual, the purpose of the *montō* session is to emphasise the *Ushumai* and *Nmi* characters' roles as representatives of the ancestors, and for the community to perform its connection with the afterworld. The ritual, being intrinsically connected to the lives of the ancestors, also has a particularly strong connection with discourses of tradition. In particular, the language used in the *montō* section – the language used by the ancestors – is emphasised heavily, and only those group members with a good command of Yaeyaman language are chosen to play the *Ushumai* and *Nmi* roles. The *fushiuta* songs that form the majority of the *Angamā* repertory likewise have a particularly immediate meaning in the context of the ritual, as the songs that the ancestors created in their worldly lifetimes. The *Angamā* ritual, in addition to serving a ritual purpose through connecting with the ancestors, thus also serves as a site through which ideas of tradition – in this case as a recreation of the music speech patterns of the ancestors – are created.

Jūrukunitsï

The importance of connecting with the ancestral spirits through music and dance can also be seen through *Jūrukunitsï* (16th day festival), another important ancestor ritual in the Yaeyaman calendar that takes place on the 16th day of the first lunar month.[23] In contrast to the more public *Angamā* ritual, where the ancestors of individual households are worshipped by members of the village youth organisation, *Jūrukunitsï* is essentially a private family event. Members of an extended family spend most of the afternoon gathered in the enclosure[24] in front of the family grave, on which a large plastic sheet has usually been spread, and spend the afternoon eating and drinking, chatting with one another and communing with the ancestral spirits. Incense, as well as food and drink, are placed in front of the grave as offerings to the ancestors, and in families containing traditional musicians it is common to perform music and dance offerings, facing towards the grave. In contrast with many Yaeyaman festivals, these performances are often very informal and impromptu, but are another important example of the use of traditional music in a ritual context.

In February 2002 I observed (and, as usual, participated musically in) the *Jūrukunitsï* ritual of the family of a local scholar and music expert Ōta Shizuo. The ritual started in the early afternoon (many Yaeyaman businesses and shops

---

[23]   The origins of *Jūrukunitsï* are unclear – the most widely accepted theory states that it derives from a Chinese agricultural ritual introduced into Yaeyama in the 15th century, which developed into an ancestral festival around the 18th century (K. Miyara 1979: 354–8). Although the ritual also exists in the Okinawan mainland, it is much more important and widespread in Yaeyama and Miyako, where prayers and entertainment are performed for all ancestors of patrilineal ascent (Miyara 1973: 301; cf. Lebra 1966: 188).

[24]   The size of these enclosures varies, but can often seat around 20 people.

shut for the afternoon to enable people to attend) and took place at Ōta's family grave in Ishigaki city. The family traces its roots back to Kohama island, and the ritual started in the early afternoon with an offering of incense, food and prayers directly towards the ancestoral spirits in the grave, followed by a similar offering of incense in the geographical direction of Kohama, followed by similar offerings to the ancestors residing in the family grave. Following this short ceremony, the offertory performances began. Most of the songs were taken from the standard Yaeyaman and Okinawan repertory, and had no particular ritual meaning in themselves – as at most Yaeyaman parties the opening song was *Akanma bushi*, and the final song was *Miruku bushi*. Nevertheless, the songs and dances were performed facing towards the family grave and, as with previous examples, were aimed ostensibly at a spiritual audience. The Kohama ancestral connection was emphasised once again as Ōta provided *sanshin* accompaniment for his elderly uncle's singing of *Kohama bushi*. Ōta's daughter, who is an accomplished *fushiuta* performer, played the mainland Okinawan instrumental piece *Tachiutushi* with her grandmother on *sanshin* and brother on *taiko*, and I was invited to play a few dance songs with Ōta, to which his family danced. As the afternoon progressed, a number of relatives dropped in to pay their respects, excusing themselves after a short time, and the ritual finally wound down as it began to get dark, and the participants returned to their daily lives.

Jūrukunitsï, like the *Angamā* ritual, once again demonstrates the way that traditional music is used as a way of 'performing' relationships with the ancestors. The music and dance at *Jūrukunitsï* is also important as a way for individual families to perform the various interpersonal relationships that exist between them. While *Angamā* can be seen as a way in which aspects of ritual beliefs are imagined and maintained at a village level, *Jūrukunitsï* can perhaps be seen as a way in which a family keeps its ancestral affairs in order. Ōta's family connection to Kohama was 'performed' on several occasions during the ritual I witnessed, spatially through the offering of incense towards Kohama, and musically through the performance of *Kohama bushi*. Individual relationships were also 'performed' in the way that different generations – Ōta and his elderly uncle, Ōta's children and their grandmother – played various traditional songs together towards the ancestors that they all share. On the several occasions that I have witnessed *Jūrukunitsï* and the similar Okinawan *Shīmī* ritual since 2002, I have been struck by the way that participants talked especially of more recently departed relations as if they were actually present, in some cases addressing comments directly to them. In many respects, the continued importance of these kinds of direct relations with the ancestors, and the continued popularity of traditional music, form a kind of symbiotic relationship – the tangible presence of the ancestors feeds into a closeness to traditional music and dance, and this familiarity with the ways of prior generations of Yaeyamans fosters a continuing connection to them.

The importance of a direct connection with the ancestors can also be seen to extend beyond particular Buddhist rituals, and applies to many aspects of daily music-making throughout Okinawa. The well-known mainland Okinawan musician Teruya Rinsuke (1929–2005) describes the importance of ancestors on musical performance in his home town of Koza:

> At celebrations, there is a tradition of asking a performer to 'bring good luck' (*karī chikite kumisōre*) ... In Okinawa, when someone dies they become a god. Gods dislike 'imperfect things' (*hanareta koto*), so if music is played for them in an incorrect way they won't listen to it. You have to play in a way where they will say 'Ah, that's my son/grandson'. This may be different in Shuri or Naha, but that's the way it is in Koza. Of course, all kinds of entertainers are important for a celebration, but they are not referred to as *karī chikiyā* (luck-bringers). A *karī chikiyā* has to be able to play the *sanshin*. (Teruya 1998: 315–16)

Again, the importance of being able to play the *sanshin* – as a traditional instrument it is one with which the ancestors are familiar – is seen as necessary to perform music that the ancestors will appreciate.

Songs for the People: The Social Meaning of Festivals

The rituals outlined in previous sections demonstrate some of the ways in which traditional music continues to be used in Yaeyama as a way of interacting with the gods from *Nirai-kanai* and the spirits of the ancestors visiting from *Gusō*. In addition to the strong ritual meaning that these and many other Yaeyaman festivals continue to hold, they also serve an important social function as a context through which social cohesion is achieved and identities are constructed. I often heard discussions related to the social function of ritual and ritual music as a context through which social groups are imagined, and I present some of them here.

One of the most frequently quoted social purposes of festivals is as a way of marking off an individual's progress through village society. Katō (1986) has outlined in detail the way in which festivals in Kohama are both structured around, and are used as a way of publicly 'performing', the age of participants. Similarly, Akiyama has shown how *hōnō geinō* are influential on the social advancement of children through Taketomi society, with almost all children taking part in the festival in some way (1997: 30–32). Particular dances or ritual drama roles in Taketomi, for example, are designated for performers of a certain age – very young children in Taketomi begin their festival career accompanying the Miruku deity on the *Tanadui hōnō geinō* stage, and they progress through various *kyon'gin* and dance roles. Being chosen to play Miruku himself is seen as an honour within Taketomi society, in the same way that playing the *Ushumai* or *Nmi* roles in the Angamā holds the highest status in that tradition, and is only permitted once a certain age has been reached. Even the tradition of elder members of society sitting in front of the stage during *hōnō geinō* performances is a kind of performance of their acquired social status. Haeno Kisaku, a well-known *fushiuta* performer from Kabira, remembers how 'when you reached the age of 49 you joined the *fudanugā*, or what would now be called an "old people's club" (*rōjin kurabu*). Even people who had played in the *jikata* of festivals like the *Ketsugan-sai* would stop playing when they reached this age, and simply watch the festival with the rest of the old people's group' (in Yaeyama Koten Min'yō Hozonkai 1997: 45). In this way, the various musical and dramatic roles in a festival act as mini coming-of-age ceremonies through which participants announce to the village society their arrival at a particular stage of life.

Another important role of festival performances is their context for the formation and delineation of social relationships within society, particularly regarding the way that performing arts are transmitted from generation to generation. Prior to the 2001 *Tanadui* festival, I observed rehearsals for the *hōnō geinō* of Hazama village, which are performed by the Ishigaki-based Hazama Minzoku Geinō Hozonkai (Hazama Folk Performing Arts Preservation Group). Practices started about a month before this in the house of the *hozonkai* president, Ishigaki Hisao, in Ishigaki island. While these practices were largely relaxed and good-natured affairs, they seemed to serve a number of specific purposes, besides merely running through the repertory. First, the presence of several village 'elders' who had 'retired' from active performance at the festival was an important way in which traditional 'correctness' was ensured. These elders were frequently (and purposefully) consulted on a number of aspects of performance, such as the correct pronunciation of Taketomi dialect, the meaning of words, or the phrasing of particular songs. I interpret this public and formalised process of asking elder group members for their advice and approval on certain aspects of performance as a kind of social performance in itself – creating a 'discourse of transmission' from older to younger generations. In an age where the repertory has been extensively recorded in written, audio and video format, this kind of formal transmission process is perhaps not a practical necessity, but the performative act of asking for personal approval from the village elders is a way of imbuing the performance of the songs and dances themselves with cultural authenticity. Second, the practice sessions created a strong sense of ritual identity among participants. One week before the *hōnō geinō* (on day one of the *Tanadui* festival), for example, the practice session involved a formal pledge (*Turukki*) to carry out the *hōnō geinō* at the festival. This ritual pledge was led by Arai Kiyoshi, the most senior member of the *hozonkai*, and attended by most of the elder non-performing members, as well as all members of the Hazama group who were participating in the festival. The ceremony was also used as an occasion to emphasise the ritual nature of the performances themselves – in a speech to the group, Ishigaki Hisao spoke about the importance of the festival as a way of communing with the gods, in contrast to the commercial performance of traditional music in the town's folk-song bars, which was played for money. This official commitment to the *hōnō geinō* group lasted for the duration of the festival until it was eventually released in a similar ritual (known as *hajiri*) on the day after the festival finished, again in Ishigaki Hisao's house, and was a tangible way of making a formalised commitment to the festival performance group.

Festivals are also an important way in which societies themselves are constructed and imagined, especially in the context of the late 20th century population exodus from the smaller Yaeyaman islands to Ishigaki and beyond. In Taketomi I often heard *Tanadui* associated with a social concept known as *utsugumi no kokoro*, which can be roughly translated as 'the spirit of mutual co-operation'[25] (see e.g. Akiyama 1997: 13; Kinenshi Sakusei Iinkai 1993). Ōyama told me:

> You used to see *utsugumi* every day of the year. People would help each other in the fields or with other work. Nowadays those old ways of working together are not so common. But you can still see *utsugumi no kokoro* in *Tanadui*. That's when everyone comes together and works as a community. That's what *Tanadui* was in the past, and the idea hasn't changed at all. It's a way for people to reaffirm (*saikakunin suru*) their identity as Taketomians once a year. (Ōyama, pers. comm. September 2001)

In this way, rather than being simply a relic from an agricultural way of life that has disappeared, *Tanadui* is seen to hold a particular purpose in the modern world, when the festival is one of the few annual opportunities for the community to 'perform' itself in one place.

While the *utsugumi no kokoro* ideal, as expressed through the performance of *Tanadui*, applies to some extent to Taketomi island as a whole, the festival continues to place importance on the old village and sub-village divisions within Taketomi. The performance of *hōnō geinō* at *Tanadui*, for example, continues to be divided between Hazama[26] and Nakasuji, and both villages maintain organisations that are responsible for the performance of *hōnō geinō* at the festival. Village identities are also maintained to some extent in certain musical aspects of the *hōnō geinō* repertory. While many of the performances of Hazama and Nakasuji villages are identical between day one and two, especially those of the *niwa no geinō* section in the morning, there are some overt differences which act as indicators of which village is performing. Each village has an instrumental melody (*gaku*), which is played to introduce certain parts of its *hōnō geinō* performances, and acts as a kind of signature tune (see Example 4.1). Ōyama Takeshi, a Hazama village member resident in Ishigaki, told me:

> As soon as we (Hazama villagers) hear the Hazama tune we know it's 'our day' and we get excited (*hotto suru*). If we hear the Nakasuji tune we don't feel anything in particular. (pers. comm. September 2001)

---

[25]   The word seems to have existed in Taketomi since the 16th century (Akiyama 1997: 13), and is strongly connected with the *bafu* and *yuimāru* communal work traditions prevalent in Yaeyama until the 1960s.

[26]   There is also a division between East Hazama, which performs its *hōnō geinō* on day seven, and West Hazama, which performs on day eight along with Nakasuji village.

Example 4.1 *Gaku* – instrumental melodies identifying a particular village
(Hazama or Nakasuji) at Taketomi's *Tanadui* festival

Source: Adapted from Sakiyama (1997: 118–19).

The practice of dividing the performance of festivals between different parts of a village or island community is found all around Yaeyama, and often leads to a certain amount of competition between each side to outdo each other. Akiyama has written that the performance of *hōnō geinō* reinforces a feeling of solidarity in a particular village, rather than working against other villages (1997: 35). Karimata (1999: 133–7) also cites the competition between rival villages to outdo each other as one of the impetuses behind strong performing arts traditions in Yaeyama. In many cases, village identities seem to be far stronger than island ones, even among the Taketomi diaspora. After *Tanadui* in 2001, I travelled back from Taketomi to Ishigaki by boat together with Hazama and Nakasuji village members who had taken part in the festival. Both groups had worked hard on their performances and were eager to go out drinking to celebrate. On reaching the port in Ishigaki, I was surprised to find that the two groups set off in different directions to drink in different bars. One member of the Nakasuji group told me: 'These days we get on quite well at the festival. Especially compared to the old days. We used to have really bad arguments between villages in the old days though. Sometimes they would get quite serious. We don't do that now. We don't go drinking together though' (Miyara, pers. comm. November 2001).

In this way, village identities can be seen to be maintained despite the dispersal of the Taketomi community to Ishigaki, Okinawa and beyond – both the Hazama and Nakasuji organisations are largely based and carry out practices in Ishigaki, as few of the prominent members live in Taketomi itself, while performances are also organised by Hazama and Nakasuji groups based in the Okinawan and Japanese mainlands. Thus *Tanadui*, along with the music and dance performed at the festival, serves as one of the most important yearly events through which members of the Taketomi community throughout Japan comes together in Taketomi itself. This phenomenon can be seen in islands all around Yaeyama, and in extreme cases entire island societies are effectively maintained outside the islands to which they maintain their roots, returning only to perform major ritual events. A good example is Aragusuku island, which maintained an average population of around 10 people throughout the early 21st century, a population which mushroomed to several hundred participants during the Harvest festival that I witnessed in 2002.

Another topic that frequently arises in discourse surrounding Yaeyaman festivals concerns the conflict between ritual performance as an essentially private affair for village insiders, and an increasing interest from scholars, tourists and other outsiders to experience local rituals. Uesedo Yoshinori, a folk crafts scholar resident on Taketomi, for example, has commented (in Tada 2008: 252) that: 'Performing arts are fundamentally something performed for the gods. They are for the pleasure of the gods. I don't want to use those performing arts just as a way to make money from tourists – everyone agrees that it's not right. We can certainly increase the number of tourists by [using performing arts], but do we really need to? There is a strong feeling against desecrating the gods, even at the expense of financial gain.' In Taketomi's case, despite statements such as Uesedo's, tourists are now mostly seen as an inevitable part of ritual life. In contrast, some villages have exhibited an explicit policy to limit the participation of outsiders in certain festivals, a policy that can be seen as a way of emphasising both the ritual meaning of festivals, and the group identities that these rituals create. One of the most obvious examples can be seen in the *Akamata-Kuromata* rituals performed at the Harvest festivals of Kohama, Miyara, Aragusuku and Komi. From dusk until the early hours of the morning during these ritual events, young village men parade around the village houses accompanying the masked gods *Akamata* (red god) and *Kuromata* (black god),[27] played by young male villagers dressed in billowing gowns fashioned from palm leaves, singing a repertory of ritual songs.

The *Akamata-Kuromata* ritual has been described by the Japanese ethnologist Miyara Takahiro (1963) as fostering 'secret societies' (*himitsu kessha*), and retains a strong aura of secrecy into the 21st century. While tourists (and researchers) are tolerated, they are bound by strict rules. In particular, video and audio recording and even note taking are strictly prohibited – when I saw the ritual in Aragusuku in 2002, all outside participants were subjected to a body search to check for hidden cameras or recording devices. The situation in Miyara was somewhat less severe, with visitors merely being told to turn off their mobile phones (many of which include cameras and recording devices), although of course recording was still

---

27   Komi also has a 'white' god *Shiromata*.

strictly prohibited. This attitude seems to be at least partly a reaction to tourist interest in rituals. At the Aragusuku *Akamata-Kuromata* ritual that I attended in June 2002, one of the village elders who had been appointed to take care of the 'outside' spectators made a speech to the following effect:

> Some villages in Yaeyama want people to publicize their festivals around Japan. In Aragusuku we don't want any publicity. We are happy for you to come and see our ritual, but we ask that when you leave the island, you forget everything you have seen and heard here.

In fact, the secrecy surrounding *Akamata-Kuromata* predates the recent tourist boom, and can also be seen as a reaction to attempts by Japanese and Okinawan scholars to document the festival. The Okinawan journalist Arakawa Akira, who himself observed *Akamata-Kuromata* in the mid-1960s, describes one mainland Japanese scholar[28] whose attempts to study the ritual in Kohama in the 1930s were rebuffed by local ritual participants, and whose death shortly after returning to Tokyo was 'proof' to the islanders of the revenge of the gods for his blasphemy in attempting to study them (Arakawa 1987: 165). The Yaeyaman scholar Miyara Kentei caused a minor sensation in Kohama after a partial account of the Kohama *Akamata-Kuromata* ritual was published in 1940 (Arakawa 1987: 166; K. Miyara 1979: 261–8).

The specific ban on audio and video recording seems to date from the 1960s when, with increasing tourism and availability of cameras and tape recorders, the issue of widespread dissemination of information about the *Akamata-Kuromata* ritual became more pressing. Tamashiro Kōichi, a native of Hateruma who worked as a school teacher of (Western classical) music in Komi in the 1960s, told me how he had been one of the few Yaeyamans interested in recording Yaeyaman songs from outside his own village for his own private study. While living in Komi he had been given permission by the village head to record the *Akamata-Kuromata* (*shiromata*) repertory, but the journalist Arakawa Akira's publication of a picture in the press the previous year had led to heightened tensions in the village. Although Tamashiro managed to record the festival, there was a strong reaction from some villagers, and in subsequent years all recording and photography were banned, as they remain today.[29]

With relatively little detailed information on the *Akamata-Kuromata* ritual, it is difficult to make firm analyses, but, in addition to the ritual purpose of the event, the formation of strong group identities through performance seems to be

---

[28]   Probably Kawamura Tadao who visited Kohama in 1938. Kawamura died in 1941. See Kawamura (1999: 179–82) for his own account of the ritual, which includes no hint of major hostilities.

[29]   Nevertheless, a recording of the Aragusuku repertory made for teaching purposes was obtained by researchers from Tokyo University of the Arts in the 1970s, and several songs from the ritual were notated in Koizumi (1981).

one of the ritual's prime objectives. Hateruma (1999: 396–7) notes that, while the requirements for taking part in the *Akamata-Kuromata* ritual in Komi have been relaxed in recent years, for much of the 20th century the ritual was only open to residents with a blood connection to the village through both parents. Like many other Yaeyaman festival performances, in addition to being a way of performing ritual relationships with the gods, *Akamata-Kuromata* is a way of imagining and maintaining social group identities at a (sub-)village level. Perhaps because of this secrecy, and the high level of group identity that it seems to produce, the level of seriousness with which the musical performance is undertaken was probably the highest of any musical genre that I experienced in Yaeyama. A number of informants commented to me about the effect that the festival has on the continuation of traditional culture in general. Miyara village, for instance, is one of the few places in Ishigaki island where the local dialect is still spoken on a daily basis – a fact which several informants put down to the very strong village bonds formed by the *Akamata-Kuromata* ritual. Miyara also has one of the largest *koyō* preservation groups in Ishigaki island, with a number of comparatively young members – also a possible result of the wide exposure to tradition which the *Akamata-Kuromata* festival provides.

A further aspect of many Yaeyaman festivals is that they frequently schedule a part of the festival period for the performance of songs specifically for a human audience. Kohama's *Kitsugan* festival, for example, is similar to Taketomi's *Tanadui* in being the island's main ritual event at which *hōnō geinō* are performed. The main *hōnō geinō* performances take place in front of the Kabuni-wan shrine in the centre of the village and, as in Taketomi, are taken fairly seriously as performances for the gods. The status of these *hōnō geinō* as ritual offertory performances is further emphasised by the fact that the entire performance is repeated on the following day (by the north and south divisions of the village separately), in a secular context for a human audience in the respective municipal halls of each village division. This event, known as Tundumi (e.g. Katō 1986: 54), is an intrinsic part of the festival despite its apparent lack of literal ritual meaning.

Many villages around Yaeyama include these kind of semi-formal music and dance performances on the evening after a major festival. In August 2002 I attended a drinking party in Hatoma following the Hatoma Harvest festival. The event started inside the village hall with performances from a group of amateur musicians of Hatoma origin (Hatoma has a population of around 60, and performers included those living in Hatoma, Ishigaki and Okinawa who had returned for the festival). I was invited to perform a song, followed by the father-daughter duo of Hatoma Takeshi and Hatoma Kanako, who had recently found fame through her collaboration with the Okinawan performer/producer China Sadao. After several more performances by local musicians, including traditional and more modern musical genres, the party moved outside into the garden of the village hall at around 11 p.m. where it split into three groups, each playing their own songs in close proximity to one another until the early hours. This informal concert and outdoor music-making event, while having no intrinsic ritual meaning, is an integral part of the festival programme, and apparently takes place in more-or-less the same format every year at this festival. Part of the reason for the event, obviously, is because it is enjoyable for the participants and audience as pure entertainment. These secular performances can also be seen as a kind of counterbalance to the *hōnō geinō* part of the festival, emphasising its sacred meaning.

Conclusions

Festivals and ritual events are one of the most important contexts for the performance of traditional music in Yaeyama, and these events hold a number of ritual and social meanings. At one level, comments by many informants showed that traditional belief systems such as *Nirai-kanai* continue to be relevant to modern-day life. Rituals such as Taketomi's *Yūnkai* are a way of 'performing' ritual beliefs of *Nirai-kanai*, and in particular of imagining them in a spatial context within the geography of the island.

Ancestral belief systems, too, continue to be highly relevant to modern Yaeyaman life. The *Angamā* ritual provides a tangible way of socially imagining the presence of the ancestors, particularly through the *montō* part of the ritual, and also provides a way of linking to their cultural lives through musical repertory and language use. In a similar way the *Jūrukunitsï* gives individual families the opportunity to commune with the ancestors through the context of traditional music and dance. The strength of ancestral belief systems and traditional music can be seen to be self-supporting – the presence of the ancestors is imagined through traditional music, and the performance of traditional music is likewise maintained through ritual beliefs.

The performance of ritual music is also culturally important for a number of social reasons. First, it provides a context through which membership of society is achieved – songs and dances are performed by people of a certain age, and these performances are often a way to mark out progress through society. Festivals are also a way in which island and village societies continue to be maintained and imagined. The widespread emigration of inhabitants from smaller islands to Ishigaki, Okinawa and Japan has meant that festival participants live predominantly outside their 'ancestral home town', returning only for major ritual events.

With the increase of tourism since the reversion of Okinawa to Japan in 1972, festivals have been used to some extent, as in towns all over Japan, to promote tourism. Some islands, such as Taketomi, have been proactive in promoting their culture outside Yaeyama, and have used their *Tanedori* festival very skilfully as part of a tourism campaign. Yet there has still been a discourse concerning the proper balance between tourism and the original ritual meaning of festivals. In other rituals, such as *Akamata-Kuromata*, tourism and other outside participation has been actively discouraged in an effort to retain the ritual nature of the event and emphasise group identity.

今に残しょーり

Chapter 5
Nama ni nukushōri –
Lineages and Preservation Groups

Ōhama Anpan's well-known *Tubarāma* verse at the beginning of Chapter 1 describes the importance of 'preserving in the present' (*nama ni nukushōri*) the ways of the ancestors as an expression of Yaeyaman heritage (*sïma nu takara*). In this chapter, I examine several ways in which traditional music genres are preserved and passed on in modern Yaeyama, and outline some of the discourses concerning tradition, authenticity and group identity that accompany these contexts. The first section deals with the *fushiuta* world, which has seen the establishment of formal lineage (*ryūha*) organisations partly based on Japanese classical performing arts models. In the second section, I consider the preservation groups set up on a village level to disseminate the *yunta* and *jiraba* repertory, and which have taken a somewhat more informal approach. I also consider the role of the Yaeyaman school system in preserving and disseminating traditional music, and analyse how the teaching of music in schools has interfaced with the more established lineage organisations. Finally I look at the performance of traditional music in the context of the Yaeyaman tourist industry, including staged events at tourist locations, and the performance of traditional music in the many folk-song bars and clubs in the main settlement of Ishigaki island, which cater to both local and tourist audiences.

The Formation of Classical *Fushiuta* Lineages

Fushiuta are probably the most widely-known Yaeyaman music genre, and are actively learned and performed all around Yaeyama, as well as in the Okinawan and Japanese mainlands. Part of the success of *fushiuta* has been prompted by the formation of formal lineages and organisations that coordinate the teaching and performance of the genre. From 2002, I studied with one of the leading teachers in Ishigaki, Ōsoko Chōyō, as well as a period of two years from 2004 to 2006 with Ōsoko's student in the Okinawan mainland, Ōtake Zenzō, and I base my description of teaching practices largely on these experiences. Both of these teachers are members of one of the largest *fushiuta* organisations, the Yaeyama Koten Min'yō Hozonkai (Yaeyama Classical Folk Song Preservation Society), of which I have also been a member since 2002. In addition to these formal lessons, I have informally observed and participated in the lessons and activities of several other teachers in Ishigaki, the Okinawan mainland, and the Japanese mainland in this period. Between 2001 and 2002 I also studied for a short period with the veteran Yaeyama recording artist Yamazato Yūkichi, who also lives in the Okinawan mainland, and informally with his student Asato Isamu in Ishigaki. Both of these performers are affiliated with an organisation called the Yaeyama Koten Ongaku Amuro ryū Hozonkai (Yaeyama Classical Music Amuro-lineage Preservation Society), but are somewhat outside the mainstream *fushiuta* world within Yaeyama.

Several studies (Blasdel 2005: 15–31; Fujita 2008: 141–2; Keister 2004) have commented on the importance of amateur performers and aficionados in the performance and dissemination of traditional music in Japanese society, and the role of music lessons as a primary site in which traditional music exists. Keister, for example, writes that the 'heart of *nagauta* music is not to be found in the extensive repertoire of compositions … but is embodied in individual performers … transmitting their experience of the music to students directly through social interaction' (2004: 1). In many cases, the formation of social relationships, between a teacher and student, between the students of a particular teacher, or between members of larger affiliations such as a *ryūha*, are potentially as important as actually learning to perform the music itself (cf. Keister 2004: 36). As a tradition with almost no professional performers, one of the most important ways that *fushiuta* exist, likewise, is through amateur performance and apprenticeship, and the social relationships that are formed through these learning experiences are often taken at least as seriously as is the music itself. I consider the history and development of the modern *fushiuta* lineages and the way they operate today, likewise, as one of the primary methods through which the 'heart' of *fushiuta* is realised and socially performed.

Fujita (2002: 767) has written of the importance of genealogy charts throughout Japanese musical traditions as a way for performers to achieve cultural authenticity by situating themselves at the end of a long historical chain, and almost any Japanese music genre, from the *shakuhachi* or *shamisen* traditions, instruments of the *noh* ensemble, to more modern instruments such as the *Taishō-goto*, are controlled by *ryūha* (lineages) that control many aspects of a performer's musical life. In some cases, *ryūha* are founded around a repertory of compositions deriving from a particular performer – the Tozan-ryū of *shakuhachi*, for example, is based around the early 20th century solo compositions of the performer Nakao Tozan, and performers in this lineage are unable to formally learn the more famous classical *honkyoku* pieces of the Kinko-ryū.[1] In other cases, such as the instruments of the *noh* ensemble, the various *ryūha* perform a more-or-less common repertory, while each lineage has particular performance characteristics and traits which mark it out from other lineages. The creation or

---

[1]   The reverse is also true, and Nakao Tozan's compositions are only performed by members of the Tozan-ryū.

development of a notation system, in particular, is one way in which lineages have asserted their distinctiveness.

In common with most Japanese genres, the issue of lineage is prominent in the discourse surrounding the modern *fushiuta* world. One of the first questions I was often asked when discussing musical issues with Yaeyamans was who my teacher was, and subsequently, to which lineage I belonged. While the idea of studying by oneself is not unheard of, it is frowned upon and often described using the derogatory term *jikoryū* ('personal' lineage), suggesting that a performer has not undergone sufficient 'traditional' training. On several occasions I heard criticism, especially of older performers, that while they were talented singers and musicians, they could not position themselves on one of the main *fushiuta* lineages, and were thus considered less 'authentic'.

Fushiuta performers are usually divided into two broad lineages, based on the geographical distinction between the traditions of the adjacent villages of Ishigaki and Tonoshiro on Ishigaki island. Both of these lineages perform almost identical repertories and, apart from relatively trivial melodic differences, transmit almost identical performance versions of songs. In addition, the Ishigaki lineage is in practice divided into around four separate *ryūha*-like organisations, all of which transmit almost identical repertories and performance versions as each other. Given these obvious similarities between lineages and organisations, many newcomers to the *fushiuta* tradition are bewildered by the social complexity of the *fushiuta* world, and the necessity for so many different groups. I offer no definitive answers, but in the following sections present some of the historical reasons for the formation of particular *ryūha*, and consider some of the social purposes that they serve.

The origins of modern Yaeyaman *fushiuta* lineages are fairly recent, and can be traced to the late 19th century, and the activities of a small group of musicians from the *yakunin* (government official) class in Ishigaki and Tonoshiro villages. In particular, the formation of lineages went hand-in-hand with a movement to standardise the Yaeyaman repertory through the production of the first Yaeyaman *kunkunshi* notations. An early example of the rationale behind the formation of standardised lineages can be seen from a quote by a Tonoshiro-born government official Ōhama Yōnō (1841–1916), complaining in the late 19th century that:

> although Yaeyama has many fantastic folk songs and virtuoso singers, because
> of its lack of a notation system, and thus due to the lack of standardization
> of song performance, people had trouble playing together at parties and
> celebrations. (In Makino 1988: 63)

In 1884, Ōhama was assigned to a government post in Naha[2] where he also studied the *kunkunshi* of the Nomura school of Okinawan music with the mainland Okinawan performer Kabira Chōrin, helping Kabira to publish two collections of

---

[2]   While Yaeyama, like Okinawa, became a part of the Japanese nation in 1879, the old

Yaeyaman song lyrics,[3] and also beginning to create his own *kunkunshi* notations of Yaeyaman *fushiuta*. At the same time, a movement to create a Yaeyaman *kunkunshi* was also under way in Ishigaki village, led by the performer Amuro Sonshi (1848–1899) and his student Kishaba Eisei (1855–1919), who later also recalled that 'due to the different playing styles of individuals at that time, it was difficult to play together ... we must make a *kunkunshi* so that people can learn the correct style' (Makino 1988: 66). Initially, there seems to have been a movement to combine the efforts of Ōhama Yōnō and Amuro Sonshi into a single standardised *kunkunshi* that could be used by performers from all villages. In 1894 Yōnō gathered together the leading players of the time, including Sonshi and Ishigaki Shin'en from Ōkawa village, to exchange ideas and with the intention of producing a standardised *kunkunshi*. Within five months of this meeting Yōnō had completed his *Yaeyama-uta kunkunshi*, and prepared to distribute it to performers from around Yaeyama. With the realisation that Yōnō's way of singing would perhaps become the standard across Yaeyama, Ishigaki village elders began to pressure Amuro Sonshi not to compromise the 'Ishigaki' singing style in favour of that of 'Tonoshiro', leading Amuro to withdrew his support for Yōnō's *kunkunshi*. A separate Ishigaki *kunkunshi* was completed some years later, although its exact date of completion is contested (see below).

The wrangling over the 'social control' (Attali 1985: 87) to be gained by 'recording' versions of songs in *kunkunshi* notations led directly to a formal division between what came to be seen as the 'Ishigaki' singing style, subsequently known as the 'Amuro' style, and the Tonoshiro, or 'Ōhama Yōnō', style. The distinction between Ishigaki and Tonoshiro performance versions seems originally to have been expressed using the term *fū*, roughly translatable as 'style', but by the mid-20th century this rather 'rustic-sounding' (*inaka-kusai*, see Kinenshi Henshū Iinkai 1987: 22) term had largely been replaced by the more prestigious *ryū* or *ryūha* (lineage), almost certainly under the influence of mainland Japanese *ryūha* examples.[4] The prestige and cultural authority provided by the status of belonging to a 'lineage' meant that the 20th century saw continued attempts to establish control of these organisations. A 1935 newspaper article reveals that the Yaeyaman *ryūha* were already vying for cultural power in the pre-WWII years:

---

nintōzei taxation system continued until 1903, and the old divisions in peasant and ruling classes was very much alive in the late 19th century.

[3]   Yaeyama-uta Ryūki Mokuryoku and Shima-fū Yaeyama-uta kunkunshi fushi mokuhyōki. The first of these contains the lyrics of 31 Yaeyama fushiuta.

[4]   A similar process can be seen in the mainland Okinawan classical song tradition, which developed its two main '*ryūha*' (Nomura-ryū and Afuso-ryū) in the early 20th century. The Nomura and Afuso ryūs which, like the Yaeyaman ryūs, share a common repertory but are divided according to performance style, were also known in the 19th century as '*fū*' but began to use the more respectable '*ryū*' in the early 20th century.

Each *ryūha* exists in its own little world and cannot see past its own limits. They must clearly put aside their personal quarrels and hatreds and, in a spirit of peace, give each other mutual help and encouragement in order to work towards the unification of Yaeyama *min'yō* and the building of an everlasting treasure. (Urasaki 1935)

Despite the desire for 'unification' in this early criticism of the Yaeyaman *ryūha*, sectarian attitudes have continued to predominate, and the original division between Tonoshiro and Ishigaki villages has further expanded so that the performance of modern-day *fushiuta* is controlled by a number of organisations, the largest of which are the *Yaeyama Koten On'gaku Amuro ryū Kyōwakai* (hereafter YKOARK) established in 1949, the *Yaeyama Koten On'gaku Amuro ryū Hozonkai* (YKOARH, 1958), the *Yaeyama Ongaku Ōhama Yōnō ryū Hozonkai* (YOOYRH, 1970), the *Yaeyama Koten Min'yō Hozonkai* (YKMH, 1977), and the *Yaeyama Koten Min'yō Dentō Kyōkai* (YKMDK, 2009). With the exception of the YOOYRH, which transmits the Tonoshiro tradition, all of these organisations are descended from the original Amuro-ryū of Ishigaki village, and have almost identical performance practices. While a comprehensive history of all of these organisations is impossible here, in the next section I give an outline of the history of one organisation, the YKMH, focusing in particular on the activities of its founder Ōhama Anpan.[5] Through the activities of this musician, we can see some of the forces that shaped the performance of Yaeyaman *fushiuta* over the 20th century.

Ōhama Anpan and the Yaeyama Koten Min'yō Hozonkai

Ōhama Anpan[6] (1914–2001) was brought up in the Mafutanē district of Ishigaki village, a district known for its performing arts, in an upper-class family that had fallen on hard times since Yaeyama's incorporation into the Japanese state, and had resorted to farming to make a living (see Kinenshi Henshū Iinkai 1987 for details of Anpan's life). Anpan's family were not actively involved in performing arts, but his mother, who had been brought up in a musical family, wanted Anpan to learn *fushiuta*, and Anpan was sent to study with Ameku Yōritsu (1888–1945) in 1929 (a chart of performers and organisations is given in Figure 5.1). Ameku was one of the first teachers to teach on a monthly fee (*gessha*) basis, another cultural import from the Japanese traditional arts system, and Anpan's mother reportedly struggled to pay the 3 yen fee. Ameku had revised his teacher Kishaba Sonchi's *kunkunshi* and published his own, the first *kunkunshi* in the Ishigaki lineage to be printed rather than hand-copied. Anpan made slow initial

---

[5]   Similar figures in other organizations include Ōhama Tsurō in the YOOYRH or Tamayose Chōden in the YKOARH.

[6]   Also pronounced 'Anhan'.

progress and went to his lessons grudgingly – he described (Kinenshi Henshū Iinkai 1987) how, in a pattern familiar around the world, his mother would wait near Ameku's house listening to the lessons, and make Anpan repeat what he had learned when he got home. This pushiness on the part of his mother during his early years was to be crucial in his eventual mastery of and enthusiasm for Yaeyaman music. Ameku eventually moved to the Okinawan mainland, and assigned responsibility for Anpan's musical education to another of his students, Ishigaki Gibo.

The destruction caused during and in the aftermath of WWII took a heavy toll on the Yaeyaman population, and a large number of the older generation of Yaeyama *fushiuta* performers, including Ameku Yōritsu and Ishigaki Gibo, lost their lives during this period. In the post-war years the responsibility for continuing the tradition was quite suddenly placed on a much younger generation of performers, including Anpan. Anpan's career was given another boost through his winning the first *Tubarāma* singing contest in 1947 (see Chapter 6) and, on the back of this sudden fame, he was encouraged to open a teaching studio in Ishigaki. In 1949 Anpan was instrumental in forming the first organised society dedicated to disseminating the Amuro-ryū, the YKOARK.[7]

Just as *kunkunshi* had played a large part in the early formation of Yaeyaman *ryūha*, the creation of notations continued to play a further divisive role throughout the 20th century. In particular, an event that was to have broad repercussions across the *fushiuta* world was Anpan's discovery, in the mid-1950s, of a *kunkunshi* manuscript that has come to be known as the '*genpon*' (original document). In the early 1950s Anpan had been offered for sale a *sanshin*, included with which was a hand-written *kunkunshi* manuscript[8] that he quickly realised was an earlier and less accurate version of his teacher Ameku Yōritsu's published notation. Anpan initially believed the document to be the lost *kunkunshi* of Amuro Sonshi, founder of the Amuro-ryū, and thus of huge significance to the lineage's history. The discovery of the document sparked a heated and drawn-out debate, as Sonshi's grandson, a priest at the Tōrin temple in Ishigaki, insisted that, as Sonshi's direct descendent, he was the rightful owner of the *kunkunshi*, and demanded its return. It has subsequently transpired that the document is probably not the work of Amuro himself, but his student Kishaba Eisei.[9] An inscription at the beginning of the document 'Written by Amuro Sonshi' (*Sakusha Amuro Sonshi*) is in a different ink and style to the rest of the *kunkunshi*, and was likely added soon

---

[7]   The organization was initially called simply the Amuro-ryū Kyōwakai.

[8]   Anpan's partial account of this story is told in an interview with Tōyama Yoshitaka, published in Kinenshi Henshū Iinkai (1987). Much of the story remains unpublished, however, and I received additional information from Tōyama Yoshitaka in an interview in June 2002.

[9]   Opinion is still divided, with members of the YKOARH maintaining that the document was produced by Amuro Sonshi, while the YKMH follows the Kishaba Eisei theory.

after it had passed to Amuro's grandson, as a way of confirming his ownership. (See Hughes 1985: 246 for a similar case in the mainland Japanese *minzoku geinō* world.) As a direct result of this disagreement, a breakaway group, the Amuro-ryū Hozonkai (subsequently the YKOARH) was formed in 1958 around Amuro's grandson, splitting the Ishigaki lineage into two factions. Feelings surrounding the *genpon* ran so high that Anpan was effectively unable to continue teaching within Yaeyama and in 1960 he moved to the Okinawan mainland where he lived the rest of his life and carried out most of his innovations in the Yaeyaman music world from afar.

Following his move to the Okinawan mainland, away from the infighting of the Yaeyaman music world, Anpan set to work creating a new *kunkunshi*. He had been dissatisfied with Ameku Yōritsu's (1943) *kunkunshi*, especially the way the rhythm had been notated, and he set out to make a *kunkunshi* with accurate rhythmic notation of the *sanshin* line, one that could theoretically be used for learning a song without the aid of a teacher. In 1966, as a result of this work, he published his *Yaeyama min'yō sanshin kunkunshi*. Perhaps due to a fear that Anpan's new *kunkunshi* would enable students to bypass the teacher completely and learn by themselves, Anpan was heavily criticised by many at this time for being a 'destroyer of tradition' (*uta nu ushā*), but the publication was understandably extremely popular and the first edition quickly sold out. Anpan's relations with the Yaeyama *fushiuta* world were further strained in 1974, when the Amuro-ryū Kyōwakai (of which he was a leading member) independently published another *kunkunshi*, incorporating many of Anpan's rhythmic revisions. Anpan subsequently broke off links with this organisation and formed a new organisation, the YKMH, further fracturing the Ishigaki lineage into three separate organisations. The story continued in 1976 with Anpan's second major achievement, the publication of his *Seigakufu-tsuki Yaeyama Koten Min'yō Kunkunshi*, a revision of the 1966 *kunkunshi* with the added improvement of a notated vocal line. Although the Tonoshiro musician Ōhama Tsurō had published the first volume of a *kunkunshi*[10] including notation of the vocal melody as early as 1952, Anpan's 1976 *kunkunshi* was the first to contain vocal notations for the entire *fushiuta* repertory. As is the case with the Nomura-ryū of mainland Okinawan classical music, which was revolutionised by the introduction of notated vocal melody in the 1930s (see Garfias 1993/1994), Anpan's 1976 *kunkunshi* was also extremely influential in the *fushiuta* world. All the other major organisations have since produced their own *kunkunshi* incorporating notation of the vocal line, but Anpan's 1976 *kunkunshi* has been decisive in making the YKMH the largest *fushiuta* organisation in the modern *fushiuta* world.

While the various Yaeyaman *ryūha* show obvious influences from Japanese organisations for traditional music, there are also some important differences. Most importantly, while Japanese *ryūha* are usually organised around an *iemoto* (household head) figure, who is often a direct blood descendent of the founder

---

[10]   *Seigaku-fu tsuki Yaeyama Min'yō Kunkunshi.*

of the *ryūha*, Yaeyaman *ryūha* have no such figure who wields absolute control. In the case of the YKMH, the presence of a single performer, Ōhama Anpan (1912–2001), as the creator of the group's notation put him in the position of a 'founder' of a certain way of playing. Nevertheless, since Anpan's death, organisation of the group has passed to a number of his students, and there is no *iemoto* figure in ultimate charge of artistic decisions. Management of the organisation is carried out by a board made up of experienced musicians, who are led by a fixed-term president. According to Ōsoko Chōyō, one of Anpan's primary students, Anpan was explicit in his wish that the term '*ryū*' should not be used for his organisation, as it had connotations of a founder who had *composed* the majority of the group's repertory (also Tōyama, pers. comm. June 2002).[11]

The Yaeyaman *fushiuta* organisations operate on a more-or-less autonomous basis, depending entirely on membership subscriptions (about $30 per year in 2010) for their survival. Local government recognition, if not financial sponsorship, has also played a part in the success or failure of certain organisations. In 1983 the Okinawa prefectural education board (*Okinawa-ken Kyōiku Iinkai*) appointed a new genre, *Yaeyama Koten Min'yō*, as a Prefectural Intangible Cultural Asset. Ōhama Anpan and Tamayose Chōden, both players of the Ishigaki style, were appointed as the official holders of this tradition. As in countries such as Korea (Howard 2004), the process of designation of a traditional musical style by an outside body (in this case by the prefectural government based in Naha), has a strong effect on preserving music in a local context, and giving certain performers a degree of respectability that they could not gain solely through local recognition. The fact that no representative of the Tonoshiro lineage was appointed has almost certainly been an influence in the sudden downturn in its popularity since the 1980s.

---

[11]   In January 2009, hearing of the plans of a breakaway group from the YKMH to use the term '*Ōhama Anpan ryū*' in the name of their new organisation, the remaining members of the YKMH consulted a lawyer and drew up a document threatening legal action if the phrase was used (Ōsoko, pers. comm. March 2009). The new organisation eventually became the *Yaeyama Koten Min'yō Dentō Kyōkai*, avoiding the use of the offending term.

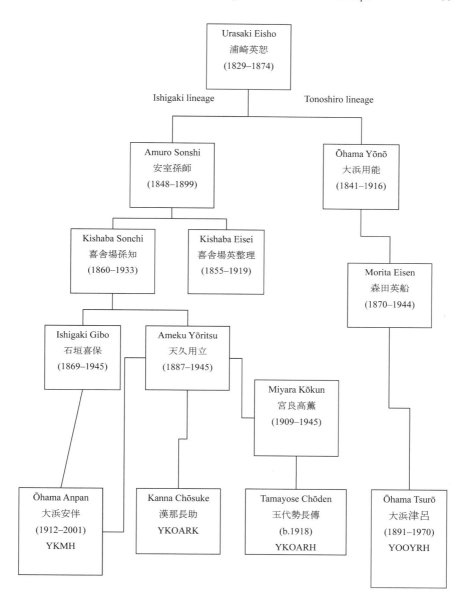

Figure 5.1   *Fushiuta* lineages

Notes: YKMH: Yaeyama Koten Min'yō Hozonkai 八重山古典民謡保存会
YKOARK: Yaeyama Koten Ongaku Amuro-ryū Kyōwakai 八重山古典音楽安室流共和会
YKOARH: Yaeyama Koten Ongaku Amuro-ryū Hozonkai 八重山古典音楽安室流保存会
YOOYRH: Yaeyama Ongaku Ōhama Yōnō- ryū Hozonkai 八重山音楽大浜用能流保存会

Learning *Fushiuta*

In this section I discuss some aspects of the process of teaching and learning in the modern *fushiuta* world. I outline some of my lesson experiences, as well as experiences of the concerts and grade tests that are part of the lineage's activities, and consider some of the social functions that these activities hold. As is the case with most Japanese traditional musical traditions (e.g. Fujita 2002: 769–70), *fushiuta* students usually have a direct relationship with only one teacher, and that relationship is maintained formally for the entire career of both players. It is uncommon for a student to change teachers except in the early years of study, unless one of them moves due to work or family commitments. The fact that students study with a single teacher for their entire career, attending regular lessons at least until they receive a teaching licence themselves (which usually takes at least five years), means that the group bonds between students of a particular teacher are continually being reaffirmed on a social level.

Fushiuta are usually taught in the form of group lessons with between two and eight students, usually at the teacher's home (Figure 5.2). Lesson fees are fixed by the organisation to which the teacher belongs, and a monthly fee (*gessha*) of around $50 entitles students to attend two classes a week. In the very early stages of learning, lessons are sometimes held on a one-to-one basis until the student has mastered the rudiments of reading the notation and tuning the instrument, but after a few weeks the student generally joins a group lesson. Groups are usually divided according to skill level, based on the grade a student has achieved at the yearly *konkūru* (grade tests) sponsored by the two local newspapers (see below).

My lessons with Ōsoko generally lasted around two hours, during which around six songs were studied, at least two of which were from the *konkūru* set pieces (one in the *hon-chōshi sanshin* tuning, and one *niagi*). The structure of the lessons usually involved all the students playing and singing in unison with Ōsoko, repeating one verse (or one section of longer songs) several times until the students could perform it reasonably well, before moving on to the next. At this stage there was not a major emphasis on minute details of the melody, and students would try to memorise each song well enough to play along with Ōsoko without recourse to the *kunkunshi* notation. In common with most mainland Japanese traditional music genres (e.g. Fujita 2002: 770; Keister 2004: 43), the method of teaching *fushiuta* focuses very heavily on the practical act of performing, rather than through overt analysis or theoretical discourse. If there was a particularly difficult passage in a song, that passage might be singled out and repeated in isolation until it was performed to Ōsoko's satisfaction, but I never encountered the phenomenon of 'exercises' designed to develop a particular technique, as might be found in European classical traditions.

Figure 5.2   *Fushiuta* lesson with Ōsoko Chōyō

In the months before a *konkūru*, the emphasis would change to performing only the first verse of each song (only the first verse is required in *konkūru*), and Ōsoko would begin to ask each student to perform individually. At this stage, every element of performance began to be analysed in minute detail by Ōsoko – small details of rhythmic nuance, pronunciation, posture, melody and feeling began to be pointed out in order to produce a more and more polished performance.

In addition to the *konkūru* set pieces, a certain amount of lesson time was set aside for songs that students might have been asked to play at social events – friends' weddings or family celebrations etc. – or songs that students simply wanted to learn for fun. While the objective in learning these songs, as with the *konkūru* set pieces, was to perform as faithfully as possible to the *kunkunshi* notation, there was none of the minute dissection of the nuances of the song that was devoted to the *konkūru* songs.

The twice-weekly schedule and the group lesson format mean that there is a strong sense of camaraderie and group identity among students of a particular teacher. In my lessons with Ōsoko, in addition to studying the actual performance of *fushiuta*, probably around one-third of each two-hour lesson was taken up with non-music-related talk – often Ōsoko's reminiscences of his youth, gossip about other musicians and acquaintances, or discussion of the latest confectionery gifts that the constant stream of students from mainland Japan to visit Ōsoko brought with them. This social aspect continues outside lessons too, and Ōsoko's group organises a range of 'extra-curricular' activities throughout the year. In an effort to instil a sense of the background of many *fushiuta* lyrics in agricultural ritual, Ōsoko maintains a paddy field in his home village of Komi where his students experience the yearly cycle of planting and harvesting rice by hand. Another yearly event is a two-day trip to one of the smaller Yaeyaman islands, consisting of a concert given by all of Ōsoko's students, followed the next day by a sightseeing tour of the *fushiuta* related landmarks on that island. This social aspect of lessons is an integral part of learning *fushiuta*, and is a way of strengthening the bonds between the 'insiders' of the group.

The demographic makeup of Ōsoko's students reveals several profound changes in the *fushiuta* world since the late 20th century. One of the most immediately noticeable aspects was the very large percentage of students from the Japanese mainland. In 2008 Ōsoko had 58 students, of whom approximately half were from mainland Japan. Many of these had moved to Yaeyama on a semi-permanent basis, while many more travelled to Yaeyama whenever possible for occasional lessons. In contrast, out of approximately 20 students who had been studying for more than 10 years, only one was from outside Yaeyama, demonstrating a sudden burst of interest from the Japanese mainland in the late 1990s.

Part of the reason for the very large number of mainland Japanese *fushiuta* students undoubtedly comes from the effects of media images of Okinawa such as those presented in the television series *Churasan* or in films such as *Nabi no koi*. One opinion that many of my fellow students expressed was an initial urge to find a 'simpler way of life' than they had experienced in the big cities. One informant (who studied with a different teacher) told me how he had worked in a company in Tokyo for 10 years, but had become dissatisfied in his early thirties with the constant grind of city life and, attracted by the music and the 'slow life' image, had moved to Yaeyama where after studying *fushiuta* for a few years he eventually opened a bar offering introductory *sanshin* lessons to mainland Japanese tourists (Kubota, personal communication, 2007).

The large number of students moving or travelling from the Japanese mainland to learn *fushiuta* has been equally matched by the number of *fushiuta* classes being set up in the Japanese mainland. The YKMH has operated a Kantō area branch since 1980 (see Figure 5.3), and branches also exist in Fukuoka and the Tōkai region west of Tokyo. Other performers such as Daiku Tetsuhiro, who has been particularly influential in introducing Yaeyaman and Okinawan music to Japan, makes frequent trips there both to perform and as a mentor/teacher for the many Okinawan music circles which have sprung up all over the Japanese mainland from Hokkaido to Kyushu. In March 2004 I observed the activities of the 'Osaka *Sanshin* Club', a group consisting of upwards of 50 members, most of whom have no family connection to Okinawa, at which Daiku holds teaching workshops several times a year. Daiku also runs classes in Okinawa which are popular with students who come from the mainland specifically to learn from him.

Figure 5.3   Concert by Kantō branch of YKMH, Tokyo 2009

Another conspicuous aspect of Ōsoko's student profile was that 39 out of 59 learners in 2008 were female. Until at least the 1960s, the playing of *fushiuta* was very much a male domain, and the already low status of the *sanshin* was many times worse for female performers. While there are isolated historical examples of female *fushiuta* singers such as Nakamoto Masako (b. 1885),[12] they were often associated with the *sakanayā* (drinking/entertainment establishments somewhat analogous to Japanese geisha houses), and were somewhat outside 'respectable' society (Yamazato Setsuko, pers. comm. September 2002). As in the Okinawan and Japanese mainlands, the post-WWII years saw a rapid increase in the number of women studying and teaching traditional dance, to the extent that traditional dancers in modern Yaeyama are almost entirely female. But it was not until the 1990s that a significant number of women began learning *fushiuta*. One of the few female *fushiuta* performers born before WWII that I encountered, Takamine Mitsu (b. 1924), told me that although she had learned to sing a number of songs in her youth, she was unable to learn the *sanshin* until the 1960s (November 2001). The increase in female learners since the 1990s has yielded a number of female

---

[12]   From the French *concours*. *Konkūru* in Yaeyama are somewhat different from European classical music *concours* in much of the world, in that there is no overall 'winner', and entrants either 'pass' or 'fail', and I have thus translated the term as 'grade test'.

performers with teaching licences, and the large number of female students currently learning *fushiuta* means that the number of female teachers will surely increase in the future. Many traditional music genres in mainland Japan, particularly those for the *koto* and *shamisen*, saw a profound gender shift from male to female from the early years of the 20th century, and it seems likely that Yaeyaman music will see a similar transition in the near future. An obstacle to the advancement of women in *fushiuta* performance, as with mainland theatrical genres such as *nagauta* or *noh* chanting, is the continued preference for male singers to accompany dance performances. It is relatively uncommon to hear female singers accompanying dance, and a number of informants commented to me that female voices lack the necessary power and *gravitas* (*omomi*) needed on such occasions.

Konkūru

Together with the establishment of a *ryūha*-like system, another influential feature of the Yaeyaman traditional music world has been the establishment of *konkūru*[13] (grade tests) to assess a student's progress. One of the first questions I was asked when people heard I was studying *fushiuta*, was what level I had achieved in the *konkūru*, and the considerable prestige gained by attainment of these certificates, for teacher and student alike, means that most teachers spend a large proportion of lesson time preparing for these annual events. *Konkūru* are organised by the two Yaeyaman newspaper companies, *Yaeyama Mainichi* and *Yaeyama Nippō*, and are theoretically independent of the *ryūha* organisations. In practice, the *Yaeyama Mainichi* tests are dominated by the YKMH, and almost all the judges and entrants to this event are also members of the YKMH.[14] The *Yaeyama Nippō konkūru* includes entrants from the three large remaining schools (including both the Tonoshiro-based YOOYRH and the Ishigaki YKOARH and YKOARK).

The *konkūru* of both newspapers follow broadly similar procedures. Application is made a few weeks before the date of the *konkūru* to the newspaper office. There is a fixed repertory of songs which a candidate must learn; for the Elementary level (*shinjinshō*) at the *Yaeyama Mainichi* newspaper, for example, the songs in 2002 were *Basï nu turï bushi*, *Hatoma bushi*, *Tsukï ya hama bushi* (all in *honchōshi* tuning), *Asadoya bushi*, *Yuruami bushi* and *Chidori bushi*

---

[13]   The judges also include a handful of non-performers – traditionally a European classical music specialist and a Yaeyaman linguistics specialist – who assess aspects such as the correct use of dialect, and the (classical) musicality of entrants.

[14]   Prior to WWII, there was no standardised system of issuing teaching licences to pupils at all. Ameku Yōritsu was given a 'teaching licence' by his teacher, Kishaba Sonchi, in 1931 at the end of Sonchi's career, with the meaning that Ameku would succeed Sonchi as the single transmitter of the lineage. The first licences to be issued to students by an organisation were those awarded to Ōhama Tsurō and Ōhama Anpan by the Ishigaki Cultural Association (*Ishigaki-shi Bunka Kyōkai*) in 1956.

(all in *ni-agi* tuning). One week before the *konkūru*, two of these songs (one in each tuning) are designated at random for performance in the *konkūru*. On the day of the *konkūru*, the candidates, wearing traditional (Japanese-style *montsuki hakama*) formal dress, play the first verse of each song alone on a stage in the city auditorium before a panel of judges, who award points on criteria such as faithfulness to the notation, pronunciation, voice quality, loudness, and rhythm. Members of the public are also allowed into the hall, sitting in darkness and silence behind the judges. The sense of tension is usually very high, and it is not uncommon for contestants to grind to a halt in the first few bars of a song through nerves – prompting a buzzer from the judges that alerts them to their disqualification.

The second part of the *konkūru*, and one that is at least as important as the first, is the successful candidates' recital (*happyōkai*). This recital takes place in the Ishigaki city auditorium about two months after the *konkūru*, and is an extremely popular event – on each of the five occasions that I have attended *konkūru* recitals since 2001, the 1,000 seat hall was filled beyond its capacity. In common with similar concerts in mainland Japan (see e.g. Hesselink 1994: 52–3; Keister 2004: 55–60), the financial underwriting of these recitals in Yaeyama is taken on by the performers rather than the audience, although the sums involved are considerably less than is common in Japan – performers pay around 5,000 yen (US$60), for which they receive a number of free entrance tickets for friends and family.

Konkūru for the performance of the Okinawan classical song tradition were first established in the Okinawan mainland by the *Okinawa Times* newspaper company in 1954, with a rival event sponsored by the *Ryūkyū Shinpō* newspaper from 1966, and the Yaeyaman events were formed largely following the Okinawan model. The first Yaeyaman *konkūru* was organised in 1975[15] under the sponsorship of the *Yaeyama Mainichi* Shinbun newspaper. The early history of these *konkūru* is entwined with the struggles I outlined above between the various lineages to develop increasingly accurate *kunkunshi* notations, and the *konkūru* also seem to have had a profound effect on the continued development of lineage organisations.

Initial attempts to establish *konkūru* by the YKOARK in the early 1970s were apparently hampered by a realisation that the variety of different performance versions even within that organisation made it difficult to establish a fair and impartial judging system (Yaeyama Koten Min'yō Hozonkai 1997). Various attempts were made to provide a standard by which *konkūru* entrants could be judged – Ōhama Anpan's students encouraged the use of his new *kunkunshi* showing the vocal line, while the president of the organisation, Kanna Chōsuke, recorded a cassette

---

[15]　Prior to WWII, there was no standardised system of issuing teaching licences to pupils at all. Ameku Yōritsu was given a 'teaching licence' by his teacher, Kishaba Sonchi, in 1931 at the end of Sonchi's career, with the meaning that Ameku would succeed Sonchi as the single transmitter of the lineage. The first licences to be issued to students by an organisation were those awarded to Ōhama Tsurō and Ōhama Anpan by the Ishigaki Cultural Association (Ishigaki-shi Bunka Kyōkai) in 1956.

of 'model examples' for entrants to copy. The *konkūru* system was established in 1975 and worked satisfactorily for the first two years, but in 1977, when a new *saiyūshūshō* ('top' prize) level was introduced, all entrants at this level were failed by the judges. Dissatisfaction over the result, and concerns over the partiality of some of the judges, caused a breakaway group to be formed in 1978 around some contestants who had failed the 1977 test. This breakaway group, which came to be known as the Yaeyama Koten Ongaku Kyōkai, was a blanket organisation for the YKOARH, YKOARK and YOOYRH groups, and this group organised a new *konkūru* under the sponsorship of the *Ryūkyū Shinpō* newspaper company. The *Yaeyama Mainichi* Shinbun-sponsored *konkūru* was left as the domain of Anpan's circle of students, which renamed itself the YKMH in 1979.

The introduction of *konkūru* in the 1970s also seems to have had a noticeable effect in standardising performance variants, and in some cases prompting performers to abandon existing affiliations to join more prominent organisations. Maehana Tomohiro, who started out in the Tonoshiro-based YOOYRH, describes his difficulties in the early *konkūru*:

> When it came to singing together at the *happyōkai*, our way of singing didn't match everyone else's. Then the opinion arose [among our teacher's students] that we should all join with Ōhama Anpan's group. Our group had about 80 students, mostly from Tonoshiro, but an argument broke out between those who wanted to stay [in the Tonoshiro tradition] and those who wanted to leave [to Ōhama Anpan] ... Thinking of the future, we felt that, unless we used Anpan's *seigakufu-tsuki kunkunshi*, we could get marginalized, and from the point of view of performing with other players, it was vital to unify our singing style. (Yaeyama Koten Min'yō Hozonkai 1997: 43)

Following this deliberation, Maehana, together with his teacher Tomoyose Eiki and his students, moved over to the YKMH way of singing. As a measure of the seriousness with which they took this decision, Tomoyose describes having prayed for forgiveness from the spirit of his deceased teacher (Ōhama Tsurō), whom he felt that he had betrayed by moving to the *utaikata* of another lineage (ibid.: 44). Although the Tonoshiro tradition is still taught, and is still used in Tonoshiro-based rituals and festivals such as *An'gama*, it has been largely overtaken by the various Ishigaki lineages, and one of the most immediate reasons for this can be seen to be the development of a *kunkūru* system from the 1970s.

Yunta and *Jiraba* Preservation Groups – Singing the Village

Compared to *fushiuta*, which were from the beginning an 'art song' genre and thus adapted relatively easily to the social changes in Yaeyama over the 20th century, *yunta* and *jiraba* suffered a huge loss of performance context with the disappearance of the communal agricultural work patterns in the 20th century. One of the ways in which this repertory has continued to survive is through the establishment of preservation groups (*hozonkai*) at a village level. Like the *fushiuta* lineages, these village groups have been active in publishing standardised canons of their repertory in lyric collections for sale locally. While the *fushiuta* lineages have largely replaced village affiliations with more formal *ryūha* organisations, attempts to produce a unified Yaeyaman canon have been less successful, and remain firmly rooted in a village context. In this section I look at the history and activities of these *hozonkai*, and consider their role in village musical identities.

The term *hozonkai* has a variety of connotations in modern Japanese musical society. While it is sometimes used for more classical traditions (we met the term earlier in this chapter used to describe some of the *fushiuta* lineages, and there are examples of its use in mainland Japanese classical traditions such as the *Dentō Kabuki Hozonkai*, a large organisation of Kabuki performers), *hozonkai* more often refers to amateur groups preserving 'folk' genres, often at a village level. The first mainland Japanese folk song *hozonkai* were formed in the early 20th century (Hughes 2008: 214) and Yaeyaman *hozonkai* can be seen as part of the same cultural pattern. Hughes has written extensively about *hozonkai* in mainland Japan (1981, 1985: 224–40, 2008: 212–24), and many Yaeyaman groups fit into the picture that Hughes describes, with some important differences. As in the Japanese case, Yaeyaman *yunta hozonkai* have been set up and run largely on village or private initiative, and are run on a fairly informal basis. While the local government has been influential in encouraging the formation of the groups through organising singing competitions, it gives no direct support or funding to *hozonkai*. In contrast to the mainland Japanese case, where *hozonkai* are often dedicated to preserving a single song or dance (Hughes 1985: 224), Yaeyaman *yunta hozonkai* typically have around 30 to 40 songs in their repertory, most of which are *yunta* and *jiraba*, but usually including a few *yun'gutu*, *ayō* and ritual songs. The Yaeyaman *hozonkai* that I observed did not usually have a formal teacher as such, but operated on a cooperative system where lyrics and melodies were discussed by all participants. The opinions of elder members, of course, are generally held in higher esteem than those of younger members, but the strict 'teacher–disciple' (*sensei–deshi*) relationship found in *fushiuta* organisations was not to be seen in *yunta hozonkai*.

Yunta hozonkai have long functioned as a way in which village identities could be fostered and maintained. An early example was the formation of a so-called 'agricultural promotion group' (*kōnōkai*) in Ishigaki village in the 1930s, in which veteran singers taught *yunta* and *jiraba* (Ishigaki aza-kai koyō henshū iinkai 1985: v). As the name implies, the primary aim of this group was to increase agricultural production through the group bonding that songs provided. After a hiatus during WWII, the club was re-formed with the aim of increasing morale in the aftermath of the war, and again one of the activities providing a focus for the group's meetings was the teaching/learning of *yunta/jiraba*. An important aspect of both of these groups was that their official *raison d'être* was not the performance or preservation of music per se, but rather they acted as sites for the construction and maintenance of social ties, in this case on a village level, through the context of music.

While the main purpose of these *hozonkai* was the promotion of village identities, these local identities were often constructed within the context of more general events in Yaeyaman society. An important stimulus to the development of *hozonkai* came, in June 1965, with the organisation of a *koyō* concert (*taikai*[16]) by the Yaeyama education board. This festival was an early opportunity for *koyō* groups from villages around Yaeyama to perform in front of each other at one event, and seems to have prompted the formation of many of the currently active *hozonkai* – a Tonoshiro *hozonkai* was founded in 1968, while similar groups were formed in Arakawa (1967) and Ishigaki (1971), for example. The *yunta taikai* continued annually until 1982,[17] after which it has continued on a more sporadic basis, roughly once every five years, and the event continues to be one of the most important contexts for the performance of *yunta* and *jiraba*. The 2001 event included performances of *koyō* from Tonoshiro, Ishigaki, Hirae, Ōhama, Shiraho, Arakawa, Ōkawa and Miyara, all villages from around the main settlement area of Ishigaki island. During my extended fieldwork trip between 2001 and 2002 (I arrived shortly after the 2001 *taikai*), most of these groups were not meeting on a regular basis, and in some cases only met up to practice the few weeks before a big performance event such as the *taikai*. Thus, the 'village' identities fostered by the singing competition can be seen to be constructed largely in the context of this concert organised at a 'Yaeyaman' level. While the concert format was ostensibly 'non-competitive', the fact that groups from different villages shared a stage with neighbouring villages inevitably led to an incentive to produce a polished repertory.

From the autumn of 2001 until summer 2002 I participated regularly in the practices of a well-established *hozonkai* known as the Tonoshiro *Kayō no Kai*, a group consisting almost entirely of women in their sixties and above, with two occasional male members. The group has been meeting on Tuesdays ('*kayō*' can mean both 'song' and 'Tuesday') since its formation in 1972, and exists as a subsection of the official Tonoshiro *Koyō Hozonkai* (see Figure 5.4), which meets on a more sporadic basis, but which gives regular performances at village events. The *Kayō no kai* consisted of a core of older members, most of whom were born in the 1920s and 1930s, and two of whom told me that they learned at least part of their repertory in a work-song context. There was also a younger generation of members who were in their sixties (in 2002), and a few younger members in their fifties. While the ostensible reason for the group's existence is to teach and perform *koyō*, its continued success is also probably largely to do with its

---

[16]   The Japanese word *taikai* (lit. 'big meeting') can have a number of meanings. In Chapter 6 I have translated it as 'competition' due to its competitive nature in that case. The 1965 *taikai* for *yunta* and other *koyō* was non-competitive and I translate it as 'concert' here.

[17]   From 1974 to 1981 the event was organised by the Ishigaki city education department.

function as a kind of social club, with frequent 'outings' to the local countryside, or to practice the members' real passion of 'ground' golf. As was the case with the very early *hozonkai*, the social aspect of most modern *hozonkai* often carries equal weight to musical considerations. All the members were born, raised or married in Tonoshiro and most had lived there all their lives. The two or three central members of the group could sing most songs in the Tonoshiro repertory from memory, and also had an extensive knowledge of Yaeyaman *fushiuta* and mainland Okinawan songs. The older members often complained, however, that since the publication of a book (Ishigaki 1992) of song lyrics, the younger members rely too much on the printed page, and are unable to memorise songs. During the practices that I observed, the group didn't usually sing a song right to the end (often 20 or 30 verses) but typically shortened songs to four or six verses in both the *funku* and *tōsï* sections – even though this obviously disrupts the flow of the original narrative content.

Almost all the Yaeyaman *koyō hozonkai* that I observed were marked by a lack of younger members. The Miyara *hozonkai* had gained some prestige among other groups by having a high school student member, but it was rare to find members in their forties or younger, and most members were over 60.

Figure 5.4   Tonoshiro *koyō hozonkai* performing in 2002 at Tonoshiro's harvest festival (*on-pūrï*)

The gender mix, with the exception of the Tonoshiro women's group, was fairly even – the antiphonal structure of *yunta* and *jiraba*, most often divided into male and female groups, has meant that most *hozonkai* are reliant on members of both sexes to provide an even balance in performance. In contrast to the *fushiuta* genre, which has traditionally been male-dominated, and has only seen a significant number of female performers since the 1990s, *yunta* and *jiraba* always seem to have had a significant number of female performers (communal work groups in the pre-WWII years were made up of both men and women), and this tradition was reflected in the *hozonkai* that I observed.

The existence of most *koyō hozonkai* as social institutions, in addition to their role as sites for music-making, has meant that the strict teacher–student relationships found in many Japanese performing arts genres (and in Yaeyaman *fushiuta* lineages) were mostly absent from the *koyō hozonkai* that I observed. On the other hand, I did hear a number of comments concerning the way these groups acted as an extension of existing social relationships, and in some cases excluded the participation of certain members. Again, age seemed to be an important factor. An informant from Taketomi in his late fifties complained that although he played a prominent part in the performing arts of his island, he was not allowed entry to the *koyō hozonkai* on the grounds that he was too young, and did not have a deep enough understanding of the repertory. Another informant, who was very active both in *fushiuta* and the traditional life of his native Arakawa village (he was a key member of the Arakawa *An'gamā* group), told me that he was refused entry to the Arakawa *koyō hozonkai*, again because he was considered to be of the 'wrong generation' to learn *yunta* and *jiraba*.

Many informants commented that the formation of *hozonkai* at a village level had not been without issue, as in practice there had been no concept of a unified 'village' repertory or style in the years after WWII. Villages continued to be divided by affiliation to *utaki* (shrine), and the songs that were sung in each village division, although similar, were sufficiently different in form to prevent members from each division singing easily with each other. In some cases these differences have prevented unification, and a number of different *utaikata* exist in a single village or island. Uesedo Tomoko, a music specialist in Taketomi, told me:

> we've tried making *hozonkai* in the past, but they've all ended in failure. The trouble is that Taketomi people are so stubborn (*ganko*). They just won't accept a leader – everyone wants to sing in their own way. Whenever we try to get together to sing, it always ends in an argument. (pers. comm. August 2001)

The examples that have succeeded have usually involved efforts to create a compromise version from the styles of a number of different singers. In 2002, Miyara Jitsuan, president of the Miyara (village) *koyō hozonkai*, told me how the first meetings of the village *hozonkai* in the mid-20th century had resulted in chaos as members of the east and west parts of the village had attempted to sing together.

His solution was to form a 'unified' style which took elements of the songs of both sides of the village and melded them into one 'Miyara version':

> At that time we used to have a group made up of members from the west and east parts of the village, but when we tried singing together it was just a mess, so the group broke up. We decided we couldn't unify the [songs of the] two parts of the village. At that time, if one person sang, so-and-so wouldn't be satisfied, so-and-so would complain. I was only twenty then ... Later [around 1975] some of the village elders came to us and asked us if we couldn't work out a single version, and that's what we've got today. It took us three years to work out a version which everyone was satisfied with. At that time we also had requests coming from Okinawa and Japan to record our repertory onto cassette tape [for the *Nihon Min'yō Taikan* project and others], but nobody had the confidence to record the correct version. One person sang this way. Another person sang that way. After we made the unified (*tōitsu*) version, we had the confidence to sing for the researchers. (Miyara Jitsuan, pers. comm. September 2002)

Miyara's identification of 'requests from Okinawa and Japan' for recorded versions of local songs also reveals another impetus on the formation of unified village repertories and canons. The 1970s had seen increased fieldwork expeditions by leading mainland Japanese musicologists such as Koizumi Fumio, the results of which were eventually published in staff notation collections (Koizumi 1981; Nippon Hōsō Kyōkai 1990a, 1990b). Publication of village repertory in these prestigious documents, and the attention of these prominent scholars from the Japanese mainland, seems to have acted as a strong impetus to produce standardised 'official' village versions of songs. Similar 'unification' processes took place in other Yaeyaman villages (see e.g. Arakawa Kōminkan Bunkabu 1986: introduction; Ishigaki Aza-kai Koyō Henshū Iinkai 1985: v). This influence of mainland Japanese scholars on the formation of very regional repertories and performances is something we also encountered in the early 20th century in Chapter 3. A similar phenomenon has been outlined in other parts of Japan by Hughes, who describes the production of a standardised version of the Hokkaidō song *Esashi Oiwake* in the early 20th century as 'ambassador for the town' in the face of interest in the song from other parts of Japan (2008: 113).

In 2002 I witnessed an interesting attempt by the Ishigaki-shi Bunka Kyōkai (Culture Association), an organisation sponsored by the Ishigaki city government, to create a centralised group for the performance of *koyō* from around Yaeyama. The aims of this club were to provide a place for the teaching and study of *koyō* that was not restricted by affiliation with a certain village, but to create a 'pan-Yaeyama' repertory for the genre. The group met once a month in the association's offices in Ōkawa and, for the time that I observed it from April to September 2002, had a participating membership of about 15 (the official membership list numbered 30). Members were dominated by the four central villages of Ishigaki island, but also included members from Taketomi and Aragusuku islands.

Of the 15 regular members, the majority were male, with three regular female members. I was actively encouraged to participate in this group as a singer and, on one occasion, guest speaker – as an outside researcher I was one of the few members of the group to have had access to songs from more than one village tradition, and, more importantly, my status as a foreigner and interest in Yaeyaman music were both a source of curiosity and lent a cosmopolitan air to what is usually seen as a very old-fashioned musical genre.

During the six months that I observed the group, the first three months were spent studying two songs from the Arakawa repertory. Other months saw a presentation from a Tonoshiro resident Yamazato Setsuko, one of the few Yaeyamans to have actively studied songs from more than one repertory, and my own presentation. In September, after much persuasion, a member of the Ōkawa *koyō hozonkai* was persuaded to come and teach the group the Ōkawa village version of the song *Shūritsu yunta*, but the group seems to have experienced difficulty in finding teachers to fulfil its 'pan-Yaeyama' objective. For example the group repeatedly asked Yamazato to teach them some songs from the Tonoshiro repertory. Her response was that if the group wanted to learn this repertory then they would have to go through the head of the Tonoshiro *hozonkai*. While Yamazato is an accomplished singer with a deep understanding of the repertory, she told me (August 2002) that, as a junior member of Tonoshiro's *hozonkai*, and with no experience of singing songs in a work situation, she felt she was not qualified to teach. A further problem which the group faces is that many people with a good knowledge of their own traditions either do not want to share their own repertory with outsiders, or feel that their command of their own repertory will be somehow damaged by learning to sing different versions of the same songs. One member of the Tonoshiro *hozonkai* remarked that his way of singing a particular song had become corrupted (*yabureduru*) through his learning of the Arakawa version of the song during the first few months of the group. While the Ishigaki culture association continues to organise concerts featuring *yunta/jiraba hozonkai* from particular villages, the activities of the pan-Yaeyaman group have become more sporadic. When I visited Yaeyama in March 2009, the group was 'resting' and, like many of the other local *hozonkai*, only seemed to gather together in the weeks before a performance.

Song Monuments

The imagination of local songs and song versions in the construction of local identities at a village level has been achieved in several ways. At the level of performance, the construction of *hozonkai* groups, and their participation at events such as the *yunta taikai* have been ways of 'performing' village identities. Cultural identities have also been imagined through attempts to form a village musical canon through the publication of lyric collections. Another way in which the connections between villages and individual songs have been publically imagined in a tangible form is through the construction of 'song monuments' (*kahi*). The phenomenon of constructing monuments honouring songs or poems with a particular regional affiliation can be seen all over Japan, and monuments can be found commemorating a wide variety of music and poetry genres: verses from ancient poetry collections such as the *man'yōshū*; *haiku* poems by the 17th-century poet Matsuo Bashō; local folk songs and 20th-century pop songs have all been immortalised by local governments and private organisations in the Japanese regions to which they are connected.

Figure 5.5   Collage of song monuments: *Basï nu turï bushi*; *Tubarāma*;
              Akanma bushi; *Hatoma bushi*

Many of these are hewn from solid lumps of rock with the lyrics of the particular song carved into one face, while others are cast in concrete, bronze or other materials. The construction of *kahi* has been particularly vigorous in Okinawa prefecture, and they are popular enough with the musically-minded Okinawan public that several guide books have been published giving details of the location of the various monuments commemorating songs and singers from the classical and folk music traditions in the prefecture (e.g. Ishigaki and Agarie 1986). Figure 5.5 shows examples of four such monuments, all of which are situated either in the presumed place of a song's composition (*Tubarāma* in Hirae village, *Akanma bushi* in Miyara or *Basï yunta* in Ōkawa) or in the location mentioned in a song's text (*Hatoma bushi* in Hatoma island).

The cost involved in the construction of these monuments can be substantial: the *Tubarāma* monument completed in 1983 had a total budget of nearly three million yen (around US$35,000 at 2011 exchange rates), raised mostly from private donations (Iriomote and Ōta 1983: 5). These relatively large sums show the cultural importance of *kahi* as a tangible way of constructing local identities through the fundamentally intangible context of song. The financial benefits achieved by increased tourism due to the construction of *kahi* are conceivable – the original rationale for the *Tubarāma kahi* mentions tourism as an aim (ibid.: 3), and *fushiuta* groups often visit the *kahi* of songs they are learning as part of their 'extra-curricular' social activities. In at least one case, surrounding the construction of a monument for *Basï yunta* (and its *fushiuta* version *Basï nu turï bushi*) they have also been used as a way of asserting village 'ownership' of a song. In Chapter 3 I described Kishaba Eijun's attempts, prompted by requests from Okinawan and mainland Japanese scholars, to investigate composers for particular songs, and his 1912 'discovery' of the song's composer, an 18th-century ritual specialist named Nakama Sakai from Ōkawa village. In the mid-20th century, a rival theory was proposed by Miyara Kentei, another prominent Yaeyaman scholar, that the song had been composed in Kabira village by a different Nakama Sakai. There followed a lengthy and often heated public debate, carried out in the local newspapers by many of the scholars of the time (see N. Iha 1957, 1962; Kishaba 1962; Y. Kojima 1962; Miki 1963). Kishaba seems to have been particularly passionate about the issue, and in 1962 published a series of six articles in the *Yaeyama Mainichi* newspaper stating his case (reprinted in Kishaba 1967: 61–88). While the issue was never conclusively decided, as a way of consolidating their 'claim' on the song, the descendants of the Nakama family in Kabira subsequently erected a memorial stone stating its origins in that village, a move which apparently enraged Kishaba (Miki 1989: 50), and which the writer Miki Takeshi lamented at the time in a newspaper article entitled '*Semento no bōryoku* – the violence of cement' (see Miki 1963, also 1980: 226). In the 1980s Ōkawa village subsequently erected its own monument in memory of the composition of *Basï yunta* in their village. The monument (see Figure 5.5), in the shape of an eagle, stands in the main shopping mall in downtown Ōkawa emitting a tape loop recording of the song.

Traditional Music in the School System

One of the most important contexts for the performance and dissemination of traditional music in modern Yaeyama has been the school system. While formal music education in Yaeyama, in common with schools in the rest of Japan, continues to be focused on European classical music (for an overview of the teaching of music in Japanese schools see Murao and Wilkins 2001), opportunities for learning traditional music exist in many of Yaeyama's schools at all levels, both as part of the curriculum and as part of organised extra-curricular activities. Each of Yaeyama's three high schools has extremely active traditional performing arts clubs (*kyōdo geinō-bu*), and these have been consistently successful in the annual national high school performing arts club competition (*Zenkoku Kōkō Sōgō Bunkasai*). Yaeyaman schools have won the competition on three occasions since its origins in 1976,[18] showing the level of emphasis put on traditional arts in Yaeyaman schools in a national context. Many junior high schools and elementary schools have similar clubs teaching performing arts from Yaeyama and the Okinawan mainland. The formation of these clubs is a fairly recent phenomenon, dating from the mid-1960s, and the transition of the teaching of performing arts into the school system relied upon, and is representative of, a fundamental change in the social position of many aspects of Yaeyaman traditional culture during the immediate post-war period.

Following the widespread suppression of traditional culture in the pre-WWII years that we saw in Chapter 3, the post-war years saw a newfound confidence in Yaeyaman performing arts that led to a cultural reassessment of many genres at this time. Despite this renewed interest in Yaeyaman performing arts, early attempts to incorporate traditional music into schools were not without issue. Iramina Kōkichi, a leading *fushiuta* performer in the current Yaeyaman music world, currently based in mainland Japan, writes:

> In 1958 I moved to The Ishigaki Elementary School in Ishigaki village. Once a month they used to have a birthday party (*tanjōkai*[19]) and I would play the *sanshin* for the students and get them to dance. While the students were enthusiastic, I started getting complaints from the PTA, with comments asking whether [traditional music] was appropriate for schools. The head teacher often used to have words with me. I didn't actually stop playing, but I deliberately used to play quietly so as not to upset the head-teacher.
>
> Nevertheless, I started to be called things like the 'delinquent teacher' (*furyō kyōin*). I remember having a really tough time. Not only in schools but in society in general, the *sanshin*, Ryūkyūan music and classical performing arts were

---

[18] Yaeyama High School won the event in 1994 and 2002, Yaeyama *Shōgyō* High School in 2007.

[19] A combined party for all the children born in a particular month.

seen completely differently to the way they are now. People's attitude to the classical (*koten*) performing arts and music was bad enough, but there was total dismissal of other forms like *zōuta* ['popular' dance songs] and *hayabiki* [fast dance songs]. (Iramina 2002: 55–6)

An early impetus for change in the social status of traditional music came from outside Yaeyama itself, with the formation of a Yaeyaman performing arts club in 1956 at the University of the Ryūkyūs in the Okinawan mainland. This university continues to be Okinawa's most prestigious educational establishment, and the fact that traditional music was being performed within its walls by the 1950s was, thus, an important statement to schools around Okinawa that the genre was socially acceptable. By 1960, Yaeyaman graduates of this university began filtering back into Yaeyaman society, and a group of newly qualified school teachers began to think about recreating the university *geinō* club idea in Yaeyaman schools. One of these graduates was Takamine Hōyū, a young English teacher from Taketomi. Takamine also describes strong resistance from the educational establishment to his attempts to introduce traditional music into the school:

> At that time teachers didn't play the *sanshin* at all, and children who played were regarded as lazy good-for-nothings (*piratsukā*). There were comments like 'if you play *sanshin* in school, people will think it is a *sakanayā* (*geisha house*)' or 'I feel uncomfortable when I hear the sound of the *sanshin*'. (Takamine 1989: 217)

Like Iramina, Takamine's initial attempts to introduce traditional music into the school system were far from smooth. He told me (April 2002) that shortly after joining the Yaeyama High School as a teacher in 1960, he had tried to play the *sanshin* at a party to welcome new staff members to the school. The school authorities, fearful that they would get a reputation as running a *sakanayā*, ran around closing all the windows and doors and told him to stop playing immediately. In addition to the general low image of the *sanshin* in society, there were other specific problems facing the introduction of music into schools. No teaching materials dealing with traditional performing arts existed until the 1970s, and the strong emphasis on teaching only what was in the established textbooks also proved to be an obstacle to the introduction of Yaeyaman music into the curriculum (Takamine 1989: 217). Takamine also notes that, with the exception of one or two villages, the loss of dialect use in everyday life in the 1960s meant that many students had trouble understanding the lyrics of traditional songs.

The Yaeyama High School club, the first of its kind in the region, was officially founded in 1964, and gave its debut performance at the school's 'culture festival' (*bunka-sai*) in that year. In the first year, the group attracted 10 members, and the dance performances were mostly by the three most experienced female students.[20] There were no students able to play the *sanshin* well enough to accompany the

---

[20]   Ōhama Tomoko, Kana Aiko and Ishigaki Michiko.

dancers so several local *fushiuta* teachers were called in to help. Following the success of this debut performance, a public concert was organised in 1965 in the Bunka Kaikan hall in Ishigaki. The large cost of make-up and costumes was covered by sponsorship from local businesses, with a hand-written programme to keep costs down. From that year, the club became more popular and *sanshin* players also started to emerge.

From these humble beginnings, with real problems finding enough students capable of performing to a high standard, the Yaeyama High School club has grown to a high level of proficiency. I observed several practices of the club in the spring of 2002, when it had a membership of 29 – musicians were dominated by boys, while the dancers were exclusively girls, a split which mirrors the gender bias in performing arts in Yaeyaman society. The clubs of the other high schools in Ishigaki were also of a very high standard, and had roughly similar gender distributions. The *geinō* club at the Yaeyama Nōrin High School (Yaeyama High School of Agriculture and Forestry) was led by a (European classical) music teacher at the school with no previous experience of Yaeyama performing arts, and the group initially collaborated with dance/*sanshin* teachers from outside the school, or created their own dances. The dancers in the Nōrin group were also mostly female, although there were three male dancers at the time of my visit.

The main activities of high school *geinō* clubs involve performing at school and other local events, as well as participating in school *geinō* club competitions at a prefectural and national level. The *geinō* club at the Nōrin High School, due to the school's agricultural connections, was a regular participant at harvest festivals around Ishigaki – in both 2001 and 2002 I observed the club performing a series of dances at the harvest festival in the *shika-aza* part of the city. The school *geinō* clubs that I observed had no official *ryūha* affiliation – one of the reasons often given for the difficulty of incorporating traditional music into the Japanese school system (e.g. Hughes 2008: 294). The Yaeyama High School club used the YKMH *kunkunshi*, while Nōrin High School group was using a *kunkunshi* produced by the YKOARH. Most of the musicians at these high school groups also took private lessons outside school in a variety of lineages, but the similarities in performance of the three main Ishigaki *ryūha* (I encountered no students who studied in the Tonoshiro-based Yōnō-ryū) mean that musicians rarely had trouble playing together. The clubs also made attempts to incorporate ritual genres and work songs from around Yaeyama into their programmes. The 2002 programme at Yaeyama High School was based on Taketomi festival music, including *Tunchāma*, the song used to welcome the gods at the *Yūnkai* ritual in September, and *Sōji kachi*, a dance used to ritually purify the stage during *Tanadui*. The Nōrin group was also active in incorporating ritual performances from around Yaeyama, such as the Yonaguni '*bō-odori*' (sword/stick dance) they were working on in 2002.

Since the early 1970s, the move to promote local traditional music in schools has come not only from within the schools themselves, but has been actively encouraged by the local board of education. A 1969 Japanese national curriculum required schools throughout the country to teach at least one folk song each year

(Hughes 2008: 293). Influenced by this law (Okinawa became a Japanese prefecture in 1972), in 1976 the Yaeyama Education Office (Yaeyama Kyōiku Jimusho) published a collection of traditional songs in staff notation for use as teaching material in schools. The songs included in this collection included children's songs from all over Okinawa, designated for use in elementary school classes, while the intended repertory for middle school students consisted predominantly of Yaeyaman work songs such as *Mayā yunta* and *Koina yunta*, and *fushiuta* such as *Tonosama bushi* and *Agarōza bushi* (Yaeyama Kyōiku Jimusho 1976). This policy seems to have had some success, and several Yaeyaman informants who went through the school system in the 1970s and 1980s remembered learning these songs in school and, in some cases, could still sing some of them.

In some cases, schools have also established courses devoted to traditional music performance. Yaeyama High School, for example, introduced an optional course entitled 'local music' (*Kyōdo no ongaku*) in 1996, with the aim of teaching the performance of traditional music to beginners. When I visited in 2002, the course contained a predominantly Yaeyaman repertory – with the exception of a few Okinawa mainland songs such as *Nubui kuduchi* and *Haisai ojisan*, and some Japanese children's songs such as *Hato poppo* taught at the beginning of the course, all songs came from the Yaeyaman *fushiuta*, *koyō* or *hōnō geinō* repertories.[21] The course also has a strong focus on teaching local history and languages, of which most students in the 21st century have only a basic grasp. Takamine Hōyū, the course instructor, told me that in contrast to the first year, when he had trouble finding students to take the class, by 2002 it was being taught twice a year, and was so popular that entry was by lottery.

In 2002, a new national school curriculum was introduced requiring schools to incorporate some teaching of a traditional Japanese instrument into music classes. Shortly following the introduction of this new curriculum, I carried out a telephone poll of Yaeyaman schools to find out what provision had been made for the teaching of traditional music. Of the three high schools, all had *geinō* clubs, and Yaeyama High School had also introduced the teaching of traditional music into the curriculum as an optional class (*sentaku jugyō*[22]). Approximately half of elementary and junior high schools, particularly the larger ones such as the Shiraho elementary/middle school, had active *geinō* clubs, most of which had been active for a number of years. Of the schools that had no current traditional music activities, such as Taketomi and Hatoma, I was told that traditional music and dance was taught within the community and almost all children performed at the local festivals. The very small size of many schools in the outer islands of

---

21   The repertory in 2002 included Basï nu turï bushi, Hanjō bushi, Tomata bushi and Densā bushi.

22   *Sentaku jugyō* take place in the hours allocated for general studies (*sōgō gakushū*) which are often used by schools throughout Japan for 'local' studies. The teaching of traditional music in Yaeyaman schools thus takes place largely outside the teaching of the core curriculum.

Yaeyama (Hatoma elementary/middle school had an average of 10 pupils over all age groups out of a total island population of some 60 people) means that the formal teaching of traditional performing arts is still strongly connected to the local community rather than the education system. On the other hand, the extent to which active performers exist in most Yaeyaman communities has meant that, first, there is little difficulty in finding volunteers to demonstrate traditional music performance in class and, second, that there is perhaps less of a need to incorporate traditional music into formal lessons when it already survives strongly in the community.

The incorporation of traditional music performance into Yaeyaman schools seems to have been particularly successful, given the historically low social status of local genres, and considering the generally low level of traditional music in Japanese schools as a whole. One factor that allowed for the introduction of traditional music into the school system in the post-WWII years, perhaps paradoxically, was the relatively sudden loss of traditional music, and especially local language use, from everyday life at around the same time. The removal of traditional culture from the daily lives of many Yaeyamans after WWII (the original Ishigaki high school club did not include any students capable of playing the *sanshin*, for example) was perhaps instrumental in also allowing for its 'social rehabilitation' (cf. de Ferranti 2009: 279 concerning Kyushu *biwa* traditions), and thus facilitated its introduction into the school system. The influence of traditional music in the Yaeyaman education system on the production of young performers of a high standard has been considerable. Graduates of high school *geinō* clubs who have followed professional careers as performers include the dance teacher Arashiro Tomoko, and the singers Ara Yukito and Ōshima Yasukatsu from Yaeyama High School, and Daiku Tetsuhiro from Nōrin High School (see also Chapter 7). Many local *fushiuta* teachers and performers told me they were introduced to traditional music in the *geinō* club of one of Ishigaki's three high schools, indicating that the school club system feeds back into traditional music-making in the community. Another obvious effect of Yaeyaman school *geinō* clubs has been that the Okinawan traditional music major at Okinawa University of Arts in Naha has seen a very high proportion of students from Yaeyama, many of whom were introduced to traditional music through their high school club experiences. The Yaeyaman *geinō* club at the University of the Ryūkyūs in Okinawa also continues to be influential, having introduced a large number of currently active festival musicians in Yaeyama to traditional music.

Traditional Music and the Tourist Industry

Okinawa is one of Japan's top domestic tourist destinations – 2009 saw around 5.7 million tourists (the population of Okinawa is some 1.4 million), of which more than 95 per cent were from the Japanese mainland.[23] Traditional music has been an important aspect of the recent tourist industry. Walking around the central settlement of Ishigaki, it is impossible to avoid hearing Yaeyaman and Okinawan traditional music, piped through speakers from the numerous tourist restaurants and shops and, as evening draws in, performed live at the numerous folk-song bars in the entertainment district. In this section I look at some of the ways music is performed as part of the tourist industry, and consider the way these performances exist within the more local Yaeyaman musical society.

The social meaning of much of the traditional music presented in a tourist context obviously differs from that on a purely local level. Gibson and Connell have written of music tourism as 'so often one more form of "invented tradition" or "strategic inauthenticity" where what is presented to tourists is a partial, incomplete and distorted version of a past that never was' (2005: 267). Nevertheless, with tourism playing such an important part in the modern Okinawan economy, performances of traditional music in a tourist context are a very real part of the musical life of many musicians. Lau's analysis of musical performances for tourists in China shows how they are simultaneously 'intertwined with the Chinese state's perception of nationhood and modernity, and with local perception of identity' (1998: 116). Thus, while tourist performances may have different meanings from purely local performances, they still feed back to some extent on the way traditional music is viewed at a local level. In another example, Dawe has described how in Crete 'most professional [*lyra*] musicians eventually turn their back on the tourist market ... *Lyra* music is dependent on the local economy as it interfaces with international monetary systems (as subsidized by tourism) but also has to "speak" and sell itself to locals who define themselves and "the music tradition" in opposition to tourists and the non-Cretan world' (2004c: 71). We can see here, again, the way in which the existence of tourists, and the production of 'music tourism' feeds back into music-making on a local level, if only by providing a focus against which local music-making is 'opposed'.

As early as 1962, tour companies were greeting visitors to Okinawa with performances of Okinawan music within the airport terminal building (Umeda 2001: 130), a practice that was revived at the height of the Okinawa boom in the 1990s under the sponsorship of the prefectural government, with hourly performances of music and dance.[24] Private tour companies continue to use traditional music as one aspect of their business. In Ishigaki the local Azuma bus company has for several years run bus tours around Ishigaki island featuring

---

23   Okinawa prefecture Tourism Planning Division. www3.pref.okinawa.jp/site/view/ contview.jsp?cateid=233&id=22761&page=1, accessed 1 February 2011.

24   The programme was discontinued in 2005.

local songs performed at their village of origin by the driver. Since the early 21st century, a number of businesses have sprung up in central Ishigaki offering introductory *sanshin* lessons (*sanshin taiken*), teaching students an Okinawan song[25] in a 30-minute lesson (see Figure 5.6). Many of these businesses offer *sanshin*, CDs and music notation for sale, although several also double as coffee shops or bars. In the Okinawan mainland, many of the major tourist destinations in Yaeyama and Okinawa offer performances of Okinawan music and dancing. The Okinawan theme park centred around the caves of Gyokusendō in Nanjō city, for example, has reconstructions of old Okinawan houses, recreations of the old life-styles in Okinawa, and performances of the Okinawan *bon* dance *eisā* at intervals throughout the day (see Johnson 2008: 208–10). Similar examples can be found within Yaeyama. Taketomi island, for example, offers guided tours in carts drawn by water buffalo, during which the paying customers are entertained by the driver singing the local Taketomi song *Asadoya yunta* (see Figure 5.7).

One of the most immediate ways of encountering traditional music in its tourist guise is at the many folk-song clubs in the main settlement of Ishigaki. These clubs are known by many names, including *min'yō sakaba* (folk-song pub), *min'yō sunakku*,[26] *min'yō raibu hausu* (live house) and *shimauta raibu hausu* (*shimauta* live house). Within the central three blocks of the Misaki-chō downtown area of Ishigaki there were upwards of 15 establishments classing themselves along these lines in 2002, and most of them advertised, or were regularly featured in, the various tourist brochures and literature distributed at Yaeyama's main tourist destinations. These folk-song clubs range from the more traditionally oriented – such as the *Hamabe Min'yō Sunakku* which plays a large proportion of Yaeyaman songs, interspersed with songs from the Okinawan mainland and mainland Japanese popular songs from the early 20th century, to establishments such as *Ryūka*, run by Tonoshiro-born *sanshin* performer and singer Kawajō Masahiko, who specialises in his own pop-influenced compositions and Okinawan *hayabiki* (fast-picking) numbers. Folk-song clubs generally seat from 30 to 60 customers, and almost always include a stage on which the performers or customers sing, usually through an echo-laden PA system. In addition to *sanshin*, accompanying instruments always include *taiko*, and often *fue*, as well as Western instruments such as mandolin and guitar. The number and popularity of these folk-song clubs is testament to the continued importance of traditional music in Yaeyama, but also to the continued use of traditional music as part of the tourist industry, and in turn to the fascination that 'traditional Yaeyama' holds for many tourists.

---

[25]   Usually *Shimauta, Asadoya yunta* or one of the band BEGIN's songs.

[26]   A *sunakku* (from English 'snack') is a drinking establishment, usually featuring the presence of female 'companions' who provide companionship, and in this case singing, to the customers.

Figure 5.6   *Sanshin* lessons for tourists in Ishigaki

Figure 5.7   Tourist cart in Taketomi. The driver is playing a *sanshin*

An early model for the modern *min'yō sakaba* can be found in the *sakanayā* (drinking houses) that existed in Ishigaki from at least the late 19th century. *Sakanayā* were somewhat similar to Japanese geisha houses, with the staff providing musical entertainment, witty conversation, and companionship to the clientele. There is little written about *sakanayā* and, especially among my musical informants, they seemed to be regarded as having been disreputable places which were, at best, irrelevant to Yaeyaman musical history. The first Okinawan folk-song club was reputedly established by the well-known performer Kina Shōei[27] in 1962 in the Okinawan mainland, but the number of clubs increased dramatically in the mid-1970s, driven by an influx of tourists following the 1972 return of Okinawa to Japan, and the *Kaiyōhaku* expo in Okinawa in 1975 (Bise 1998: 191). Folk-song clubs had also been an important aspect of the mainland Japanese *min'yō* boom in the 1970s (Hughes 2008: 192–6) and Okinawan clubs can be seen as an extension of the nation-wide renaissance of interest in folk songs at the time.

I had extensive contact with one Misaki-chō folk-song club called Asadoya between 2001 and 2002, as well as visiting others on a sporadic basis. Asadoya is run by Kuroshima-born Asato Isamu,[28] a student of the Shiraho performer Yamazato Yūkichi. After working in a variety of jobs in Tokyo and the Okinawan mainland, Asato returned to Yaeyama, where for several years he made a living as a fisherman in Taketomi, with a sideline business taking Japanese tourists out in his boat during the day and entertaining them with his singing during the evening. As a result of a connection made through this side business, he was taken up in 1996 by the small Japanese Respect record label, which released a CD of him performing *fushiuta* in very simple arrangements with only the addition of bamboo flute to most tracks, and with ambient sound effects of the sea emphasising the 'island' aspects of the recording. The decision to use this repertory was apparently not Asato's, who told me that he favours the more lively mainland Okinawan songs during his live shows, as it gets a more favourable response from audiences (who often know little about Yaeyaman music). The record was nevertheless a success in mainland Japan, and enabled Asato to open the club in Ishigaki city.

Asadoya (Figure 5.8) owes its original existence to the popularity with which Asato's music was received in mainland Japan, and continues to cater largely to a tourist clientele. Between 2001 and 2002, when I visited the club on a regular basis, a large proportion of his customers – probably more than half – were tourists from the Japanese mainland. The club was generally occupied from 8 p.m. to 11 p.m. by a tourist audience, with a second round of Yaeyaman locals usually arriving around 10 p.m., who would make up the majority of the clientele until the club shut at around 2 a.m.

---

[27]   Father of Kina Shōkichi.

[28]   The club's name is a pun on his name and the song *Asadoya yunta*.

Figure 5.8   Asadoya folk song bar

Asato's choice of repertory was quite sharply divided between tourist oriented material, based mainly on more up-tempo songs, and the slow Yaeyaman songs such as *Tubarāma*, *Yonaguni shonkanē* and *Kohama bushi*, in which Asato specialised, and which he usually featured only in front of more knowledgeable (local) audiences. In particular, several of Asadoya's regular clientele were fishermen who had worked with Asato in his pre-professional musician days in Ishigaki. There were also frequent visits from members of the Kuroshima diaspora in Ishigaki, as well as members of Asato's extended social network throughout Yaeyama and Okinawa. Clubs such as Asadoya, while depending largely on the tourist industry for their financial viability, are thus also supported by a local customer-base, many of whom are passionately interested in the music.

I was warned on several occasions by local Yaeyamans of the potential dangers to my musical development of visiting clubs such as Asadoya. Comments ranged from outright criticism: 'they play *asobi-jamisen* (for fun, not serious, *sanshin*) and are destroying the correct way of playing'; to reluctant acceptance: 'they serve a purpose I suppose, in providing a tourist attraction'. This view was also taken by some performers in *min'yō* clubs themselves. The proprietor of one club in Ishigaki, an accomplished performer, told me that he had sent his daughter to learn with a leading member of the Yaeyama Koten Min'yō Hozonkai, so that she could learn the Yaeyama repertory 'properly'. Part of the ambivalence toward folk-song clubs comes from their historical connection to *sakanayā*, with the somewhat seedy connotations that those establishments continue to have. It also comes from a more general stigma against professional performers in Yaeyama (and Okinawa).

One (female) performer who has had extensive experience working in folk-song bars and on the tourist circuit told me:

> There isn't really a tradition of professional performers in Yaeyama. Music has always been played by ordinary people, and so professional performers aren't necessarily better than anybody else. A lot of people don't want to pay out money to listen to people playing songs that they can play themselves. (Yamashiro, pers. comm. September 2001)

Folk-song bars are thus culturally contested sites for the preservation and dissemination of traditional music in Yaeyama. Among the cultural Yaeyaman elite, in particular, these establishments are still often viewed with disdain, or at best with a kind of grudging acceptance as tourist attractions. Yet folk-song bars are also frequented by a more knowledgeable local Yaeyaman audience, and can be seen simultaneously to have an existence in Yaeyaman society outside the tourist industry. Like many other aspects of music-making in Yaeyama, the way traditional music is viewed at a local Yaeyaman level is constructed through a combination of Yaeyama's multiple cultural positions within the nation. It is unlikely that the majority of folk-song clubs could survive without the support of the tourist industry – Asadoya, at least, made the majority of its income from this market. Yet they serve a consecutive purpose as sites for the performance of local Yaeyaman communities through the context of traditional music.

言ずすどぅ主

Chapter 6
Izu su du nusï –
The Singer is Master:
Regional versus Individual Styles in the
Performance of *Tubarāma*

Tubarāma shonkanē,	*Tubarāma* and *Shonkanē*
Izu su du nusï yaru,	the singer is master

(Traditional *Tubarāma* lyric.
Translated from Ishigaki-shi Bunka Kyōkai 1999: 26)

A hot and stuffy evening in August. Summer is festival season in Yaeyama, and there is a brief respite between the harvest festival in July and *sōron* in late August. Sitting on the floor around a low table in a small traditional Okinawan house in Miyara are six men and women in their 70s and 80s who have gathered together at my request to demonstrate some of the village *yunta* and *jiraba*. The group, under the leadership of Miyara Jitsuan, a veteran of the village *yunta* preservation group (and one of the compilers of the book) sing a few unaccompanied *yunta* from the basic repertory, interspersed with earnest explanations of the finer points of the dialect used in the songs, and memories of the old work patterns in the years before and just after WWII. They are nervous, especially when I get the microphone out, and after a few instances of forgotten lyrics, someone produces a copy of the village 'song book', a collection of officially-sanctioned lyrics to all the local songs. My heart sinks. After a while Miyara produces a bottle of *awamori*, the local liquor, and pours generous helpings for the male members, including me. The women drink tea. After half an hour the mood has changed considerably, and the talk and songs begin to flow more freely. The subject changes from *yunta* and *jiraba* to another famous Yaeyaman song, *Tubarāma*, and the members almost instantly forget about my presence and their nervousness about singing 'correctly', and break into their own versions of this well-known melody. One of my closest informants, who has long been active in the movement to stop a new airport being built on the island, sings a verse protesting the planned construction, a choice that, as she informs on the way home, was surreptitiously directed at another member of the group, a policeman who had been on the other side of the long-running dispute. Others sing of unrequited love. I am also urged to sing, and manage to stumble through one of the few verses that I have memorised from a book. I have an overwhelming feeling that this is the 'real thing' – that these people aren't singing this song simply as a recreation of the past, but that the words really mean something to them. While these singers are technically less refined than the numerous entrants to the annual *Tubarāma* singing competition that takes place every autumn in Ishigaki, they seem to represent a context for singing that is rapidly disappearing on the island. They aren't singing for judges, or even for my tape recorder, and seem to care little about the correct 'traditional' form of the song. They're singing for themselves. (Adapted from my field notes/field recording, 18 August 2002)

In this chapter I focus on a single song in the Yaeyaman repertory, *Tubarāma*, and consider some of the contrasting social meanings that it holds as part of the modern Yaeyaman tradition. The title of the chapter – '*izu su du nusï*' (the singer is master) comes from the well-known *Tubarāma* verse shown above, a reference to the musical and lyrical freedom traditionally allowed and encouraged in the performance of the song. The phrase is often cited in connection with *Tubarāma* both in everyday speech, in print (see e.g. Yamazato and Ishigaki 2002), and in the context of various performance situations, as an explicit discourse of personal freedom in the performance of the song that contrasts with ideas of village or lineage ownership of repertory that we saw in the previous chapter. While Yaeyaman genres such as *fushiuta* have been concerned with creating ever more refined and standardised versions of songs, singers of *Tubarāma*, at least in the past, have been encouraged and expected to express more personal feelings in a relatively free format. This active encouragement of lyrical and musical creative freedom is one of relatively few examples within Yaeyaman musical traditions, and the possibilities for individual expression mean that the song is often described using phrases such as the true 'soul of Yaeyama' (*Yaeyama no kokoro*, e.g. Nishihara 1995). Yet despite this traditional creative freedom within the performance of the song, a separate discourse situating *Tubarāma* within the tradition of a village, island, or within a unified Yaeyaman canon has also played an important part in modern performance practice. The contrasting aspects of these ideologies, either to refine and standardise or to maintain diversity, have played an important part in the way in which discourses of tradition and musical meaning have been carried out in the Yaeyaman musical world. In the following sections, I first examine the historical background of *Tubarāma*, and consider how its modern social meanings have been constructed by historical performance contexts, as well as more modern writings by local scholars. Following this, I examine some of the musical aspects of the *izu su du nusï* concept, outlining the ways in which variation is achieved, and considering the way in which these have been used in the imagination of both local and personal identities. In the final section I examine some of the ways in which rules of performance and variation, and the more general meaning of

Tubarāma in Yaeyaman society, have been constructed in the context of local singing competitions.

Words

Until the mid-20th century, it would have been hard to avoid hearing *Tubarāma* performed in Yaeyama. The song seems to have been performed in a range of social situations, by men and women of peasant and upper-class backgrounds. Several local writers (Karimata 1999: 418–19; Kishaba 1924: 95) have described versions of the song being sung in the fields (*nū*), while walking on the road (*mitsï*) back from work, at home (*yā*), among many other social situations. Miyagi Fumi (1982: 473) describes an early 20th century practice of singing the song as a lament at the graveside of recently deceased friends or family members. Among my informants, the most commonly cited context for the performance of *Tubarāma* before WWII was while walking or (horse) riding home from work (Nakashima Tama, Tau Toki, Ishigaki Shinchi, Ikema Nae).

In contrast to the *yunta/jiraba* work songs, whose group singing style and narrative content make substantial lyrical variation difficult, most *Tubarāma* lyrics consist of self-contained verses of just two lines which stand on their own as an expression of a particular idea or emotion. A glance at a collection of commonly sung *Tubarāma* lyrics from Ishigaki island (Ishigaki-shi Bunka Kyōkai 1999) reveals lyrics concerning love, loss, yearning, war, family and old age, among many others. The vast majority of the 'traditional' (*koten*[1]) lyrics in this collection are songs about love. Another feature of *Tubarāma* is that the majority of lyrics, old and new, are explicit expression of emotions in the first person, and often seem to be addressing a particular person. To give one example:

Tsïkï tu tida tu ya, yu nu mitsï tōryōru	The moon and sun take the same path across the sky
Ura tu ban tun, pïtu mitsï ari ōra	I hope you and I also travel one path

(Ishigaki-shi Bunka Kyōkai 1999: 53)

The realisation of *Tubarāma* verses in performance (see Example 6.1) almost always involves two singers, one who sings the main lyrics, and another, usually of the opposite sex, who provides sung interludes (*hayashi*) after the first and second lines. These interludes vary according to the context, the most common being '*tsïndasā yo tsïndasā*' (how sad, how sad) after line 1, and '*makutu ni tsïndasā*' (how very sad) after line 2. The main singer then sings a final line usually containing a standardised phrase – a common example is '*nzō shi nu kanushāma yo*'

---

[1]   Defined in this work as those dating from before WWII.

(Ah, my sweetheart) sung by male singers, or '*nzō shi nu tubarāma yo*', with the same meaning, by female singers.

As with many songs in the Yaeyaman repertory, the search for 'origins' featured prominently in the 20th century discourse surrounding *Tubarāma*. Of the large number of published articles about the song over the years, especially those published within Yaeyama, many are devoted to this subject (e.g. Kajiku 1972; Kishaba 1967; Maehana 1976; Makino 1973). Several theories exist concerning the meaning of the word *tubarāma* itself, the most widely-accepted of which is that it derives from the Yonaguni dialect verb '*tubarun*' (to meet; Hokama 1995; Y. Miyara 1979), a theory backed by the fact that the song has a strong performance tradition in Yonaguni island to this day.[2] While *Tubarāma*'s exact origins are unclear, it has come to be strongly associated with a narrow lane, known in Ishigaki dialect as the *Nakadō mitsï* (*Nakadō* road), running east from Tonoshiro to Maezato in the main Ishigaki urban area. This very localised geographical association derives from one of the most famous verses of the song (see below), which is often considered the 'original' lyric. As usual, Kishaba Eijun's writings have been influential in creating an image for the song in the Yaeyaman popular imagination. In 1967 he wrote:

> Long ago a beautiful girl was born into the Nakasuji household in Maezato. Under the severe feudal class system, young upper-class men in Ishigaki had the right to take any peasant girl they fancied, by force if necessary. The peasant men were powerless to do anything about this. The upper-class Ishigaki youths fought amongst themselves to get the beautiful young girls.

> In my youth 70 years ago [the late 19th century] the Nakadō road was narrow and mysterious, and bordered on both sides by long grass. There were legends about ghostly spirits appearing, and poisonous *habu* snakes lurked in the grass. At the time *Tubarāma* was born around 150 years ago [the early 19th century] the Nakadō road was probably this kind of spooky place.

> However, true to the saying that love is blind, the young men, thinking only about who could arrive first, used to travel up the road to the Nakasuji house and wait for the girl to appear. If there had only been one of them, she would probably have come out and they could have discussed matters of the heart, but faced with the prospect of six or seven young men outside her gate, she stayed in

---

2   The presence of the word in songs from other parts of Yaeyama means that it was probably used in older dialects all around Yaeyama. The song *Tubairyāma* from the western part of Iriomote, although musically unrelated to *Tubarāma*, seems to have derived its title from the Iriomote dialect word *tubairu*, also with the meaning of 'meeting' (see e.g. Ishigaki-shi Bunka Kyōkai 1999: x; Y. Miyara 1979: 410). A rival theory proposed by Kishaba Eijun (1967: 142) derives the term from the Japanese *tonobara* – a respectful form of address from women to men.

the house every night, sleeping between her parents. Even on rainy nights, when the men surely thought that they would be alone, to their surprise there were another six or seven men waiting, clutching umbrellas and thoughts of love. Days passed, and then months, but there was no response at all from the girl. As day broke and the young men set out disappointed on the journey home, one of them suddenly broke into an improvised song:

Nakadō mitsï kara	Along the Nakadō road
nana kera kayuruke	I've walked so many times
Nakasuji kanushama	The beautiful Nakasuji girl
sōdan nu naranu	won't show her face
Ira Nzōshi	Oh how sweet
Kanushāma yo	My true love

Note: This verse was the starting point of *Tubarāma bushi*.

(Kishaba 1967: 144–5)

This lyric has become the standard to which most modern beginning students of the song learn to sing, and is the lyric notated in standard *kunkunshi* for the song. Due partly to Kishaba's writing, it has also come to be seen as the 'original' verse. While other rival theories (e.g. Maehana 1976) exist concerning the historical details of the story and the location of the girl's house, Kishaba's theory is by far the best known, and has been influential in a number of aspects. As with much of Kishaba's research, the assumed composition of the 'original verse' by an (unnamed) member of the ruling class posits a classical lineage for the song. The '*Nakadō mitsï*' lyric seems to have been popular since at least the early 20th century[3] with *fushiuta* performers, who were historically of the ruling class, and Kishaba's emphasis on this particular verse is presumably due to this connection. Likewise, the geographical connection of *Tubarāma* with a highly specific location, in this case the Nakadō road, continues to be of relevance to the way the song is culturally imagined in the present. In 1983 a commemorative stone monument was erected in Hirae on a small triangle of grass at a busy intersection on the road where the young men are assumed to have walked (see Figure 5.5). Since 1991, the monument has become the focus for an annual singing event that further strengthens the song's geographical connection with this very specific location, and which I consider later in the chapter.

A third aspect of Kishaba's account is his assertion that the song was spontaneously improvised in the context of an (in this case unfulfilled) attempt to

---

[3]   The song is referred to as *Nakadō bushi* rather than *Tubarāma* in many early 20th-century documents and *kunkunshi*. The earliest known recording of the song, made by Kishaba Sonchi for Nittō records in 1922, carries the title *Nakadō Michi* (Kishaba 1924). The song is still sometimes known in the Okinawan mainland as *Nakadō bushi* (see e.g. Noborikawa 1970: 53).

form a sexual relationship. This aspect is also one that appears, in various forms, in much of the modern discourse surrounding the song. In Chapter 3 I outlined the *utakake* (*utagaki*) tradition – the practice of antiphonal singing, often with a sexual motive – that was historically found in many parts of Japan and East Asia as a whole. Historical examples of *utagaki*-like practices in Yaeyama can be found in the writings of Iha Fuyū on the '*makuta asobi*' (Iha 1938) and the lyrics of songs such as *Yamabārē yunta* describe practices similar to the *mō-ashibi*. *Tubarāma*, with its antiphonal structure – usually sung by two solo singers of the opposite sex – and a relatively large number of lyrics connected with romantic themes, is perhaps the Yaeyaman song with a historical performance context closest to the *utakake* tradition (e.g. K. Nakasone 1998b: 30; Karimata 1999: 418). I heard several references to the use of the song in this kind of context, and many older Yaeyamans had an image of the song being used in this way, even if they had no direct experience of such practices. One informant in Shiraho remembered the singing of *Tubarāma* in the 1920s and 1930s:

> You'd go to the house of the man you liked and sing things like 'hear my song and come out, hear my voice and come out' (*uta o kiite detekoi, koe o kiite detekoi*). All these [*Tubarāma*] lyrics are like a conversation (*kakeai*). Then the man would hear the song and say to himself 'ah that's the voice of the girl I like' and he'd come out. That's how people would make relationships. Because [*Tubarāma*] is a *kake-uta* (antiphonal song). (Nakashima Tama, pers. comm. October 2001)

Tubarāma lyric collections also contain a number of examples hinting at the song's use in this kind of situation:

Yuda nu kagi kara, tsïkïn tiryōru	The light of the moon shines in the shadow of the branches
Pitumïn nukē, pari kūyō miyarabi	Without being seen by anyone, Come out and meet me, my sweetheart

(Ishigaki-shi Bunka Kyōkai 1999: 24)

Kanushama makutu nu, munu yariba	If she truly loves me,
Uta ba sïki, pari kïndara	she'll come running when she hears my song

(Ibid.: 85)

Another of the song's common cultural images was repeated to me by the Shiraho singer Yamazato Yūkichi (May 2002): 'if you went up into the hills and started singing, a reply would come floating across from somewhere, even though you didn't know where it came from'. I heard several similar comments about *hayashi* replies appearing as if out of nowhere, although not all singers had this experience. On the subject of women adding *hayashi* to his song as he walked, the well-known *Tubarāma* specialist Ishigaki Shinchi (b. 1916) commented:

> No way – who's going to do that? I was just singing, just walking … the only time we worked together with the women was at weeding times. Then we used to sing *yunta* and *jiraba*. (Interview in *Yaima*, September 2002)

Many people remembered the social restrictions in early 20th century Yaeyama. Ishigaki Shinchi remembered how:

> We did have yū-asobi, but it was only singing together, you know. These days they all hold hands and do all kinds of things. We couldn't do that kind of thing then. No way. (Interview in *Yaima*, September 2002)

Other informants also commented on the social restrictions between men and women, which could partly be broken down through singing. Tau Toki told me (October 2001):

> In Shiraho people would sing as they were riding home [on horseback] after working in the fields. They'd sing songs such as:

Sa tida iriba	When the sun goes down
Yama nu pa ni kakusu	It hides itself behind the mountains
kanusha miyarabi	The young women
Birama nu sudi kakushi	hide in their man's sleeve

> These days, young people do all kinds of things like kissing [in public], but we never even used to hold hands in public when I was young. People never held hands like they do today, even if they were married. People would laugh at them. I'm jealous of young people nowadays! (pers. comm. October 2001)

While a large number of *Tubarāma* lyrics are connected with matters of the heart, the song has also been used throughout the 20th century to express a wide variety of emotions. As one of the few traditional songs in which active composition of new lyrics is considered appropriate, *Tubarāma* has been a rare example of traditional music used in explicit expressions of political dialogue. A well-known example came in 1956, when a group of Yaeyaman musicians was invited by the Japanese education ministry to perform in Tokyo. The occasion came 11 years after WWII, amid a growing movement throughout Okinawa prefecture for a reversion to the Japanese nation. Performers on the tour included the famous names of the day such as Ōhama Tsurō and Ōhama Anpan, and there was a sizeable Tokyo-based

Okinawan contingent in the audience. The highlight of the performance was Ōhama Tsurō's performance of *Tubarāma*, in which he sang:

Pai nu kazema nu suru suru sugubashuya	If you feel the southern wind blow,
Ukīnā nu fa nu nakiunde umui tabori	know that it's because your Okinawan children are crying
Nama nu ittuki, kunu kurishan shōru	At this time we are suffering so much.
Yagati uyamutu muduridusï	Soon we will return to our parents' side,
Ira nzō shi nu, Yamatu nu uyaganashi	to the motherland, Yamato (Japan)

(Makino 1988: 144; Ōshima 1996)

Ōhama's *Tubarāma* performance was an unequivocal expression of a growing movement in Okinawa at the time for reversion to Japanese rule that is still remembered fondly by many Yaeyamans. The participation of the troupe from Yaeyama seems to have had considerable political significance on a national level too, and was enthusiastically taken up by the leading daily newspapers. The *Mainichi* newspaper, for example, covered the story on the front page of its morning edition on 27 October 1956 with the politically unambiguous headline 'Performing arts returned to the motherland' (*Geijutsu wa sokoku e fukki*). The verse is also particularly interesting because of its geographical context – the fact that it was sung in Tokyo in front of a mixed audience of Yaeyamans, Okinawans and Japanese mainlanders – and that Ōhama Tsurō chose to deliver his message of allegiance to Japan in the Yaeyaman language. Far from being a stranger to standard Japanese, Tsurō had been active since the 1930s in 'updating' Yaeyaman songs into the standard Japanese language, producing songs such as *Yaeyama sodachi* which incorporated a standard language version of *Tubarāma*, as well as participating in the 1934 Columbia recordings that produced the famous Japanese language version of *Shin-Asadoya yunta* (Chapter 3). His explicit choice of the Yaeyaman language in this context, unlike the linguistic 'concessions' of *Shin-Asadoya yunta*, seems to be an early post-WWII example of a movement to imagine Yaeyama (Okinawa) as a Japanese entity, but to do it on explicitly Yaeyaman terms.

Another example of the political use of the song is the verse I mentioned in the introduction to this chapter, protesting the construction of a new airport in Ishigaki. In the late 1970s a plan was proposed to build a new airport on the coast in Shiraho, which would have had disastrous consequences for the marine life in the area. A local protest group was formed in Shiraho, which fought for many years to stop the planned construction.[4] One of the arguments used by the protestors for stopping construction was the importance of protecting local traditions against the effects of the mass tourism that an enhanced airport threatened, and *Tubarāma* was

---

[4]   Construction is going ahead in 2011, although at a different site from the original plan.

an important symbol of this tradition. One informant, who has a long history both as an activist and researcher of local traditions, composed a series of *Tubarāma* lyrics concerning the planned construction:

Anera Toubuni paru mitsï kusairunde	As you clear a path for the flying ships
Atara Karadaki sukuttsashi sïtirundena	Don't tear down *Karadaki* hill

(Yamazato 1982: 72)

Other Yaeyamans have used the song to express more ambivalent opinions regarding the return to mainland Japan in 1972. A collection of *Tubarāma* lyrics by an anonymous author from 1982, entitled *Yamato-yū* (the age of Yamato[5]), bemoans the changes that took place after the 1972 reversion:

Yamato-yū nari ushidagirarē	Into the age of Yamato we are dragged
Mī ba ukiri tobiri aragi	Everything has been turned upside down

(Shinjō[6] 1982: 74)

The fact that this verse was published anonymously indicates the politically sensitive nature of the statement, 10 years after Okinawa's return to Japan. In contrast to Ōhama Tsurō's 1956 verse calling for the return of Okinawa to Japan, this 1982 example, also in the Ishigaki language, addresses the social realities of the post-reversion era, with mainland Japanese companies buying up land in Yaeyama for tourist development projects. I mentioned in Chapter 4 how Taketomi islanders had formed syndicates to buy back local land from outside developers at around this time in a (largely successful) attempt to keep tourism at a locally manageable level. Through the use of local language and traditional repertory, the two verses above seem to be part of this expression of 'local' resistance to unrestrained development by Japanese companies in Yaeyama.

Variant Forms: Village and Personal Styles

Beside the freedom to create new lyrics, the *izu su du nusï* ideal also refers to the fact that singers are traditionally allowed a certain freedom in their melodic interpretation of *Tubarāma*.[7] In this section I analyse a number of versions of the

---

[5] Another name for the Japanese mainland.

[6] A pseudonym. The author worked for the local government at the time.

[7] Several theories consider the origins of *Tubarāma*'s melody. It seems likely that the song is connected to the song family known in Miyako as *Tōgani* (the Miyako song *Irabu tōgani* is the best known example), although there is no direct evidence as to which song came first. The Miyako song *Yāma Āgu* (Nippon Hōsō Kyōkai 1990b: 515), has an

song, both from my field recordings and from commercially released recordings, and consider the various melodic versions in the context of discourse surrounding the song. Variant forms can be seen in macro-form – general melodic outlines connected with a particular village for example – to more micro-variations such as the execution of certain phrases by individual singers in individually stylised ways. I heard a number of terms used to describe a particular melodic variant or singing 'style', the most common of which was the standard Japanese '*utaikata*' (lit. 'way of singing'): '*Ishigaki no utaikata*', for example, refers to the Ishigaki 'way of singing' the song. A Yaeyaman dialect word '*buriyō*' is also used with the same meaning (e.g. '*Ishigaki buriyō*'). Other common terms included *Ishigaki-fū* (Ishigaki style), or simply *Ishigaki no Tubarāma* (Ishigaki's *Tubarāma*).

The Yaeyaman musicologist Arasaki Zenjin (1992: 43) described three distinct 'macro' forms of the song by geographical location – the *Āru* (east) style connected with areas east of Tonoshiro village; the *Īru* (west) style of the western part of Ishigaki island; and the *Ishanagira* style of the main settlement of Ishigaki. This broad division was confirmed by many singers. Ishigaki Shinchi, one of the best-known Ishigaki *Tubarāma* specialists, described the variety of singing variants:

> Shiraho [east of Ishigaki] has its own *buriyō*, and there are also distinct *buriyō* in Ishigaki and Kabira [west of Ishigaki]. The *buriyō* in the Mafutanē[8] part of Tonoshiro is the same as that in Shiraho, and they sing the '*Nakasuji kanushama*' part [phrase 2] on a high note (*būn to ageru*). They sing that part on a low note in Ishigaki. In Kabira, they start the '*nakado mitsï*' phrase on a high note. (Ishigaki 2002: 24)

These broad melodic differences can easily be seen from a comparison of performances from each of these regions. Example 6.1 shows the most widely-performed Ishigaki version of the song, as notated in the standard Ishigaki lineage *fushiuta kunkunshi*.[9] This version is performed with *sanshin* accompaniment, and includes the main vocal line and a secondary *hayashi* part, shown in bars 8–10 and 15–17 (using smaller noteheads; *hayashi* lyrics are shown above the staff).

---

almost identical melody and lyrics to those commonly used in *Tubarāma* in Yaeyama today. Sugimoto (1975: 92) writes that many Miyako performers believe *Irabu Tōgani* originated in Yaeyama, while Yaeyaman theories sometimes attribute Miyoko origins to *Tubarāma* (e.g. Kishaba 1967: 139–40).

[8]   Ishigaki Shinchi (pers. comm. October 2001) and the Shiraho singer Yamazato Yūkichi (pers. comm. November 2001) both told me that the Shiraho *buriyō* was introduced to the Mafutanē division in the north of Tonoshiro by the legendary Tonoshiro performer Ōhama Tsurō, whose wife was from Shiraho. The Tonoshiro *kunkunshi* contains transcriptions of *Tubarāma* for both the Ishigaki *buriyō* and the Shiraho *buriyō* (Shikina 1979: 78–9).

[9]   The notated pitch is arbitrary and varies according to individual singers. Male singers generally sing approximately one octave lower than notated.

Example 6.1 Ishigaki village *Tubarāma*

Source: Adapted from YKMH *kunkunshi* (Ōhama 2004b: 12).

The main vocal line consists of three phrases (corresponding to lines 1 and 2 of the verse plus the final standardized phrase): the first, from bars 3–8, consists of a rising phrase over one octave from g′ to g″; the second, from bars 10–16 rises from around c″ to g″ before descending to g′; while the 3rd phrase traces an arc from c″ to g″ before falling back to end on c″.

Example 6.2   Second phrase of the 'Mafutanē' *Tubarāma* version

Source: Adapted from YOOYRH *kunkunshi* (Shikina 1979: 79).

Example 6.3   First phrase of the Kabira version of *Tubarāma*

Source: Transcribed from a field recording by the author of the Kabira performer Takamine Mitsu, December 2001, Kabira.

Ishigaki Shinchi's reference to the Mafutanē version singing the second phrase (*Nakasuji kanushama …*) on 'a high note' can be seen from a notated version of a Tonoshiro village version of *Tubarāma*. In comparison to the Ishigaki version, which begins this phrase around the pitch c″, the Mafutanē version rises almost immediately to g″, before descending to g′ as in Ishigaki.

A third example, transcribed from a field recording made in December 2001 of the Kabira performer Takamine Mitsu, highlights Ishigaki Shinchi's reference to that village's 'start[ing] the *nakado mitsï* phrase on a high note'. In this version, the initial phrase rises immediately to c″, descending back to g′ before rising to g″ as in the Ishigaki version.

In this way, these quite basic differences between performance versions are recognised by performers from around Yaeyama as being representative of the style of particular regions or villages. In particular, the 'east' style is particularly connected with Shiraho, and the 'west' style with Kabira.

Example 6.4   Second phrase of Miyara Kōrin's version of *Tubarāma*

na_   ka   si   zi_   ka nu_____   sha_   ma   so___   dan   nu____   na____

ra_____   nu_____   i   ra

Source: Transcribed from CD *Miyara Kōrin zenkyoku* (Nnarufon), track 6.

Within these larger 'village' variants forms, individual singers also seem to
have had their own particular melodic versions. Tominaga Hide, leader of the
Tonoshiro *yunta/jiraba* group, told me (September 2001) how 'at the end of the
day, all the men used to come home from the fields singing *Tubarāma*. Each
had a slightly different way of singing the song, so you could always tell who
was coming down the road by their singing'. In some cases, singers became
known for the way they sang particular phrases. Several informants commented
on the *Tubarāma* performance of the mid-20th century performer Miyara Kōrin
(1917–1959), an Ishigaki-born student of Ōhama Anpan who became famous
for being the first Yaeyaman singer to make extensive commercial recordings of
fushiuta. The Tonoshiro performer Shinjō Wataru told me in September 2001,
for example, how Miyara had a particular way of singing the descending phrase
in phrase 2 of the song that 'nobody else could imitate' (see Example 6.4 bar 4,
on the syllable '*ra*').

From this example, it is clear that, while Miyara Kōrin's *Tubarāma* performance
follows the same general pattern as that notated in his teacher Ōhama Anpan's
kunkunshi (the version shown in Example 6.1), the fine details of the performance
follow quite a different melodic path. Listening to the four verses in this recorded
version, Miyara seems to have sung this phrase with a fairly consistent delivery
each time, and this phrasing seems to have been a kind of personal trademark, as
confirmed by Shinjō's assertion.

In addition to these personal 'trademark' micro-variants, historical recordings
of *Tubarāma* reveal that individual singers would commonly use slightly
different melodic variants from verse to verse in a single performance. Example
6.5 shows a comparison of the first phrase of three separate verses of Sakiyama
Yōnō's 1934 *Tubarāma* recording made for Columbia records, and shows that
Sakiyama subtly varied the melodic outline of his delivery each time through.

Example 6.5   Comparison of three verses of Sakiyama Yōnō's 1934 *Tubarāma*
            recording

Source: From CD *Okinawa uta no Seizui* (set 2, disc 2, track 20).

These subtle variations include a lengthening of the line in example (a) to
incorporate a larger number of syllables (14 rather than the 12 in verse b[10]), but
also additional melodic material such as the high g at the end of bar 4 in example
(c). While not shown in the transcription, in this performance Sakiyama also
alternated between the so-called Ishigaki and Shiraho melodic frameworks in the
second phrase of the song, showing the melodic variety employed singers at this
time crossed the more 'macro' regional variant boundaries.

    The practice of creating personal melodic variants is far less common today
than it seems to have been in the past. There seems to have been a movement
towards standardising performance to a small number of versions from around
the mid-20th century as the song began to be accompanied more and more by
the *sanshin*. The veteran performer Tamayose Chōden (b. 1917), head of the
YKOARH *fushiuta* organisation, commented in a commercially-released DVD
(Miyara Kōsei n.d.) about the history and performance of *Tubarāma*:

> *Tubarāma* started to change after it began to be accompanied by the *sanshin*.
> When you have the *sanshin*, you have to sing to a fixed rhythm or the two won't
> match. Everyone learns [a fixed version] by copying each other. The original
> *Tubarāma* had no *sanshin* – it was sung on the way back from the fields – so
> you could start the melodic line from below like this [sings] or from above like
> this [sings]. There are all sorts of ways of starting the line – that's the original
> [nature of] *Tubarāma*.

The movement towards standardisation comes partly from this kind of practical
reason, but also from the rather strict nature of the *fushiuta* lineages where, as

---

[10]   In contrast to the majority of Yaeyaman songs, which have verses composed of
fixed mora counts, *Tubarāma* lyrics have no fixed form.

we saw in Chapter 5, melodic variants have been standardised through the use of *kunkunshi* notations. Miyara Kōsei (b. 1940), a prominent member of the YKMH, told me that he used to sing the Ishigaki outline of *Tubarāma* in a variety of 'personal' versions depending on his feelings, but that after winning the NHK all-Japan *min'yō* singing competition in 1969 he abandoned other styles of singing and concentrated exclusively on the style notated in the *kunkunshi* of his teacher, Ōhama Anpan.[11] The merits and demerits of standardising the song into a small number of performance versions has been one of the most prominent issues surrounding the song in recent years, and I deal with many aspects of the debate in the next section.

The *Tubarāma* Competition and Contested Individuality

One of the most important contexts for the construction of *Tubarāma*'s place in modern Yaeyaman society has been through the discourse surrounding the *Tubarāma* competition (*taikai*) that is held annually in a park in downtown Ishigaki on the night of the full moon in the eighth lunar month. The date of the competition, the night of the year at which the moon is believed to be at its brightest and most beautiful, and the fact that it is held outdoors, are cultural references to the historical use of the song in a *utagaki* context (Karimata 1999: 420). The modern competition is one of the highlights of the Yaeyaman cultural calendar, and attracts entrants from around Japan in sections for singing and composing original lyrics. Around 25 contestants are chosen through qualifying heats in the weeks leading up to the competition, and all perform two verses of the song on an outdoor stage constructed especially for the event, wearing traditional Yaeyaman peasant *kimono* (*muichā*), and watched attentively by several hundred spectators who show no signs of boredom listening to the same short melody repeated for several hours. Past winners of the competition include many of the big names in the *fushiuta* world such as Ōhama Anpan, Yamazato Yūkichi, Ōsoko Chōyō and Daiku Tetsuhiro, many of whom cite the event as being one of the key events of their careers (e.g. Ōhama interview in Kinenshi Henshū Iinkai 1987). Since the early 1990s, an active move has been made to promote the event at a national level, and contestants come from the Okinawan mainland, Tokyo, Fukuoka and Osaka.[12] The competition is also promoted in much of the tourist literature in Yaeyama.

There have been several critical studies of the effects of music competitions on music-making in general, many of which have relevance for the *Tubarāma* competition. Henry has described the way in which traditional music competitions

---

[11]   This statement refers specifically to the *sanshin* accompanied *fushiuta* version of the song. Miyara also sings several versions of the Yonaguni variant form *Dunan Tubarāma* and unaccompanied forms from Ishigaki such as *Nū Tubarāma* in a variety of *utaikata* (personal communication, May 2002).

[12]   The number of prospective contestants from Kansai is large enough that a qualifying round was also being held in Osaka in the early 21st century.

in Ireland 'legislate the style by the selection of winners and the enunciation of the criteria by which they are selected' (1989: 91). McCormick (2009) has summarised a number of criticisms against classical music competitions since the 1970s, in particular that they concentrate on technical aspects of performance over artistic expression, and that they discriminate against performers who are unable to deliver a 'particular kind' of performance (2009: 13–14). Barz (2000), too, has described the often complex ways in which judging criteria at choir competitions in Tanzania influence the aesthetics under which those choirs operate. The *Tubarāma* competition has likewise seen a sometimes heated debate, both in everyday discourse and in more public media such as newspaper and magazine articles, concerning the way the competition is carried out, and the subsequent effect it has on the social meaning and performance practices of the song. In particular, much of this debate has centred around a perceived detrimental effect to the idea of *izu su du nusï* in performance through an overemphasis on particular standardised performance characteristics. In this section I present a historical overview of the competition, and consider some of the ways in which in which the *izu su du nusï* concept has been actively negotiated in the context of discourse surrounding it.

Competitive singing competitions with an overall 'winner', as opposed to the grade test system (*konkūru*) that I outlined in Chapter 5, are a feature of folk-song communities around Japan (e.g. Hughes 2008: 201–3) and, like the *Tubarāma* competition, often focus on the performance of a single song. The first example of this kind of event in Japan is thought to have been the Esashi Oiwake competition in about 1910 in Esashi, Hokkaido (see Hughes 2008: 114). The *Tubarāma taikai* in Ishigaki dates back to 1947, and came as part of a more general post-WWII renaissance in Yaeyaman culture that we have seen in other chapters. In common with the *fushiuta* grade tests seen in Chapter 5, the initial *Tubarāma taikai* was initiated by a local newspaper company, in this case the *Kainan Jihō*. Haebaru Eiiku, a writer at this newspaper in 1947, told me how its editor had heard a man singing *Tubarāma* on his way home after work and organised the *taikai* in the hope of meeting him (February 2002; see also Haebaru 2002). The competition seems to have been an instant success in a period with little other organised entertainment, and quickly became an annual event. During the early years of the competition, it encompassed a variety of singing styles, with each performer singing their own version of the song, and this musical diversity seems to have been one of the reasons for the event's success. The *taikai* also seems to have been run quite informally at first – performers could choose whether or not to use the *sanshin* as an accompanying instrument, and appeared on stage in their everyday (Western-style) clothes (Ishigaki 2002: 21). The winner in 1947, Ōhama Anpan, was decided by a ballot taken among members of the audience, rather than by official judges.

Within a few years, the competition began a process of standardisation that continued over a number of years. A 1980 publication by the Ishigaki city government (Tubarāma Taikai Un'ei Iinkai Jimukyoku 1980) outlines some of the changes in format and organisation that the competition saw since its inaugural event. 1949 saw the creation of two separate categories, one for performance (singing accompanying yourself on *sanshin*) and one for the composition of lyrics, and also the abandonment of an audience poll in favour of the introduction of a panel of judges. The competition has attracted a variety of sponsors throughout its history including, at various times, the *Kainan Jihō* newspaper, two local cinemas, the Ishigaki tourist association (from 1964 to 1976) and, from 1977, the Ishigaki city government. The move away from private sponsorship, with its obvious motive to promote the competition as 'entertainment', first to the tourist association and subsequently into an 'official' local government-sponsored event with an emphasis on correct 'tradition', is often seen as one of the biggest factors leading to the standardisation of singing styles in the competition (Yamazato Setsuko, pers. comm. June 2002). In 1975, for example, a new rule stated that contestants must wear 'traditional' Yaeyaman dress (*muichā*), while 1976 saw the introduction of the '*Nakadō mitsï*' lyric as a set verse (*kadaikyoku*) to be sung by all contestants.[13]

This perceived increase in standardisation due to the influence of the local government prompted several long-running public debates concerning the running of the competition. In a 1979 article in the *Yaeyama Mainichi* newspaper, a newspaper with a large circulation throughout Yaeyama, the Yaeyaman journalist Kinjō Asao[14] states a number of problems with the competition:

> Since Ishigaki city took over sponsorship of the *taikai* two years ago, it has quickly come to be dominated by the personal tastes of the judges, and is very different from the *Tubarāma taikai* that we used to know. Historically, folk songs were not something to be protected and governed by the state, but were the product of the common people under oppression, and could be sung freely by anyone, anywhere, without interference. Because of this, it is natural that there should be differences between different regions, and nobody can properly decide which region has the 'proper' singing style.

> Recently, however, *Tubarāma* has changed to being focused only on [the style of] the main city of Ishigaki, and even in places such as Shiraho and Miyara, I've heard that the singing style has come to be sung in this style. It must be said that the responsibility for forcing the common people's song *Tubarāma* into this policy of 'performing arts unification' (*dentō geinō no tōitsuka*) lies with the organisers of the *taikai*. Looking at the judging panel, it epitomizes this centralizing approach, with nobody who wants to preserve the regionality of the song. One gets the feeling of haughtiness in the judges, who at the last contest announced that there were no lyric compositions worthy of the top prize.

---

[13] This 'set verse' requirement was subsequently abandoned in 1983, when competitors could select one verse from a list of four, with one free choice.

[14] Real name Tomoyose Eishō.

It seems that the common people's culture is becoming the exclusive property of the elite.

Tubarāma, which once had a feeling of one-ness between performer and audience, with people adding their own verses at will, has now been placed in the hands of the authorities, and the *taikai* has become a place where amateurs cannot participate. In a situation that encourages the 'stereotyping' (*mannerika*) of singers, a more open-minded approach and less monopolisation are necessary.

In this blunt article, Kinjō makes a number of points that were still being made in the early 21st century. The first of these concerns the way the competition is judged – Kinjō cites the 'personal tastes' of the judges as holding too much sway. An instruction manual that I saw for competition judges in the singing section from the early 1980s cited volume, voice quality, impact (*tanōru*), start and finish of phrases, expression of feeling, pronunciation and pitch (*chōshi*), each of which are scored from 1 to 10. Despite the fact that none of these categories specifically mentions that entrants must conform to a particular *kunkunshi* or melodic form, in practice the fact that the competition judges are all members of the four main Ishigaki island lineages, all but one (the YOOYRH) of which have almost identical versions of the song, means that the *fushiuta* version of the song as notated in the standard *kunkunshi* inevitably prevails in the competition.

A standardised singing style has also been actively promoted through the introduction, since 1987, of *Tubarāma* 'classes' (*kyōshitsu*) during the weeks leading up to the contest. These classes are run free of charge by the four main *fushiuta* lineages on a yearly rotation basis,[15] and are open to all prospective entrants to the competition. In 2002, this workshop was held weekly in the Ishigaki culture centre (*bunka kaikan*), and taught the song in a class format, using *kunkunshi* notation along with a specially designed graphic notation to show the finer points of the melody. The classes I attended focused very heavily on the accurate reproduction of the notated melody, as well as the correct Ishigaki pronunciation of the lyrics, with relatively little attention given to aspects such as artistic expression, loudness, or any of the other criteria in the judging list. The impact of these classes has been problematised by several Yaeyaman performers, including Yamazato Yūkichi:

In the past there were singing styles like the Shiraho or Kabira versions. Nowadays, if you don't attend the classes you can't even get past the trial round of the competition. It's not a good situation when the people teaching the classes are the judges of the competition. It's a situation that needs to be changed. (Yamazato and Ishigaki 2002: 25)

---

[15]   In 1987 the workshop was run by the YKMH, in 1988 by the YKOARK, and in succeeding years by the YKOARH and the YOOYRH. In 2010, the Culture Centre was also running *Tubarāma* classes once a month throughout the year.

In fact, most of the participants at the classes that I observed did not make it through to the main event, while many in the event had not been in the classes that I observed. Nevertheless, the establishment of classes has been one way in which the formal lineages have promoted their cultural authority over the competition, sending out a message of the importance of a particular version of the song.

Another point that Kinjō makes in the article is that the competition discriminates against particular kinds of performers, specifically those from outside the Shika-aza of Ishigaki, and those who have not studied formally. Henry (1989: 91) has noted a similar criticism of competitions run by the Irish traditional music organisation Comhaltas Ceoltoiri Eireann, that they standardise the music by not admitting regional genres. In the case of the *Tubarāma* competition, the complaint lies not with genres as such, but with the particular melodic versions of the song of certain villages, and the ability of performers to create their own variant forms of the song. The Shiraho-born Yaeyaman scholar Ishigaki Shigeru commented:

> *Tubarāma* has the concept of *izu su du nusï* that isn't found in other Yaeyaman songs, but the present *Tubarāma taikai* seems to be forgetting this concept. People in Kabira say that they are unable to enter the competition. They know they will be misunderstood by the judges, and they don't even enter. (Yamazato and Ishigaki 2002: 25)

The perceived discrimination against the variant versions of villages outside the Shika-aza also applies to those within the main city who have not studied the authorised version of the song notated in the *fushiuta kunkunshi*. Tominaga Hide, leader of one of the Ishigaki *yunta hozonkai*s, and a veteran singer told me (September 2002):

> I used to enjoy singing *Tubarāma* just for fun. I can't really imitate the way they sing it now though. I'm a bit embarrassed if I sing, because I know that it's not 'correct', so I don't really sing [*Tubarāma*] in front of people nowadays.

From the early years of the competition, emphasis was placed on singing in Yaeyaman languages, and standard Japanese lyrics were forbidden despite the pre-war popularity of singing traditional songs in standard Japanese versions that we saw in Chapter 3. This insistence on local dialect is another example of a more widespread renaissance in traditional culture following the suppression of the 1930s and 1940s. Nevertheless, a complaint about the competition format concerns the way it has discriminated against dialects other than that of the Shika-aza of Ishigaki city. The Shiraho singer Yamazato Yūkichi expressed a complaint commonly cited by singers from that village:

> I want [the judges] to accept [all] kinds of dialect variations. Words in Shiraho which include the sound '*shi*' change pronunciation as you go through Miyara

and Ōhama, and when you get to Ishigaki people pronounce it as '*sï*'. The idea
that '*shi*' is incorrect and '*sï*' is the real pronunciation is absurd. (Yamazato and
Ishigaki 2002: 25)

One of the main practical reasons for the focus on the dialect of the Shika-aza
part of Ishigaki seems to be that regional dialects, even within Ishigaki island,
are sufficiently different from each other for the judging panel, which is made up
mostly of members from the Shika-aza, to have difficulties assessing the relative
poetic merits of verses in regional dialects. Morita Son'ei, one of the judges of the
lyric composition part of the competition told me:

> Personally I have no objection to people writing in the dialect of their own
> village. The trouble is that most of the judges on the panel come from Ishigaki,
> so they don't know dialects from other villages very well. When we judge the
> entries, one of the things we look for is the correct use of dialect. Entrants know
> this, and to make sure that we look at their entries they tend to write in the
> Ishigaki dialect. (pers. comm. May 2002)

A final point that Kinjō Asao made in the 1979 article, in addition to the impact of
the competition on regional and personal styles, was the distinction between the
music of the 'common people' (*minshū*) and what he saw as excessive interference
by the government and the *fushiuta* lineages making up the judging panels. While
I seldom heard discussions of issues of social class in Yaeyama, Kinjō's reference
to folk songs being the product of the common people 'under oppression'
(*dan'atsu no naka de*) is a clear reference to the old class system in Yaeyama. This
anxiety about the excessive 'mediation' by the Yaeyaman cultural elite imposing
on the artistic activities of 'ordinary people' bears some resemblance to Harker's
1985 study of British folk song, in this construction of cultural meanings in the
context of issues of social class. A distinction between peasant and upper classes
continued in Yaeyaman society until the end of WWII, and Kinjō's comment is
partly influenced by the remnants of this social structure. It is also presumably
connected with Yaeyama's historical relationship with the Okinawan mainland
and Japan and, furthermore, the way Yaeyaman culture has been appropriated by
certain Japanese scholars. Later in the article, he develops the idea further:

> There are countless examples of popular culture (*minshū bunka*) being taken up
> by a small group of specialists, and being placed out of reach of the common
> people. The *min'gei* (folk arts espoused by) Yanagi [Muneyoshi] is one such
> example. This problem is not only found with *Tubarāma*, but is allowing that
> evil (*ashiki*) tradition of 'lineage' (*ryūgi*) to poison the world of folk songs that
> were born of hard work and common people's lives, and to steal that culture
> away from the people. (Kinjō 1979)

The reference to Yanagi Muneyoshi, who we met in Chapter 3, is interesting as it ties the debate about the social meaning of *Tubarāma*, once again, into the context of the way Yaeyaman culture is represented within Japan as a whole. Kinjō seems to be challenging the objectification of local culture by outside agents – in this case the mainland Japanese academic world. I return to this issue in the context of more recent pop music styles in Chapter 7.

There have been several attempts over the years to get back to what Kinjō described as the 'original' context of the song, both within the competition itself and through the establishment of alternative events. On several occasions, the judging panel has been abandoned, due to complaints of favouritism (*hiiki*) in 1951 and 1953, and in a stated attempt to encourage 'free expression' in 1964, 1965 and 1977 (Tubarāma Taikai Un'ei Iinkai Jimukyoku 1980). In an attempt to emphasise the *izu su du nusï* ideal, the mid-1960s events were completely re-structured as 'free singing' contests, with no judges, no overall winner, and no microphones. Another important initiative began in 1991, with the establishment of an 'alternative' *Tubarāma Taikai* on the night before the main competition. This event, known as the *Zen'ya-sai* ('night-before' festival), takes place in front of the *Tubarāma* monument completed in 1983 in Hirae and, like the mid-1960s events, has no judges and explicitly welcomes a variety of *utaikata* and singing styles. Several of the performers that I observed in 2001 sang without *sanshin* accompaniment, and most were dressed in their everyday (Western) clothes on the small stage set up in front of the song monument. On several occasions, members of the audience would suddenly burst forth with *hayashi* in reply to singers singing on their own on the stage. Some people sang in a Shiraho style, one sang the Yonaguni version of the song in a version he later told me he had developed himself (Tomari Eibun, pers. comm. October 2001). Several children sang, as did many more elderly participants. In this way, the *Tubarāma* stone monument, a tangible symbol of a fundamentally intangible object, was now serving as a focus for the recreation both of the song, and the perceived (at least by some) ideology behind it. Behind the stage, a prominent placard announced the ideology of this 'alternative' event with the phrase '*Izu su du nusï*'.

Conclusions

This chapter has focused on the single song *Tubarāma*, looking at some of the various musical forms it can take, and examining the way in which its cultural meanings have been actively negotiated and constructed in public and private contexts. The *izu su du nusï* ideal that encouraged singers to develop individual performance styles was gradually weakened during the 20th century, partly as a result of *Tubarāma*'s enshrinement as official 'traditional culture' through events such as the *Tubarāma taikai*. As with the genres examined in earlier chapters, the need to preserve a cultural form that had gradually moved away performance in everyday life played a big part in prompting these processes of preservation and standardisation. These processes are similar to those that have taken place in other parts of Japan, notably in the case of the Hokkaido song *Esashi Oiwake*, where one of the main preservation methods has been the use of a *taikai* (singing competition). As in Hokkaido, the *taikai* format has had the effect of forcing performers into a standard *utaikata* that will be judged favourably in the competition.

The fact that there has been a considerable public discourse of opposition to the *taikai* format shows, on one hand, that older performers are reluctant to abandon the *utaikata* of their individual villages in favour of a unified Ishigaki (Yaeyaman) *utaikata*, and also that they are reluctant to abandon the original freedom in performance of the song in favour of a 'correct' standardised *utaikata*. Beyond this, though, the concept of *izu su du nusï* has also been used as a way of expressing more personal ideas of ownership of traditional culture, and challenging what many people see as oppressive attempts by organisations such as the local government, the *fushiuta* lineages, or the Japanese academic world to objectify traditional music.

Chapter 7

The Okinawa 'Boom' –
Local Music on the National Stage

In this chapter I look at the activities of Yaeyaman musicians in the 1990s and 2000s as part of a phenomenon often referred to as the Okinawa 'boom' (e.g. Roberson 2001: 211–12), that took place through a variety of media, including recordings, television and film. The musical aspects of this boom were characterised by artists from around Okinawa (including the Amami islands to the north of the prefecture) performing new compositions and pop/rock arrangements of traditional material to audiences throughout Japan and in some cases abroad. The 1990s and beyond also saw a widespread national interest in Okinawan food, film and other cultural forms.

The presence of Okinawan music in the Japanese music industry can be seen as early as the 1970s, with musicians such as Kina Shōkichi, China Sadao, Kadekaru Rinshō and Yamazato Yūkichi being promoted on the Japanese music scene. Mainland Japanese musicians such as Kubota Makoto and Hosono Haruomi also began to incorporate elements of Okinawan music into their work around this time – Hosono, for example, recorded a version of the song *Asadōya*[1] *yunta* as early as 1978 on his album *Paraiso*. After a lull during much of the 1980s, Okinawa became a hot topic once again at the end of the decade in the context of the 'world music' (*wārudo myūjikku*) genre that became popular in Japan around this time. As part of this interest in world music styles, Japanese musicians such as Sakamoto Ryūichi, Hosono's partner in the influential Yellow Magic Orchestra, began to look not only abroad, but also to Okinawa as a kind of domestic 'other' for sources of musical inspiration. Sakamoto, for instance, included a three-piece Okinawan female chorus group in his albums *NEO GEO* (1987) and *Beauty* (1989), a line-up he also featured on his 1989 world tour. Another mainland Japanese band, The Boom, also started experimenting with Okinawan material from 1990 on their album *Japaneska* which, as the title suggests, used Okinawa as a way of investigating concepts of 'Japanese-ness' in the context of the world music movement of the period (Gillan 2009). An extension of this mainland Japanese interest in Okinawan music was that Okinawan musicians themselves also began to be promoted once again in Japan. An early example was the Rinken band, led by the mainland Okinawan musician

---

[1]   The album notes list the song as *Asatoya yunta*.

Teruya Rinken, who had struggled to survive on the Okinawan music scene through the 1980s, but found a new lease of life with Tokyo audiences from 1990 (Teruya and Matsumura 1995: 193–7). The year 1990 also saw the creation of a new Okinawan band, the Nēnēs,[2] an extension of Sakamoto Ryūichi's late 1980s chorus group, who were formed specifically to perform in the Japanese mainland (China 2006: 218–22). This four-piece female vocal group presented a pop-influenced repertory, usually including traditional elements such as the *sanshin*, accompanied by synthesizers, guitars and elements of world music styles.

From these early examples, we can see the importance of mainland Japanese audiences in providing a context for the early Okinawan music boom, and several studies have considered the multi-layered identity issues involved. Roberson (2001: 213) has described the music of this period as 'a set of sites (both sounds and sights) through which contemporary Okinawan identities are constructed, reflected, and set in contrast to – and sometimes in resistance against – powerful national and international forces'. Johnson, in his (2001) study of the Nēnēs, describes how the music of this band is 'consumed' by Okinawan, Japanese and foreign audiences, and represents various local and national identities depending on each of these contexts. Takahashi (2006) has described the music of the Nēnēs, in particular, as 'directed outward' (*soto-muki*), a reference to the fact that, rather than simply being 'consumed' within the mainland Japanese market, this group was from the beginning created largely with Japanese audiences in mind. China Sadao, the founder of the Nēnēs, has also described how a large part of the Nēnēs' early sound can be attributed to the mainland Japanese arranger Sahara Kazuki (b. 1958 in Fukuoka), who was chosen for his credentials in the world music field (China 2006: 219).

The promotion of Okinawan music in a Japanese context bears many similarities to the world music phenomenon in America and Europe. In particular, many studies have seen world music styles as a way of constructing ideas of locality specifically within the context of modernisation and globalisation processes (e.g. Murphy 2007; Roberts 1992; Taylor 1997). Despite early fears of 'cultural grey-out' (Lomax 1968: 4), many examples from around the globe have shown that the spread of 'international' pop music styles has, perhaps surprisingly, led to an increased focus on local issues. The use of globalised influences in the creation of modern Spanish flamenco music, for example, has been described by Biddle and Knights as a method of 're-regionaliz[ation]' (2007: 12–14). Similarly, the *xibeifeng* (north-west wind) genre in 1980s China used rock and pop elements combined with aspects of the folk music of Shaanxi province in northern China as a way of producing a 'national' Chinese style in opposition to imported pop music from Taiwan and Hong Kong (Baranovitch 2003: 18–26). (The specific regional connection of *xibeifeng* with northern Shaanxi Province, an area often seen as the 'cradle of Chinese civilization', also has parallels with the cultural position of

---

[2]   Also Nēnēzu. I adopt the romanisation used by the band on CD covers and other publicity.

Okinawa as a repository for ancient Japanese customs.) I consider examples of this kind of interweaving of international, national and local identities in the production of new Yaeyaman and Okinawan musical styles below.

Another dominant theme in much of the world music literature has identified a concern 'with marking out "otherness", whether linguistic, racial or ethnic' (Murphy 2007: 39). Okinawa's cultural position in Japan has been unusual in that it has featured discourses both of cultural 'connection' to the Japanese mainland (as part of the *Nantōron* for example) and difference – not least through its historical periods of separation from Japan, and also through the obvious musical and linguistic differences that we have seen in earlier chapters. These have continued to be important elements in recent Okinawan history, and both have been expressed through the Okinawan music boom. In particular, we have seen several examples in previous chapters of discourse surrounding the use of Okinawan languages, and these issues have surfaced once more as part of the Okinawa boom.

Okinawa's cultural position in Japan is also partly connected to an idea common in many 'world music' styles that Taylor describes as 'authenticity as primality', where the music has 'some discernible connection to the timeless, the ancient, the primal, the pure, the chthonic' (Taylor 1997: 26–7). Okinawa was often been portrayed in the 20th century as a link to ancient Japanese 'roots', and this cultural image has been frequently referenced in the context of the Okinawa music boom. Much of the cultural representation of Okinawa in the Japanese media has presented the islands as an antithesis to the harsh realities of modern Japanese city life – as a region rich in spirituality where gods and ancestors are still revered. Terms such as 'healing islands' (*iyashi no shima*) that became prominent in early 21st century references to Okinawan culture, can also be seen in the context of the 'authenticity as primality' idea.

Yet despite the presentation of a connection to the 'timeless and ancient' in many world music styles, many artists have not been overtly concerned with authenticity of musical traditions or lineages. New Yaeyaman music from this period has likewise made use of international musical elements alongside more traditional styles, and the conflict between tradition and innovation has featured particularly prominently in discourses surrounding the music-making of many Yaeyaman performers in this period. Taylor's idea of 'strategic inauthenticity' (1997: 143), as a way for some 'world music' performers to purposefully avoid the use of tradition to make a particular point, is relevant to some of these debates, and many Yaeyaman performers have likewise cited the use or non-use of traditional material as holding particular cultural significance. In the following sections I present an outline of some of the Yaeyaman performers who have been active in this cultural phenomenon and, through analysis of recordings, song texts and interviews, I consider some of the cultural meanings of the music-making of the period.

Yaeyaman Artists in the Okinawa Boom

Yaeyaman musicians began to play an important part in the Okinawan music boom from its early years. This sudden prominence of Yaeyaman performers was somewhat surprising given that the professional Okinawan music world up to that point had been dominated by mainland Okinawan musicians.[3] There are several reasons for the sudden success of Yaeyaman musicians, including the continued importance of traditional music in Yaeyaman ritual life that we saw in Chapter 4, and the successful incorporation of traditional music into the education system that I outlined in Chapter 5. In this section I give brief musical backgrounds for some of the Yaeyaman performers who have been successful in the Okinawa boom.

One of the first Yaeyamans to find national success throughout Japan was the singer and *sanshin* player Ara Yukito (b. 1967). Ara grew up in Shiraho, the son of a well-known *fushiuta* teacher, and was also an active member of the traditional music club at the Yaeyama High School (see Chapter 4). Because of this background in tradition, his output has made use of songs from the traditional repertory – his first album with his backing band Parsha Club, released in 1994 by the Japanese Toshiba EMI label, consisted entirely of Yaeyaman *fushiuta* in energetic funk/rock arrangements. Ara's leather-clad image and rock star appearance were also a long way from the exotic images that most other Okinawan acts at the time projected. Later 1990s albums focused more on original compositions in a funk/rock style, many of which derived an 'Okinawan' flavour from the use of Okinawan language and through Ara's performance of the *sanshin* on many tracks. A 2001 album *Acoustic Parsha* featured an 'unplugged' version of the band, performing *fushiuta* accompanied by *sanshin*, acoustic guitar and bass and he has also released a CD of *fushiuta* accompanied only by his *sanshin* and the *taiko* of his long-time collaborator Sandē (Ara Yukito with Sandē n.d. see discography). Since 2008 he has also collaborated with the Miyako singer Shimoji Isamu in a project known as *Sakishima meeting*.

Another Yaeyaman musician to find early success was the Taketomi-born singer and guitarist Hidekatsu (b. 1961). Although Hidekatsu has a family connection to traditional music through his grandmother, a ritual specialist and performer of Taketomi ritual songs, he told me (October 2001) that he had almost no interest in either traditional or ritual songs in his youth, and had moved to Tokyo in the 1980s with the intention of becoming a rock guitarist. Hidekatsu eventually began incorporating promoting himself as an 'Okinawan' performer with a debut release *Miruku Munari* on the Japanese BMG Victor label in 1993. Against a heavy, repetitive drumbeat[4] and synthesizer backing-track with a vaguely

---

3   The Yaeyamans Yamazato Yūkichi and Daiku Tetsuhiro are notable exceptions.

4   The drumbeat was enthusiastically adopted by many new Okinawan *Eisā* groups, although Hidekatsu told me that it was originally influenced by the folklore music of the Andes.

Oriental flavour, he delivers a half-spoken vocal rap[5] in the Okinawan language, interspersed with vocal *hayashi* reminiscent of the mainland Okinawa *Eisā* dance style. He has been at the forefront of the Okinawan music boom of the 1990s and beyond, providing music, for example, for the highly successful *Eisā*-influenced dance group Ryūkyūkoku matsuri daiko.

A performer who has straddled both traditional and more modern sides of Yaeyaman music is Daiku Tetsuhiro (b. 1948). Like Ara, Daiku learned *fushiuta* in a high school *kyōdo geinō* club, in his case at Ishigaki's agricultural high school. After graduating he studied with the Shiraho performer Yamazato Yūkichi and was included in the recordings and Japanese mainland performances organised by Takenaka Rō in the 1970s. Since the early 1990s Daiku has produced a string of albums containing Yaeyaman songs, both in traditional arrangements and with rock and jazz instrumentation, as well as Japanese popular songs of the early to mid-20th century. His 1994 album *Uchinā jinta*, for example, consisted predominantly of these pre-WWII Japanese popular songs, with a mainland Japanese *chindon* ensemble that was also a feature of Japanese bands such as Soul Flower Mononoke Summit at around the same period. Another example, from 1998, is *Agarooza*, an album of *yunta* that resulted from a collaboration with the saxophonist Umezu Kazutoki, a native of Sendai in the north of Japan. The album, while based on traditional repertory, runs a gamut of musical elements, from rock through jazz and Latin to African-influenced styles. Daiku has also produced a number of albums of Yaeyaman *fushiuta* in more traditional arrangements, often accompanied by his wife, Daiku Naeko, on *koto* and vocals.

The Shiraho-born singer Ōshima Yasukatsu (b. 1969), like Ara Yukito, received a grounding in Yaeyaman *fushiuta* in the traditional music club at Yaeyama High School, and moved to Tokyo in 1989 to work in a company. After participating in the developing Okinawan music scene in the capital, he released his first album, *Nishikaji Haikaji* (North Wind, South Wind) on the Polystar label in 1993, containing a mixture of Yaeyaman *fushiuta* and original compositions. Ōshima has recorded a range of traditional songs from around Okinawa, and has been active on the international world music scene, recording with the Irish band Altan and the American jazz pianist Geoffrey Keezer among others.

Nishidomari Shigeaki was born in Yonaguni in 1969 and grew up listening to his father play *fushiuta* and other *sanshin* songs in the festivals of his native Kubura village. The continuing low status of traditional music (see Chapter 4) at the time meant that his father discouraged him from playing the *sanshin* but he managed to pick up an accomplished technique practising by himself (Fujita 1998: 42). In 1994 he released his best-known composition *Kaze no donan* (The wind from Yonaguni), a song that came to be used in several television commercials (and as the theme tune for a weather programme) on prefectural networks.

---

[5]   The lyrics of the song were taken from the traditional song *Kohama kuduchi*, in which lyrics are delivered in a half-spoken style somewhat analogous to rapping.

Figure 7.1   BEGIN performing in Ishigaki, 2002

Like several other Yaeyaman artists, Nishidomari has largely avoided the use of Yaeyaman traditional elements such as scales or repertory in his work, producing an image of locality through use of Yonaguni dialect and, to some extent, the *sanshin*.

The three-piece band BEGIN (Figure 7.1) are also graduates of Yaeyama High School, and long-time collaborators with Ōshima Yasukatsu, although they were not members of the traditional music club at the school. Like Ōshima, they started their musical career in the late 1980s based in Tokyo, playing original songs and covers in a blues/pop style, and achieved success in the Japanese market, performing a number of songs in English[6] (an early hit was a cover version of Eric Clapton's *Wonderful Tonight*). The band did not really begin to promote aspects of 'Okinawan-ness' in their performances and recordings until the Okinawa boom was in full swing in the latter part of the 1990s, since when they have released

---

[6]   Okinawa prefecture, as host to a large number of American military bases, is sometimes mistakenly assumed to be a region where the residents can all speak English. The 1970s popularity of Okinawan hard rock bands such as Murasaki, who cut their teeth in front of American military audiences, and who sang in perfect American accents, gave subsequent performers a kind of cultural authority to perform English songs. The absence of military bases in Yaeyama means that most Yaeyamans do not speak English.

a series of CD singles and three albums (*BEGIN no shima-uta – Omoto Takeo*[7] volumes 1, 2 and 3) on the Japanese Teichiku label, into which they inject a strong Okinawan flavour through the use of the *sanshin*, Okinawan dialect words, Okinawan scales, and Okinawa-themed lyrics. These albums quickly made BEGIN one of the most popular and well-known 'Okinawan' bands throughout Japan in the early 21st century. The band have juggled a number of performing styles through the 2000s, maintaining their original pop/rock repertory for some performances, while performing their 'Okinawan' songs at others.

Okinawan Music in Other Media

Okinawan music was disseminated in a variety of formats during the Okinawa boom. The mainland Japanese music labels such as Columbia, Victor and Teichiku actively produced and promoted Okinawan artists in the 1990s and 2000s, as did smaller specialist world music labels such as Offnote records. Okinawan music was also presented to national audiences through a large number of film and television productions aimed at the Japanese market, incorporating incidental music and theme songs by Okinawan musicians and, in several examples, featuring musicians in starring roles. One of the most prominent and influential figures in the construction of an Okinawan cultural image in mainland Japan through film, for example, has been the Kyoto-born film director Nakae Yūji (b. 1960), who first lived in Okinawa as a student at the University of the Ryūkyūs in the late 1970s, and who has based his subsequent film-making career in the islands. Nakae's 1992 debut *Pineapple Tours*[8] emphasised the 'exotic' aspects of Okinawa, with quirky personalities and rich traditions, and included starring roles for the musicians Teruya Rinken and Ara Yukito, as well as appearances from other Okinawan musicians and actors. The film was influential in gaining national and international attention both for Okinawa and its musicians, with awards from the Japan directors' association and the Sundance film festival. Nakae's subsequent works have continued to feature traditional Okinawan musicians and music heavily. His 1999 hit *Nabi no koi* featured the veteran Okinawan singer Noborikawa Seijin as one of the male leads, with guest appearances from Kadekaru Rinshō, Ōshiro Misako and the Yaeyaman musician Yamazato Yūkichi. His 2002 film *Hotel Hibiscus* followed much the same formula of sun-drenched scenes and quirky personalities, starring the mainland Okinawan musician Teruya Masao. More recently Nakae has produced a documentary (2003) of the Yaeyaman group Shirayuri Kurabu, an ensemble of elderly Shiraho amateur musicians who maintain a repertory of mostly pre-war Japanese pop songs. The marketing of this group as a kind of 'Okinawan Buena Vista Social Club'

---

[7]　The album title *Omoto Takeo* is a pun derived from 'Omoto-dake' the highest mountain in Ishigaki, and Takeo, a Japanese male given name.

[8]　Nakae directed the second part of this three-part film.

(Nakae 2004, discography) emphasised the cultural position of Okinawan music as 'world music' within Japan. His 2007 film *Koishikute*, set in Ishigaki, continued the musical theme and featured the Yaeyaman band BEGIN and other younger Okinawan musicians. Although Nakae touches on more serious issues, such as the presence of the American bases in Okinawa, in several of his works, in general these films all have an optimistic feel-good factor which was undoubtedly influential in promoting a positive image of Okinawa within Japan. In addition, Nakae's prominent use of Okinawan musicians in most of his work was certainly influential in fuelling the mainland interest in Okinawan music in general.

Just as in the film world, Japanese television has been influential in promoting Okinawan musicians, and constructing certain images of Okinawa in the Japanese mainland. In 1993 the national broadcaster NHK set its annual historical drama series (*taiga dorama*) in the Ryūkyū of the 16th–17th centuries. The series, entitled *Ryūkyū no kaze* (The wind from Ryūkyū) seems to have played at least some role in fuelling the nationwide interest in Okinawa. As Hara (2000) points out, the impetus behind the programme came both from the 20th anniversary of Okinawa's return to Japan, and from the Okinawan music boom that was already underway in Japan by the early 1990s. The programme strongly promoted an image of the 'peaceful' nature of Okinawa, its openness to the outside world, and the fact that it had historically been a kingdom separate from Japan (Hara 2000: 157–8), and frequent use was made of traditional Okinawan musical elements such as the *sanshin*. While the programme did not draw outstanding viewing figures in comparison to NHK historical drama series in subsequent years,[9] as the first major nationally-broadcast drama set in Okinawa, it undoubtedly served to promote the national image of the region. Furthermore, the use of an Okinawan theme in this flagship NHK drama series, which presents a different 'Japanese' historical story every year, was an important statement of Okinawa's legitimate cultural position within modern Japan despite its divergent history. From a musical point of view, the programme featured the Rinken band song *Churajura* (Beauty), furthering this band's popularity throughout the country, and linking the drama in a more general way to the national interest in Okinawa at the time.

Far more important than *Ryūkyū no kaze* in boosting the image of Okinawa in mainland Japan, NHK's 2001 morning drama series *Churasan* (Beautiful) also drew on many of the same cultural images of Nakae's films. Using a mixture of Okinawan and mainland Japanese actors, the drama was set in the Yaeyaman island of Kohama, Shuri and Tokyo and, like *Pineapple Tours* and *Nabi no koi*, played heavily on the 'slow' and 'laid-back' aspects of Okinawa life. Ishigami (2005: 90–92) has noted that one of the elements leading to the programme's success[10] was its use of Yaeyaman and Okinawan musicians, with contributions from

---

9   Average viewing figures were 17.3 per cent of the national total (http://videor.co.jp, accessed 5 June 2009).

10   The series drew a respectable average viewing figure of 22.2 per cent (http://videor. co.jp, accessed 5 June 2009).

BEGIN, Kiroro, Da Pump, Miyara Shinobu, as well as informal performances from the residents of Kohama island. The drama seems to have been influential in promoting an influx of tourists to Yaeyama in particular, many of whom have made the move to live permanently in the region – in an analysis of the recent mainland Japanese immigration to Ishigaki, for example, the sociologist Tada Osamu (2008: 227–64) has cited the importance of this television programme, terming it the '*Churasan effect*' (*Churasan kōka*).

Yaeyaman Music in a Global Context

The Okinawan music boom took place largely within a national Japanese cultural context, and can be understood partly in the context of the cultural image of Okinawa within Japan. But wider forces of globalisation have also played a role in affecting the musical output of Yaeyaman artists. I have already noted the influence of a more general interest in 'world music' in many Western countries that partly prompted the Japanese interest in Okinawa. The display of Okinawan music CDs in the world music section of music stores, rather than with other Japanese traditional genres, is one example that I mentioned in Chapter 1. In addition to these kinds of media representations of Okinawa, there are also several examples of the more immediate effects of globalisation on Yaeyaman musicians, as they experience playing in front of non-Japanese audiences and interact with musicians from around the world. I give some examples in this section.

A specific example of the impact of performing in front of non-Japanese audiences on the production of 'local' musical identities can be found in BEGIN's stated reason for their abrupt change of career direction in the late 1990s to incorporate aspects of Okinawan styles into their music. The early musical output of the band made relatively little use of Okinawan musical motifs, and the members have described (BEGIN 2005) in detail their particular fascination with American musical genres, prompting them to record their 1993 album *MY HOME TOWN* in Nashville. This visit to the United States in particular seems to have had a deep effect on the band's approach to music-making. In a story which is indicative of the situation faced by many Japanese bands when interacting with non-Japanese listeners, BEGIN describe a visit they made in 1993 to the blues club of the singer B.B. King in Memphis:

> The tour co-ordinator introduced us as a blues band from Japan, and we were invited to play a song in the club ... thinking about it though, if we were going to do it what would we have played? ... [our] first thought was to do [Eric Clapton's] *Wonderful Tonight*, but if we were to sing blues music in English it would hold absolutely no interest for the [American] customers in the bar. (BEGIN 2005: 71–2)

Wishing to emphasise their status as successful professional musicians, the band insisted that they would play only if given a 30-minute set, a request that was rejected by the club (ibid.). Despite this, the incident, subsequently referred to by the band as their 'fantasy 30 minutes' (*maboroshi no sanjuppun*), is cited as being a major influence on the subsequent explicitly Okinawan musical influence that has been a feature of the band's output since the late 1990s:

> We began to think about what exactly was in our 'blood' … we've come to the conclusion that it's Okinawan music – we sometimes say to each other that some day, when we get to play on stage with Clapton, it would be cool to be able to sing in Okinawan dialect. (Ibid.: 73)

The stimulus to produce this kind of 'poetics of place' (Lipsitz 1994) in an international context has been cited by other Yaeyaman performers who have experience performing outside a Japanese cultural context. Daiku Tetsuhiro, for example, has stressed the importance of the voice:

> First of all is the voice. It may be strange for me to say it myself, but it's a voice that is only found in Yaeyama. It's a kind of nationalism [*nashonarizumu*], but I realised that it is a nationalism that can communicate throughout the world. I think young people are making a mistake, as Okinawan music these days has become 'pop music', and the singers' voices have changed a lot. It's not an Okinawan style any more. It may be easy to listen to, and if you limit yourself to Japan it may be OK, but it just doesn't get accepted abroad. Foreign audiences can't understand what you're singing about [anyway], and the thing they find enjoyable is the sound of the voice.
>
> When we sang *Tubarāma* (in Mali during a concert tour of Africa) I couldn't believe the applause of the audience. It was just like singing back at home. (Interview in DeMusik Inter 1998a: 87–8)

Like BEGIN, Daiku specifically cites the experience of playing abroad as an influence on his production of a specifically 'Yaeyaman' vocal style. As Daiku states, a common dilemma for many Japanese J-pop singers is their inability to be accepted in Western countries singing what is often dismissed as (a bad imitation of) Western pop music (see also Stevens 2008: 146–7). The use of 'local' Okinawan imagery as a way of accessing foreign markets has not been confined to Okinawan artists. Ogawa has noted that the use of Okinawan musical styles by artists from the Japanese mainland has also enabled them to find success in Asian markets: the Japanese band The Boom's forays into Okinawan music, for example, provided them with the 'ethnic' credentials to participate in a pan-Asian pop opera written by the Singapore-based musician Dick Lee in 1992, that they wouldn't have had simply by being a Japanese rock band (1995: 169; see also Kawamura 1993: 124–30 for a discussion between Miyazawa and Lee on various aspects of Asian pop music). Similarly, of 13 representative 'Japanese' musicians or groups listed in Ohsuga's (1993) book *Asian Pop Music* (*Eijian poppu myūjikku*), four (Rinken band, Kina Shōkichi & Champloose, Nēnēs, Ara Yukito) are from Okinawa, and three others (Sakamoto Ryūichi, Hosono Haruomi and Kubota Makoto) have had a long association with Okinawan music.

The musical connections of Okinawa with other Asian countries have also been explored by a number of Yaeyaman performers. Hidekatsu has described his own music not as Okinawan music, but as 'Progressive Asian Music' (*purogureshibu eijian myūjikku*; in Isoda and Kurokawa 1995: 73). Nishidomari Shigeaki presents Asian connections in a number of ways on his 1997 album *Hibi dandan*, including a song about Genghis Khan and an inlay card filled with pictures of Shanghai and the surrounding countryside. Musical connections with South-east Asia have also been referenced by several artists. The Nēnēs recorded a version of the Okinoerabu song *Sai sai bushi* on their 1995 album *Nārabi* accompanied by a Balinese *jegog* bamboo gamelan ensemble. Likewise, Daiku Tetsuhiro's 2009 album *Gamelan yunta* consists of Yaeyaman *yunta* and *fushiuta* performed in collaboration with a Balinese gamelan ensemble. In an interview in 2010 regarding this album, Daiku cited the similarities of the [*pelog*] scale in Bali with the *ryūkyū* scale, commenting that 'sometimes when I heard Balinese music, it was just like I sometimes felt like I was listening to Okinawan music'.[11] The Asian connection has also been utilised at the level of local government. In the spring of 2002, for example, the Okinawan education office (*kyōiku jimusho*) organised a series of concerts around Okinawa demonstrating the musical links, through the use of three-stringed plucked lutes, among China, Okinawa and Japan, with performances by a Chinese *sanxian* player, two *tsugaru-jamisen* players from the north of Japan, and Ara Yukito representing the Okinawan *sanshin*.

The 'Weight of Tradition'

The construction of local identities in new Yaeyaman compositions has been accomplished through a variety of musical approaches, sometimes drawing on traditional repertory, instruments or other musical material, while at other times ignoring these elements almost entirely, constructing 'Yaeyaman-ness' in other ways, such as through costumes or language. Many performers, such as Daiku Tetsuhiro, Ōshima Yasukatsu and Ara Yukito, had extensive training in *fushiuta* traditions and incorporated this material into some of their recordings. Others, like Nishidomari Shigeaki, have largely steered away from traditional forms despite their experience as traditional musicians. Another type of musician, such as Hidekatsu or the members of BEGIN, have little or no formal training

---

[11] http://ryuqspecial.ti-da.net/e2656662.html, accessed 4 February 2011. Despite the similarities between the scales used, in the same interview Daiku also cites the differences between the two musical cultures as a 'border that must be crossed'.

in Yaeyaman traditions, but nonetheless drew on aspects of traditional repertory and musical forms in their recordings. All of these performers have been involved to some extent in a public discourse surrounding the conflict between the use or non-use of tradition in new musical forms, much of which has taken place in the context of published interviews. I also heard the issue mentioned frequently in my own interviews with performers. In this section I consider some examples of the musical construction of Yaeyaman identities in new music, and analyse some of the cultural meanings behind these musical forms in the context of the debates surrounding tradition.

One of the reasons Yaeyaman performers have taken innovative approaches in recent musical output has obviously been the simple desire to be artistically creative – as Timothy Taylor (1997: 143) has put it, 'they make art, and in art, anything goes'. Taylor has also described a second reason for many world music performers' 'lack of concern with authenticity', one he terms a 'strategic inauthenticity', that is sometimes used to dispute the world music industry's implied 'demands that they and their countries remain premodern, or modern, while the rest of the globe moves further toward a postindustrial, late capitalist, postmodern culture' (1997: 143). While the cultural power relationships involved in the largely domestic (Japanese) Okinawa boom are different from those between Africa and the West that Taylor describes, the use of non-traditional musical aspects by Yaeyaman musicians has nevertheless arguably been 'strategic', and has challenged some of the existing images of 'Okinawan-ness' both inside and outside the prefecture. Okinawan musicians, too, have on occasion expressed a feeling of pressure from the Japanese mainland to project certain images of Okinawa. Concerning the release of Parsha Club's debut album in 1994, the band's arranger Uechi Masaaki has commented:

> When we released the CD there were a lot of things said about us by the Okinawa enthusiasts and critics in Tokyo, things like 'that's not Okinawan music' or 'Okinawans shouldn't be making this kind of music'. (Isoda and Kurokawa 1995: 63)

The Okinawa boom was already in full swing by 1994, and groups like the Nēnēs and Rinken band had released albums of music that mixed Okinawan traditions with 'world music' elements. The particular complaint of many Tokyo commentators, perhaps, concerned Parsha club's use of aggressive rock and funk styles that were at odds with the more friendly and accessible images of other Okinawan bands at the time – it was OK to mix traditional and modern styles, but rock music was not what audiences were looking for in Okinawa at the time.

BEGIN, despite their comments about Okinawan music being 'in their blood', have explicitly avoided playing songs from the traditional repertory, and have commented on their uneasy relationship with tradition in interviews and through song lyrics. Unlike many other Yaeyaman performers, the members of the band came to traditional music quite late in life, after they were already established musicians. Lead singer Higa Shōei explains how his initial idea of introducing an Okinawan element into the band's repertory was rejected by the other members:

> After the other two had been so against my idea of learning the *sanshin* and Okinawan songs, I was searching around for some way to proceed. I bought some instructional videos and CDs and tried learning by myself, but it never really felt right … I started using the *sanshin* at a few gigs, but I was very dissatisfied for quite a while. If Okinawan *sanshin* players saw me playing, for example, they might be angry with me for making fun of Okinawan music … Then it suddenly hit me – what I can do is play 'amateur *sanshin*' [*asobi*[12] *sanshin*]. I can't play in the classical [*koten*] style at all, and anyway there are plenty of people who are preserving the classical style. So what can we do? From the very start we wanted to be a bridge between Okinawa and the mainland. In that way, the songs we sing are still 'island songs' (*shima-uta*), but they're also modern pop songs. They're '*asobi*' *shimauta*. The *sanshin* style is '*asobi*' *sanshin* … It's not related to any lineage (*ryūha*), it's something which just arises naturally from the common people [*shomin*]. It doesn't matter if people criticize me for holding the *sanshin* wrongly or using the incorrect plucking technique. (BEGIN 2005: 119–20)

In their explicit non-use of tradition, BEGIN's 'strategy', in this case, was thus to avoid the perceived danger of criticism from *within* Okinawa for not being sufficiently schooled in traditional performance. Their answer was to utilise various traditional elements, like the *sanshin*, while bypassing the 'guardians of tradition' by creating their own repertory. In a similar way, Daiku Tetsuhiro has also cited the conservative nature of traditional music circles as one of the impetuses for his use of his incorporation of pre-WWII mainland Japanese pop songs into his repertoire since the early 1990s:

> There was a way of thinking (when I was growing up) that classical (*koten*) and traditional songs should be learned properly from a teacher. But these [Japanese popular] songs could be sung freely. There was a feeling that they were 'our' songs so we could relax. The weight of tradition (*dentō no omosa*) can sometimes get in the way, can't it? (Interview in *Myūjikku Magajin* (October 1994), reprinted Matsumura 2002: 205–6)

Many performers who have attempted to innovate within the traditional repertory have reported friction within their lineage organisations. Ara Yukito told me in November 2001:

> I studied the tradition quite hard. There's nobody who can play in a more correct or traditional way than me. But on my recordings, I play in my own personal

---

[12]   The term *asobi* literally means 'playful', i.e. 'for fun', as opposed to the classical (*koten*) style which must be taken seriously.

way. The old teachers in my lineage [*ryūha*] hate this. Even though I received the top prize in the *fushiuta* grade tests, my lineage has effectively disowned me. They are not interested in what I'm doing.

Ōshima Yasukatsu, likewise, despite his success and popularity as a performer of *fushiuta*, has cited a lack of formal training as a reason for refraining from formally teaching the repertory: 'Never, I can't do that. I think it's great that people do teach, but I didn't study formally, so I can't teach formally. Anyway, I'm still studying' (in Fisher 2002).

In addition to the conservative nature of the traditional music world, Daiku has also cited the excessive 'mediation' of Yaeyaman traditions by local government as a reason for his 'strategic' incorporation of new approaches:

> Not only in Okinawa, but in Japan as a whole, people are stuck on this idea of the 'traditional form' (*dentō to iu katachi*). I want to break that down. Groups such as the government culture department try to support certain aspects of culture. They say that folksongs (*min'yō*) or *yunta* are great, but songs are not the property of these academics. They're supported and made by the common people. Yaeyaman music also has to get back to this idea ... Rather than making music that the academics praise, I make music for the common people, and I intend to continue doing so. (Fujita 1998: 13–14)

Daiku's reference to a conflict between government mediation of traditional genres, and in particular his positioning of the 'common people' in opposition to this 'official' culture, is similar to BEGIN's reference above to their music being of the 'common people' (*shomin*), and also resembles the discourse we encountered in Chapter 6 surrounding the song *Tubarāma*, and its relevance for some as a symbol of the Yaeyaman 'common people' (*minshū*). In reality, Daiku is no outsider to local government – he worked for many years as an official in the Naha city government, and in 1998 (the year of the above quote) was appointed as a 'holder' (*hojisha*) in the Okinawa prefectural government's designation of Yaeyaman folksong as an Intangible Cultural Property, a cultural distinction that he advertises on his website.[13] He has also released numerous recordings of *fushiuta* and other Yaeyaman genres in more strictly traditional versions. This quote, then, is perhaps not a criticism of traditional approaches *per se*, but seems to be a way of arguing for a particular approach toward tradition, one that allows for innovation and experimentation. Of all the Yaeyaman artists of the Okinawa boom, Daiku has perhaps found the most consistent success in combining traditional and innovative approaches in his music-making, and one of the reasons for this is his articulate negotiation of these matters in interviews such as the one above.

A further discourse surrounding tradition and modernity has also been carried out partly in the lyrics of songs themselves. In Chapter 1 we saw the Ishigaki band

---

[13]   www.daiku-tetsuhiro.com/profile.html, accessed 3 February 2011.

BEGIN's song *Shimanchu nu takara* (Treasures of the island people), released in May 2002 in commemoration of the 30th anniversary of the return of Okinawa prefecture to the Japanese nation. The song, a collaboration between the band and students of their old junior high school in Ishigaki, discussed many issues facing modern-day Okinawans, such as the loss of traditional ways of life and a lack of knowledge about distinctly local issues, yet concluded that Okinawans (Yaeyamans) continue to maintain pride in their distinct cultural identity – the 'treasures' of the song's title. The song, while hardly confrontational, seemed to be addressing a number of issues inherent in the Okinawa boom at the time. The song's status as a 'commemoration' of the return of Okinawa to Japan was, at one level, an explicit statement of Okinawa's political membership of the Japanese state. Higa has described one of the motives behind the song:

> I wasn't so much trying to project a certain image of Okinawa, but to say that thirty years ago these islands had finally come back [*kaette kita*] to Japan and could be visited without a passport. We wanted people from all over Japan to celebrate that fact. We wanted to say to people 'Okinawa, with such amazing scenery, has become *your* property. Okinawa is *your* islands'. (Hayashi 2002: 14–15)

The song also seemed to be questioning both the relevance of Yaeyaman traditions to modern life, and the extent to which Yaeyama should be defined by those traditions. In one verse, the singer states that he doesn't understand the words to traditional songs, and in other verses admits that he doesn't know the details of the blue seas and starry skies for which Okinawa is famous, yet still understands what it is to be an 'island person' (*shimanchu*). At another level, the song also seemed to be commenting on the nature of the Okinawa boom itself. One line, 'I understand better than anyone' (*dare yori mo shitteiru*: BEGIN 2002 liner notes), despite a lack of knowledge of local tradition, is presumably a reference to the widespread dissemination of Okinawan culture around Japan, with Okinawan 'experts' springing up throughout the nation. Another line notes that island life contains something that 'can't be captured on the television screens' (*terebi de wa utsusenai*) that broadcast a particular version of 'Okinawa' to the Japanese nation during the boom. The song thus posed the question of cultural ownership in an age when Okinawan music is actively being performed and appropriated by enthusiasts from outside Okinawa.

Another example of a 'strategic inauthenticity' that has questioned the nature of Okinawa's relationship with Japan is Daiku Tetsuhiro's performance since the early 1990s of the song *Okinawa o kaese* (Return Okinawa!), recording it on his 1994 album *Uchinā jinta* and also on the 1997 compilation album *Chibariyō Uchinā* (Fight! Okinawa) (see also Roberson 2001: 233–4). The song, composed in 1956 by the Fukuoka-born topical songwriter Araki Sakae, was created as a focus for the movement within Japan and Okinawa to return the islands from American administration to the Japanese nation. As Daiku writes in the liner notes to the 1997 release, it had been widely sung at pro-reversion demos in Okinawa in the years leading up to the 1972 return, but had suddenly disappeared once its political purpose had been satisfied. Daiku's revival of the song seems to have had a number of meanings. From 1995, Daiku changed one line of the song's refrain from '*Okinawa o kaese, Okinawa o kaese*' (Return Okinawa! Return Okinawa!) to '*Okinawa o kaese, Okinawa e kaese*' (Return Okinawa! Return it to Okinawa!), a change he explains in the liner notes (1997) as a way to emphasise the continued burden of American bases on the islands due to Japan's continuing security treaty with the United States. Nevertheless, Daiku's use of this song, with its ostensible message of allegiance to the Japanese nation (at least up until Daiku's 1995 lyric alterations) would at first seem to be at odds with the expression of a specifically Okinawan identity. Daiku's original recording of the song in 1994, furthermore, was on an album of Japanese pop songs from before WWII – a period when Yaeyaman traditions were being actively suppressed. The use on the 1994 *Uchinā jinta* album of a *chindon* ensemble, another representative of mainland Japanese culture from the early 20th century, also seems to destabilise the Okinawan cultural identity of the album, challenging audiences' understanding of the 'ethnic' aspects of Okinawan culture in the context of the Okinawa boom.

Daiku's use of this material has not been uncontroversial. In a 1998 interview about *Uchinā jinta*, he commented 'It's been five years since then and I've only just been forgiven. But if I hadn't stepped out, we'd never have got where we are now' (in Fujita 1998: 14). As we saw in Chapter 3, from the very early 20th century a large section of Okinawan society has been concerned with promoting Okinawa's status as a full member of the Japanese nation, while simultaneously stressing its cultural distinctness. The reaction to the Osaka exposition incident in 1903 is one example, as is the production of the 'national' version of *Asadōya yunta* in 1934. Ōhama Tsurō's Tokyo performance of *Tubarāma* in 1956, in which he called for the return of Okinawa to Japanese rule, singing entirely in Ishigaki dialect, held multi-layered meanings – expressing Okinawa's allegiance to Japan, but at the same time stressing its cultural difference to the mainland. Daiku's recordings of this material can also perhaps be seen as a way of exploring the multiple cultural meanings of Okinawa in a Japanese context. By singing these specifically Japanese songs, or *Okinawa o kaese*, a song about Okinawa's membership of the Japanese nation, but doing it in an 'Okinawan' context, simultaneously stressed Okinawa's right to cultural independence and freedom from military bases, but also reminded listeners that solutions must be found within a Japanese framework.

Daiku's association with this mainland Japanese repertory has continued in the 2000s: a 2006 release *Jinta Wonderland*, for example, again featured pre-WWII Japanese popular songs, with *chindon* accompaniment provided by the Osaka group Chindon Tsūshinsha. Recordings of the same repertory have also been released by the veteran *fushiuta* performer Yamazato Yūkichi, for example on his 1997 album *Yaeyama Shosei-bushi*. More recently, in 2003 the director Nakae Yūji released a documentary film featuring the Shiraho group Shirayuri kurabu, who after some 50 years of performing these songs on an amateur basis within their home village, were thrust suddenly into the Tokyo spotlight. Yet another hitherto unknown singer of pre-war popular songs, Arashiro Nami (usually known simply as Namii), found national fame at the age of 85 in 2006 when a biography was published by the major Japanese publisher Iwanami shoten (Kyō 2006), followed by a documentary film in 2007. The nationwide popularity of these artists, singing early 20th century Japanese pop songs with *sanshin* accompaniment, is one of the more intriguing aspects of the Okinawa boom. Yaeyama's culturally ambiguous position within the Japanese nation has perhaps paradoxically allowed them to perform this dated repertory with more contemporary cultural and political meanings, as a musical exploration of cultural diversity within the nation.

Musical Aspects

A discourse concerning tradition and modernity can also be seen to some extent in the use of musical scales in new compositions. In Chapter 2 I outlined the use of musical scales in traditional Yaeyaman music, noting the uniqueness in a Japanese context of the *ryūkyū* scale. Despite its potential use as a symbol of cultural identity, the scale has been used relatively infrequently by Yaeyaman musicians during the Okinawa boom. Hidekatsu's music, for example, mostly eschews both the *ryūkyū* scale and traditional instruments (his first instrument is the guitar). In his 1994 song *Marebito den*, for example, the vocal melody mostly uses the pentatonic *d, f, g, a, c* (similar to the mainland Japanese *min'yō* scale) with a synthesizer backing track. This pentatonic scale was used surprisingly often in much 1990s Yaeyaman music, in songs such as Hidekatsu's *Miruku munari*[14] and Sakieda Hiroshi's *Hai nu yūshi*, among others. On the rare occasions when Hidekatsu has used the *ryūkyū* scale, it has been as part of his incorporation of a song from the traditional repertory into his music, as in the 1994 song *Nirōsuku*, which uses the Taketomi ritual song *Tunchāma*.

Nishidomori Shigeaki, who grew up in a traditional music environment, also makes relatively little use of either the *sanshin* or *ryūkyū* scale in his music. In *Kaze no donan* (Example 7.1), for example the melody is based in a-minor/c-major, with a backing track played mostly on the synthesizer. Nishidomari's *sanshin* makes an appearance from the second verse but is not given prominence in the mix.

---

[14]   The scale is used in the first part of the instrumental introduction. The vocals are performed in a pitch-less rhythmic-spoken style.

Example 7.1 *Kaze no donan*

Note: Music: Ameku Kazuya; lyrics: Hakudou.

Of the performers of new music, BEGIN have made perhaps the biggest use of traditional Okinawan scales. *Shimanchu nu takara* (Example 7.2) from BEGIN's 2002 album *Omoto Takeo2*, is a good example of the band's style. The song starts with a *sanshin* introduction (a) using the ryūkyū (*f*, *a*, *b-flat*, *c*, *e*) scale played against a background of drums, guitar, bass and keyboards. As the vocal line enters (b), the scale changes to a predominantly anhemitonic pentatonic *f*, *g*, *a*, *c*, *d* scale[15] with the occasional use of the 4th degree (*b-flat*). The chorus (c) sees a return to a predominantly *ryūkyū* scale, before a return to the *f*, *g*, *a*, *c*, *d* scale of the verse in the final bars.

Example 7.2 *Shimanchu nu takara*

Note: Words and music: BEGIN.

For many artists, the use of traditional scales or repertory has been of relatively little importance in producing a sense of local identity, and many musicians have gone so far as to avoid using it. Uechi Masaaki, musical arranger for Ara

---

[15]   Anhemitonic pentatonic scales are five-note scales containing no semitones. This particular scale, containing the 1st, 2nd, 3rd, 5th and 6th degrees of a major scale, is often described in Japanese as the '*yona-nuki*' ('4th and 7th removed') scale.

Yukito's band Parsha Club and former bass player with the Rinken band, told me in November 2001 that he had been dissatisfied with that band's over-use of the Okinawa scale in its original compositions.[16] Likewise, the mainland Okinawan producer and songwriter Bisekatsu commented to me in a March 2008 interview that compositions by Okinawans tended to sound Okinawan without trying:

> Many mainland Japanese musicians have used the ryūkyū scale in their music, but I never found [their music] so interesting. *Shima jima kaisha* [by the Okinawan musician Fukuhara Tsuneo] doesn't use the ryūkyū scale, and it's in waltz time, but it still sounds Okinawan. Only Okinawan musicians can do that.

BEGIN's guitarist Shimabukuro Masaru has also described their musical approach on one song on their first 'Okinawan' album (2000):

> In one way, if you just take away the notes re and la [from a major scale], then it sounds like the *ryūkyū* scale. But with *Ganbare bushi* we wanted to try to get the feeling of 'Yaeyaman-ness' (*Yaeyama rashisa*) without using that sound … During the recording, [vocalist Higa] Shōei kept asking to do 'just one more take' … I knew that he wanted to get that 'Yaeyaman feeling' (*Yaeyama-pposa*) … that is something only a Yaeyaman would really recognise – it's something you can't really explain in words. (BEGIN 2005: 134–5)

Both of these comments thus show an ambivalent attitude towards the use of the Okinawan scale, and both reference the idea of an Okinawan or Yaeyaman 'feeling' that doesn't rely simply on using a particular scale, but expresses something that cannot be replicated by 'outsiders'.

Dialogues with the Past

A recurring theme in earlier chapters of this book has been the construction of a modern Yaeyaman identity based on discourses of history. These discourses have functioned both at a local level, in the context of issues of tradition and lineage, and on a national level, connected partly with Yaeyama's assumed cultural status as a repository for ancient Japanese traditions, for example. A feature of much of the new music created by Yaeyamans since the 1990s has been that, while it has often updated Yaeyaman musical traditions, lyrics have nevertheless continued to maintain a strong dialogue with the 'past'. In this section I examine some uses and meanings of historical imagery in these songs, and consider them in relation to other 'world music' genres.

---

[16]   Uechi's comments were also directed towards Rinken band's use of synthesized *sanshin* sounds which, he told me, failed to express the correct intonation of the *ryūkyū* scale due to their use of equal tempered tuning.

Lipsitz (1990) has described the way pop music can be used as a way of constructing 'collective memories' of particular histories, and many new Yaeyaman songs seem to be fulfilling this kind of function. At a local level, the depiction of historical events in new songs has coincided with a continued discourse of local history in other areas of Yaeyaman life that has often been concerned with 'set[ting] the local area in opposition to centralized authority, [and] providing a counterpoint to the rhetoric of unified nationalism' (Schnell 1999: 53). In Chapter 2 I outlined some of the major events in Yaeyaman history, the best known of which are the Oyake Akahachi uprising of 1500 and the history of the *nintōzei* taxation system imposed by the Ryūkyū government on Yaeyama until the early 20th century. As in Schnell's example, both of these historical events set Yaeyama in opposition to 'centralized authorities' (Ryūkyū and Japan) to some extent, and they continue to be important in local Yaeyaman identity constructions. One of the ways that collective memories of these events have been maintained is through their imagining in cultural forms including music.

Several examples of the use of historical aspects of the *nintōzei* in modern music-making can be seen in the recordings of the Yonaguni-born musician Nagama Takao.[17] Yonaguni seems to have had a particularly harsh administration of the *nintōzei*, and the cultural policies of the Ryūkyū government are well known by all modern Yonaguni islanders. An example is the infamous Kubura-bari,[18] a narrow crevice in the cliffs on the outskirts of Kubura village, across which pregnant women were reputedly forced to leap in an attempt to limit the island population (e.g. Ikema, Eizō 1972). Nagama's composition *Kubura-bari*, included on an eponymous cassette album from the mid-1980s, revisits this story. The song, in a mixture of Japanese, Yonaguni and mainland Okinawan dialect,[19] was recorded with a mainland Okinawan backing band (including members of Kina Shōkichi's group of which Nagama was a member) in the 1980s, and is one of the earliest examples of a new composition by a Yaeyaman musician in an 'Okinawan pop' style. The cassette album from which it comes was still hugely popular in Yonaguni in the early 21st century, and I heard many of the songs performed at informal musical events in the island. *Kubura-bari* and other of Nagama's songs[20] deal with one of the more unpleasant aspects of the *nintōzei*, but one that is still very much a part of the modern Yonaguni collective memory.

---

[17]   In 2011 Nagama was based in the Japanese mainland.

[18]   *Bari* (*wari*) = split, crack.

[19]   The first line, for example, contains the Yonaguni dialect word 'Donan' (cf. Okinawan dialect 'Yunōn'), the Okinawan/Japanese word 'shima' (cf. Yonaguni dialect 'chima'), and both the Yonaguni/Okinawa dialect 'nu' and standard Japanese 'no' particles. Lines 3 and 4 are standard Japanese. 'Washiriti nayumi' in line 4 is in the mainland Okinawan mainland dialect.

[20]   A 1998 song *Tun'guda* also describes the harsh population control policies in Yonaguni in the Ryūkyū kingdom period.

The reincorporation of Nagama's compositions back into Yonaguni music-making practices shows their social role as a context for collective memory formation.

The Oyake Akahachi legend, likewise, was a favourite topic for cultural reinterpretation from the early 20th century in Yaeyama, and has been depicted in an epic poem by the writer Iha Nantetsu, several films, and a number of musical projects. Miki (1992: 117–22) has pointed out how the spirit of Yaeyaman resistance inherent in the story was strong enough for early 20th century book and film (1937) versions to be suppressed in the pre-WWII years for fear of inciting anti-Japanese feeling in the Japanese colony of Taiwan, but was also used positively as a symbol for the freedom of Okinawa from American administration in the post-WWII years. One of the more recent reimaginings of the story was the release in 1996 of the song *Hai nu yūshi* by Sakieda Hiroji (b. 1953, Arakawa[21]), in which he describes how Akahachi 'united the people, united the island' (*tami nu kutu sundi, sïma nu kutu sundi*) (words and music: Sakieda Hiroji. CD liner notes). *Hai nu Yūshi*, released on the Okinawan Kokusai Boueki label, can be seen as a way of identity building through collective memory at a specifically local level. The Akahachi legend has also been used in the construction of broader Okinawan identities. In 2000 I saw a musical drama version of the story in Tokyo produced by the Kohama-born musician Hirata Daiichi, and performed by school children from Ishigaki (see also Hirata 2008: 196). The performance, which drew a full house in the 2,000-seat hall, featured performances by Ishigaki musicians, as well as the Peruvian-Okinawan singer Alberto Shiroma, playing new compositions composed for the drama. Listening to the conversations in the foyer before and after the concert, it was obvious that a very large part of this audience was made up of the Japanese mainland Okinawan community. The reimagining of local histories in new musical productions such as this can thus be seen to play an important part also in the maintenance of links between Yaeyama/Okinawa and its diasporic communities.

As well as these more specific historical tales, the representation of a more general sense of the 'timeless and ancient' (Taylor 1997: 26) has been a prominent aspect of modern Yaeyaman music, and one that can be partially related to the presentation of the 'past' in the so-called 'Southern-island theory' (*Nantō-ron*) that I outlined in Chapter 3. This theory was founded on the historical cultural connections between Okinawa and mainland Japan, and often saw Okinawa as a region where aspects of 'ancient' Japanese culture survived as part of everyday life. Hidekatsu's 1994 song *Marebito Den* (Legend of the 'Other'), for example, describes how 'from three thousand years of darkness, from the other world in the sky, from a sleep of seven thousand years, the *marebito* opens his eyes' (*Sanzen nen nu yamiyu kara, tin nu gama nu nīru kara, nanasen nen nu nemuri kara, nama*

---

[21]   Sakieda's mother was a ritual specialist, and a specialist singer of the unaccompanied vocal genres of Arakawa. When I met him in 2002, he was earning a living making and selling *sanshin* in Naha, and was an active member of the YKMH, although the musical aspects of this recording bear little relation to the *fushiuta* tradition.

mizamitaru marebitu ya) (music: Hidekatsu; lyrics: Iramine Takanori. Hidekatsu CD 1994 liner notes). The concept of a spiritual being that visits from a mythical otherworld, bears similarity to many of the indigenous Yaeyaman ritual beliefs that we saw in Chapter 4. The term '*marebito*', however, is not commonly used in Yaeyaman traditional society, and is particularly connected with the mainland Japanese folklorist Orikuchi Shinobu (1887–1953), one of the Japanese scholars influential in developing theories of Okinawa's historical links with Japan in the early 20th century. In a 1929 essay entitled *The Birth of Japanese Literature* (*Kokubungaku no hassei*) Orikuchi outlined the importance of similar ritual beliefs throughout historical Japan on the development of Japanese literature, drawing much of his evidence from research on extant practices in Okinawa, including several pages on Yaeyaman rituals (Orikuchi 2003: 3–65). Hidekatsu's use of the term *marebito*, and the historical imagery in the song, can thus perhaps be placed in the context of these early 20th century cultural images of Okinawa as a historical link to a 'Japanese' past propound by Orikuchi and others.

Attempts to locate modern Okinawa as a region largely untouched by the modern world can be found throughout the Okinawan boom, both in music and other media. The Yaeyaman novelist Ikegami Eiichi (b. 1970[22]), for example, began his 1994 book *Bagajima nu Panasu* (Stories from My Island):

> The warm breeze blew in from far away in the Southwest. If you listened carefully you could hear the sounds of a *sanshin*. Whatever else happens in the world, the beauty of this island will never change, as long as the island people (*shimanchu*) are living there. (Ikegami 1994: 5)

Ikegami's novels (e.g. 1994, 1997), aimed largely at a national Japanese audience, have frequently referenced Yaeyaman traditions, including music, local dialect and ritual beliefs. This passage, with the wind blowing in from mainland Asia, the sound of tradition in the form of the *sanshin*, and the suggestion of a community where the troubles of the outside world are irrelevant, displays many of the stereotyped images of Okinawa that prevailed through the Okinawa boom of the 1990s and early 21st century. The idea of Okinawa as a site for the preservation of a more 'human' society that was subsumed in the post-WWII rush for modernisation, in particular, is referenced by much of the media output of this period. The 2001 NHK drama *Churasan* drew heavily on this kind of imagery. Okada Yoshikazu, the writer of the drama, has commented:

> In *Churasan*, I portrayed the deep human relationships and quality of life that used to exist everywhere [in Japan]. The place where those things remain best is in Okinawa, isn't it. Family values, or the honesty of the leading female

---

[22]   Ikegami was born in the Okinawan mainland, but grew up in Ishigaki from the age of three. His first novel, *Bagajima nu Panasu* (*Stories from My Island*, 1994) was written while studying at Waseda University in Tokyo.

character. They were a kind of nostalgia for Japanese people as a whole. (Quoted in Tanaka 2002: 188)

Likewise, many Yaeyaman and Okinawan performers have referenced Okinawa's (real or imagined) cultural position as preserver of the ways of the Japanese past. Songs such as *Kaze no Donan*[23] by the Yonaguni-born musician Nishidomari Shigeaki, which states 'you idiots without dreams, who say that the old stories of our ancestors hold no interest. The words of the elders, they are the words of God, never forget them', tap into this kind of discourse. The image of Okinawa as a culture that can rescue Japan from the stresses of a modern capitalist world runs through much of Nishidomari's work. In the title song of his 1997 album *Hibi dandan*, for example, he asks the question (in standard Japanese): 'Japanese people, why are Japanese people so busy? Why are Japanese people so sad? Why can't Japanese people live freely?' The implication, again, is that Okinawa represents some kind of answer to the mundane modern Japanese urban existence – a return to a simpler way of life.

Language

Another way in which issues of regionality have been constructed in new musical compositions within Yaeyama, Okinawa and Japan during the Okinawa boom is through the use of local languages. The widespread use of local languages in new Yaeyaman compositions of the Okinawa boom contrasts with examples of pre-WWII compositions that we saw in Chapter 3 that very often favoured standard Japanese. It also runs counter to the use of Okinawan language in daily life – the use of Okinawan language in the songs of the 1990s came at a time when most of the Yaeyaman population had long since switched to using standard Japanese in daily communication. Although the Okinawan mainland record industry had continued to release new songs in the dialect of Naha in the Okinawan mainland throughout the post-WWII period, it was only in the 1990s that dialects from outlying parts of Okinawa began to feature in the recorded output of the prefecture. Why, then, this sudden re-emergence of highly localised language patterns?

A number of studies on the use of language in regional pop musics (e.g. Berger and Carroll 2003; Sparling 2007) have noted that while language is important as a cultural marker, the literal meaning of lyrics is often less important. In some cases meaning may even be derived *specifically* from a non-understanding. Writing about the perception of local languages in Hawai'ian music, Szego (2003), has described an 'aesthetic of (in)comprehensibility', where the fact that the lyrics of a song cannot be easily understood becomes one of its attractions. In many

---

[23]   The local dialect word for the island name of Yonaguni is pronounced variously as Donan and Dunan. Nishidomari uses Donan in the title of the song, but sings 'Dunan'.

cases, these derived meanings are connected with many of the issues of history and cultural difference that we have seen in earlier sections. Concerning the use of Scottish Gaelic by the Cape Breton singer Mary Jane Lamond, Sparling has suggested that for the majority of her listeners, with little or no knowledge of the Gaelic language, 'Lamond's fluency in Gaelic is associated with authentic origins and a pure, ancient tradition' (2007: 37).

The use of local languages in new compositions has taken a number of different forms. We saw in earlier examples such as Nagama Takao's song *Kubura bari* how artists have often mixed dialects from several Okinawan regions with standard Japanese in a single composition, a phenomenon that mirrors to some extent the everyday language patterns of many Yaeyaman communities. Kumada (1998: 148) has noted that many Yaeyaman performers have often used mainland Okinawan, rather than local Yaeyaman dialects, as for example in Parsha Club's 1996 song *Gokoku Hōjō*. This may be an attempt to appeal to audiences across Okinawa – most mainland Okinawans have trouble understanding Yaeyaman dialects, for example, or due to Parsha Club's status as an 'Okinawan' rather than 'Yaeyaman' band – the group's output has incorporated lyrics from several mainland Okinawan lyricists such as Shinjō Kazuhiro. It may also be due to the fact that many younger singers have learned a large part of their dialect through traditional songs from the Okinawan mainland, and use this vocabulary in their new compositions.

Despite this mixing of Yaeyaman and mainland Okinawan dialects by some artists, other songs, such as Nishidomari Shigeaki's *Kaze no Donan*, in the Yonaguni dialect, use the language patterns of an extremely localised part of Okinawa that are barely understandable even to other Okinawans, let alone mainland Japanese listeners. In the context of the explicit targeting of mainland Japanese markets, this use of local dialects played quite a different role to that of the earlier recorded Okinawan music of the mid-20th century. Whereas older examples, aimed solely at a local Okinawan audience who used the Okinawan language in their daily lives, were using the (almost exclusively Okinawan mainland) language as an expression of literal meaning, examples from the Okinawa music boom were in many cases using Okinawan languages and dialects as a marker of regionality or cultural difference, as in Sparling's example, rather than as a method by which literal meaning was transmitted from singer to audience. The result in this shift of emphasis was that suddenly it was acceptable for a singer to sing in any dialect, or about any subject matter, as long as the right image was transmitted. Songs such as *Kaze no donan*, containing large segments in Yonaguni dialect which are totally incomprehensible to almost all Okinawans and Japanese mainlanders alike, have nevertheless found popularity, perhaps through this very semi-comprehensibility (Japanese translations are provided in the liner notes to this CD).

This sudden acceptance of regional Okinawan dialects in the 1990s and 2000s can also be seen through performers from other parts of Okinawa. Since 2002, one of the most successful Okinawan musicians inside and outside the prefecture has been the Miyako-born Shimoji Isamu (b. 1969), a singer and songwriter in a blues/folk style who sings almost entirely in the language of the largest Miyako island. As with Yaeyaman dialects, the Miyako language in which Shimoji sings is mostly incomprehensible even to mainland Okinawan listeners, let alone those in mainland Japan where he has a large fan base. Yet for many it seems to be this incomprehensibility itself that is one of Shimoji's selling points. An anonymous reviewer on the Japanese Amazon.co.jp website of Shimoji's 2006 album *Ataraka*, from Aomori in the north of Japan writes:

> My first impression was 'is this really [a branch of the] Japanese language?' I have no idea what he's singing, but that's what makes it good [*soko ga iin desu*]. It's all in the dialect of Miyako. I get the impression that this CD is full of feelings that can only be expressed through dialect. All the songs have a strong sense of humanity that will have you hooked after one listening. (www.amazon. co.jp/ATARAKA, accessed 16 June 2009)

As in Szego's study, this listener's 'strong sense of humanity' seems to derive specifically from an 'aesthetic of incomprehensibility' – it is expressible only through 'dialect', and the fact that the literal meaning is not understandable only increases the symbolic meaning of the song. The reference to the lyrics being in the 'Japanese language', and the use of the word 'dialect' (*hōgen*) also seem to be significant. In contrast to earlier 20th century examples in Chapter 3, where national unity was stressed through the use of standard Japanese, the celebration of linguistic diversity in the context of the 'Japanese' language is now a source of cultural pride.

The sudden rebirth in Okinawan language songs in the 1990s and beyond should thus also be seen as a rethinking of Japanese linguistic or cultural diversity that is connected with a more general reassessment of ideas of *Nihonjinron* within a 'multicultural Japan' in recent years. Condry (2006), for example, has described the use of language in Japanese rap music as a way of breaking down 'the hegemonic understanding of the Japanese as one people with one language' (2006: 135). Likewise, in a study of regional identity construction through rap in France, Brian George notes the way this musical genre has been 'embraced by some of those challenging the linguistic and cultural hegemony of Paris and working towards the recognition of linguistic diversity in the nation' (2007: 110). The use of Okinawan dialects in new songs (directed at least partly at a nation-wide audience) should also be seen in the context of this discourse of multiculturalism, as a way of redefining what it means to be Japanese.

Summary

In this chapter we have seen some of the meanings that new music by Yaeyaman performers have held in the national Okinawan music boom of the 1990s and 2000s. The prominence of Yaeyaman performers on the national music scene in this period is remarkable. After years of relative inactivity, it was as if the region had suddenly come alive with musical creativity. Yaeyama's prominence in the Okinawan music world is partly due to the continued importance of traditional music in everyday life that we have seen in the rest of this book. The importance of traditional music in village ritual contexts explored in Chapter 4 has undoubtedly been of importance in producing performers with knowledge of traditional genres. Ara Yukito, for example, still performs at Shiraho ritual events such as *sōron* and the harvest festival (pers. comm. November 2001); Nishidomari Shigeaki grew up as the son of a dance accompanist at local festivals; Hidekatsu is the son of a ritual music specialist in Taketomi; Daiku Tetsuhiro is also sporadically involved in festival music in his native Arakawa, and has included ritual music such as the Arakawa *mishagu pāsï* in his recordings. The performing arts clubs at Yaeyaman schools likewise seem to have been influential on many of these artists. Daiku, Ara, Ōshima Yasukatsu and other performers started learning music in local schools before embarking on professional careers.

Despite these 'local' reasons for the success of Yaeyamans in comparison to other parts of Okinawa, the Okinawan music boom of the 1990s and beyond cannot really be understood without considering its meaning in a Japanese context. The Okinawa boom functioned on a variety of levels in positioning Okinawa culturally and politically within the Japanese nation. The image of Okinawa as Japanese 'roots' that has existed since the early 20th century continued to be important in the context of the Okinawa boom, and an image of the past, and of the old traditional family values which are seen as disappearing in the Japanese mainland, was one of the major themes of the new Okinawan music of this period. This kind of image has been actively appropriated by Japanese media and music industries, and enthusiastically received by many parts of Japanese society. The depiction of Okinawa as a kind of tropical time-slip, where the problems of the real world do not apply, is of course far from the very real social problems of unemployment and domination by American bases that face modern Okinawa, and several commentators have criticised the romanticised treatment of Okinawa in much of the material from this period. The mainland Japanese writer Hanamura Mangetsu, for example, describes the hit film *Nabi no koi* as a 'colonialist movie' (*shokuminchi eiga*) due to its over-sentimental depictions of old-fashioned Okinawan life (2007: 162). Sogabe Tsukasa, in a book on the Okinawan comedian and musician Onaga Būten, has described his feelings of resistance to the reliance on 'exoticism' in much Okinawan music of the boom, as well as criticising the 'mainland Japanese business approach of commodifying Okinawa[n music]' (Sogabe 2006: 20; see also Tanaka 2002).

Despite these criticisms, the music of the Okinawa boom has also played an important role within Okinawa itself by providing a context for the reappraisal of aspects of tradition, as we saw in the extensive discourse surrounding the subject. Going into the second decade of the 21st century, Okinawa continues to have a thriving local musical scene that mixes elements of tradition and modernity to an extent that cannot be found in any other Japanese prefecture. This musical creativity is largely an extension of the musical activities of many of the artists mentioned in this chapter in forming new musical expressions of Yaeyama and Okinawa's position at the edge of Japan.

とーすぃ

Chapter 8
Afterword

This book has looked at some of the different ways that traditional music-making has been used in the construction of a variety of Yaeyaman cultural identities. These various 'Yaeyaman' musical identities have been connected with social units as small as the family, in the case of some of the ritual music-making contexts that we saw in Chapter 4, or even the individual, as in the performance of *Tubarāma* in Chapter 6. They have also often been implicitly bound up within Yaeyama's larger webs of affiliation with Okinawa, Japan and the rest of the world. I began with two very different ideas of modern Yaeyaman identities, expressed by Ōhama Anpan and the group BEGIN as 'island (people's) treasures' (*shima (nchu) nu takara*). Over the course of the book I have tried to analyse some of the ways that ideas of *shima/sïma* as 'place' have been imagined musically, and presented some of the diverse range of music-making that continue to make Yaeyama, as Iha Fuyū described in 1912, the 'land of song' (*uta no kuni*).

At one level, traditional music-making in modern Yaeyama has continued largely independently of the outside world. In the early 21st century, the performance of ritual song continues to play an important part in traditional life at a village level, and is one of the main ways that local ritual belief systems are performed and socially imagined. The performance of music and dance in front of the household Buddhist altar in the *Angamā* ritual, in front of the grave at *Jūrukunitsï*, or facing towards the mythical otherworld of *Nirai-kanai* at Taketomi's *Yūnkai* ritual were all examples of the construction of very specific spiritual notions of place (or spatial notions of spirituality) through musical performance. The connection of Yaeyaman spiritual beliefs with ancestral systems and village creation myths has also meant that ritual music continues to be deeply implicated in modern imaginations of village and intra-village cultural identities. We saw how rituals such as *Tanadui* are often a site through which intra-village cultural identities are constructed, and that these identities are often carried over to diasporic communities in Ishigaki, Okinawa and Japan. In some cases, such as in the Aragusuku community which essentially survives only in the diaspora living outside that island, ritual music performance provides one of the main contexts for the performance and maintenance of Aragusuku cultural identities.

The *fushiuta* tradition presents a slightly different case to these more specific geographical imaginations of place, as the old affiliations with Ishigaki and Tonoshiro villages have been replaced by more ephemeral conceptions of place situating modern performers, through lineage charts, in relation to historically important performers. The group identities involved with these lineage organisations are usually very strong – the majority of musical activities of most *fushiuta* performers take place within the context of their own lineage, for example. They have also been remarkably successful at promoting *fushiuta*, and this genre is booming in the early 21st century, with perhaps more performers and students than have existed at any time in the past. There are several reasons for the modern popularity of *fushiuta* since the mid-20th century – a release from the cultural oppression of the pre-WWII years, coupled with the effective end of the class system (*mibun seido*) that had continued to divide Yaeyamans into a (*sanshin*-playing) upper class and a (*yunta/jiraba*-singing) peasant class, meant that *fushiuta* were reinvented as a classless symbol of Yaeyaman culture in general. This reinvention of the cultural image of *fushiuta* and the *sanshin* prompted profound changes to take place in its performance practices. In particular, the relaxation of the stigma against women and children playing the *sanshin* since the late 1960s has meant that the social demographic of the *fushiuta* community has changed drastically since earlier times. Another of the biggest reasons for the popularity of *fushiuta* has been the shift of affiliation in music-making away from the original village contexts towards a system that has allowed *fushiuta* to become a 'classical' genre with less-strong regional ties. Individual *fushiuta* lineages such as the YKMH now have branches in Yaeyama, the Okinawan mainland and several Japanese cities such as Tokyo. The high level of standardisation brought about by the *kunkunshi* notations used in these organisations has meant that it is easy for their members to play together with each other, and has fostered a sense of community among members around the country.

Local and national governments have also been influential in prompting the reappraisal of local genres – the designation of Taketomi's *Tanadui* festival as an Important Intangible Folk Cultural Property by the national government has had a profound effect on the way in which songs in this festival are now transmitted, for example. Likewise, the designation of Yaeyaman 'classical folk song' (*koten min'yō*) as an intangible cultural asset by the prefectural government was influential in promoting certain lineages and performers in the *fushiuta* tradition. The development of *hozonkai* for the preservation of the *yunta* and *jiraba* repertory was partly stimulated by the activities of the local Yaeyaman government in setting up performance events for this genre, and the Ishigaki government's sponsorship of the *Tubarāma* singing competition, too, has been highly influential on the way that village performance variants are favoured or rejected.

In contrast to these efforts of *fushiuta* lineages and government groups, there has also been a simultaneous discourse contesting the extent to which aspects of tradition should be formalised and standardised. In Chapter 6 I outlined the way that ideas of individual creativity in the context of the performance of the song *Tubarāma* have often been the focus of debates about the extent to which traditional culture should be officially mediated. These debates have related in particular to the annual singing competition for the song, and have taken place in local newspapers and magazines, as well as through the creation of 'alternative' singing events. More recently, the issue of the 'common people' (*shomin, minshū*) has appeared in several quotes from Yaeyaman performers such as BEGIN and Daiku Tetsuhiro (Chapter 7) or Kinjō Asao (Chapter 6) as part of a discourse surrounding the mediation of tradition by local government or *fushiuta* lineages.

In many cases, music-making in Yaeyama has taken place simultaneously at a range of cultural and spatial levels, as a combination of the local, regional and national. The Okinawa boom of the late 20th and early 21st centuries was only the most recent manifestation of a long cultural process situating Yaeyama within the context of Okinawa and the Japanese nation, one that has often taken place in the context of music. In Chapter 3 I showed how the development of 'local' ideas of a Yaeyaman 'folk song' canon were influenced by Iha Fuyū and other scholars' developing concepts of Okinawa's position within Japan, as well as the more general ideas of folk music and culture being developed in the Japanese mainland in the early 20th century. The concepts of 'local' Yaeyaman musical culture developed by Kishaba Eijun and other Yaeyaman scholars at this time were thus developed through the combined activities and interests of the Japanese academic and political worlds as a whole.

The new Yaeyaman music of the 1990s and beyond was likewise functioning not only within Yaeyaman or Okinawan society, but also served as a way of negotiating ideas of Okinawa's position within the modern Japanese nation. In Chapter 7 I considered several reasons for the continued popularity of Yaeyaman and Okinawan musical styles with mainland Japanese audiences, from an image as a kind of exotic 'roots' music, to the role of Okinawan music as 'healing islands' (*iyashi no shima*). Much of the music of this period can be analysed within models of the world music phenomenon in North America and Europe. In particular, forces of globalisation have acted in a quite immediate way on some Yaeyaman performers – the members of BEGIN cited a crisis of confidence when faced with performing blues music styles to an American audience as being a direct impetus to 'go back' to their Okinawan 'roots'. This was perhaps an extreme example, but the influence of global music markets has been felt by many Yaeyaman performers – on the subject of collaborating with musicians from around the world, Daiku Tetsuhiro commented in a 2010 interview, for example, that 'I'm aiming for something like the Buena Vista social club'.[1] Comments such as these highlight the way in which Yaeyaman traditional musicians operate under a variety of globalised cultural influences, and are part of a larger international 'world music' culture. To give another example, on recent trips to Yaeyama several Yaeyaman performers have commented to me that my own interest in Yaeyaman music, and my activities as a performer, prompted them to take lessons in *fushiuta* performance so that they wouldn't be 'outdone' (*makenai yō ni*) by a foreigner. The impetus of outsiders from mainland Japan and abroad thus often seems to have stimulated a feeling of cultural responsibility to learn more about local Yaeyaman traditional culture.

---

[1]   http://ryuqspecial.ti-da.net/e2656662.html (accessed 21 February 2011).

The re-emergence of local languages as symbols of local identity must also be seen in the context of Yaeyama's cultural position within Japan. The widespread suppression of Yaeyaman languages in favour of standard Japanese (*hyōjungo*) in the early 20th century was supported partly through the activities of Yaeyaman composers' creating standard-Japanese versions of traditional songs, as well as new compositions promoting standard Japanese. Ōhama Tsurō's 1956 *Tubarāma* performance, singing of Okinawa's allegiance to Japan, but doing so in the Yaeyaman language, was an early example of another approach, one that stressed the importance of Yaeyama's 'difference' within the context of the Japanese nation. The use of local languages and dialects in more recent musical output, such as that of Nishidomari Shigeaki or the Miyako singer Shimoji Isamu, can also be seen in a similar way. While the literal meaning of lyrics are often lost on listeners (both Okinawan and Japanese) with no knowledge of these very localised dialects, the 'aesthetic of incomprehensibility' on which many of these compositions play can be seen as one way of exploring ideas of Japanese diversity.

Okinawan music has also been part of a more general cultural discourse in Japan in recent years concerning cultural and ethnic diversity in the context of the nation. In several instances there have been attempts to link ideas of Okinawan minority culture in a Japanese context. To give one example, the Charanke matsuri, an annual festival held in Tokyo's Nakano district since 1994, was established to promote cultural links between Okinawan and Ainu groups in the Japanese capital, and features performances of traditional music and dancing, food and crafts from both regions.[2] In 2010, the event also featured performances from a Korean *Nongak* percussion ensemble, further emphasising its role as a context for the imagination of Japanese cultural minority groups. This kind of exploration of cultural links between distinct and very different Japanese minority groups can also be seen through the work of the *zainichi* Korean musician Pak Poe, who has performed a number of collaborations with Okinawan artists, or the Kansai band Soul Flower Union, who have also been active in presenting images of Japan's cultural minority groups, incorporating Okinawan, Korean and Ainu elements into their recordings and live performances.

While the influence of mainland Japan has appeared throughout the genres and music-making contexts that I have examined in the book, I certainly draw no essentialist conclusions concerning Okinawa's 'true' status – culturally, politically or ethnically – in the Japanese nation. Modern Okinawans, of course, hold a variety of opinions on the islands' relationship with the rest of Japan. A small, but relatively vocal minority regularly calls for political independence for the islands. A larger number want increased autonomy and, in particular, clarification regarding the future of the American military presence in the prefecture, a topic that, due to Yaeyama's relative isolation from the issue (Yaeyama has no American military bases), has unfortunately been largely absent from the discourse presented in this book. The majority of Okinawans, perhaps, feel allegiances to Japan

---

[2]   http://charanke.com/index.html (accessed 13 February 2011).

while simultaneously maintaining strong local identities. A 2006 opinion poll of prefectural residents by the *Ryūkyū Shinpō* newspaper showed, for example, that 43 per cent of Okinawans as a whole (and 56 per cent of Yaeyamans) expressed a 'closeness' (*shitashimi*) to the Japanese emperor, and the prefecture's return to Japan was ranked as the second most important event in 20th-century Okinawan history[3] (Ryūkyū Shinpō-sha 2007: 35, 85). At the same time, 84.8 per cent expressed pride in being 'Okinawan' (*Uchinānchu*, ibid.: 22), while 98 per cent of Yaeyamans expressed pride in traditional Yaeyaman culture (ibid.: 28). Clearly these various different cultural identities are not mutually exclusive, but co-exist and, in many cases, influence each other. As many recent studies have shown, music is not used as a way of 'expressing' pre-formed identities, rather it is one of the ways in which those identities are imagined and negotiated in the first place. Music in Yaeyama has been one of the ways in which these kind of multiple identities, of region and nation, have been constructed. From the early 20th century compositions of Miyara Chōhō, through the mid-20th century *Tubarāma* performance of Ōhama Tsurō in Tokyo, to the commercial releases of BEGIN, Daiku Tetsuhiro and others in the early 2000s, we have seen many examples of the way in which Yaeyaman music has been part of an ongoing process to negotiate ideas of belonging and difference relating to Yaeyama's place in Japan.

Japanese cultural 'booms' come and go. The nationwide interest in Okinawan music has subsided since its heights in the early years of the 21st century, with subsequent 'international' booms such as the 'Korean wave', as well as a brief craze for learning the Chinese *erhu* prompted by the early 21st-century success of the Chinese female group Twelve Girls Band, and several others. Yaeyaman music nevertheless still has a very solid fan-base throughout the country, and Yaeyaman performers continue to visit the large Japanese cities on a regular basis. Writing this in February 2011, BEGIN, Ara Yukito, Daiku Tetsuhiro, Nagama Takao and many other Yaeyaman performers continue to schedule regular performances in Tokyo and the rest of Japan, as well as in Yaeyama and the Okinawan mainland. In addition to the success of Yaeyaman performers in Japan, there have also been a large number of Japanese mainlanders learning, and subsequently teaching, Yaeyaman *fushiuta*, as well as other Okinawan musical genres. In terms of active learners, Okinawan music is certainly one of the most popular 'traditional Japanese' musical genres in Tokyo in the early 21st century. A concert celebrating the 100th anniversary of the birth of the *fushiuta* performer Ōhama Anpan took place in Tokyo in the middle of February 2011, with performers coming from Yaeyama and Okinawa to join the Tokyo branch of the YKMH organisation that Ōhama founded. Most of the other *fushiuta* organisations also have a presence in the Japanese mainland, with students and teachers from the Tokyo Yaeyaman community as well as many with no family connection to the region.

On a short visit to Ishigaki at the end of February 2011, nearly 10 years after my initial fieldwork trip, I met up with members of the Taketomi community who

---

[3] WWII ranked number one.

were already excitedly talking of the *Tanadui* festival, scheduled for October of that year. One informant told me how he was looking forward to seeing members of his family who would be travelling from Tokyo and the Okinawan mainland for the event. My *fushiuta* teacher Ōsoko Chōyō continued his busy schedule, teaching students from all over Japan as well as his long-standing local circle of performers. The popularity of *fushiuta* shows no sign of abating, and in comparison to only two *sanshin* shops in Ishigaki in 2001, I counted upwards of six in 2011, showing the continuing popularity of the genre. The Tonoshiro *yunta* group continues to meet on Tuesday every week. The deaths of many of the older members in recent years were a serious blow to the group, but an influx of spritely younger members seems to suggest that the group will continue. Traditional music-making in Yaeyama seems set to continue its cultural importance for the time being.

Appendix 1:
Glossary of Japanese, Yaeyaman and Okinawan Terms

Akamata Kuromata	赤また黒また	Masked gods at harvest festival
Akanma bushi	赤馬節	*Fushiuta* title
Angamā	アンガマー、母子、姉子	Ancestor ritual at *bon* Festival
Asadōya yunta	安里屋ユンタ	Song title
Ayō	アヨー	Yaeyaman song genre
Bafu	バフ	Communal work pattern
Basï nu turï bushi	鷲ぬ鳥節	*Fushiuta* title
Bari nōshi	（疲れ治し）	Party after a festival/event (lit. 'recover from tiredness)
Bōhan kyōkai	防犯協会	Crime prevention association
bon (o-bon)	盆	Ancestor festival
Bunka-sai	文化祭	Culture festival
Buraku	部落	Village sub-division
Buriyō	ブリヨー	Singing style/version
Buzā	ブザー	Yaeyaman peasant class
Chīga	チーガ	Body of *sanshin*
Chūkan-on	中間音	Infix (in tetrachord)
Chūzan seikan	中山世鑑	1650 history of Ryūkyū
Dentō	伝統	Tradition
Deshi	弟子	Pupil, disciple
Dōkōkai	同好会	Appreciation society
Fāmā	子孫	Angama dancers
Fū (e.g. Tonoshiro *fū*)	風（登野城風）	Style, lineage
Fushi chūshin (no maki)	父子忠臣之巻	*Kumiodori* play
Fushiuta	節歌	*Sanshin*-accompanied song genre
Gessha	月謝	Monthly fee (for lessons)

Gokoku hōjō	五穀豊穣	Five staple crops
Gongche (pu)	工尺 (譜)	Chinese notation system
Gun	郡	District (county)
Gusō/Gushō	後生	Afterlife
Hanjō bushi	繁昌節	Song title
Happyōkai	発表会	Recital
Hayashi	囃子	Sung syllables (often meaningless) inserted between the main lyrics of a song
hikujima	低島	Low island
Hōgen ronsō	方言論争	Dialect controversy
Honchōshi	本調子	Sanshin tuning
Hōnensai	豊年祭	Harvest festival
Honku/funku	本句	Main part (of song)
Hōnō geinō	奉納芸能	'Offertory' performance
Iemoto	家元	Head (of *ryūha*)
Ishigaki-shi Bunka Kyōkai	石垣市文化協会	Ishigaki city cultural association
Iyashi no shima	癒しの島	'Healing islands'
Jikata (also jiutē)	地謡	Dance accompaniment
Jikoryū	自己流	'Personal' lineage
Jinruikan	人類館	'Human race hall' at 1903 Osaka exposition
Jiraba	ジラバ	Yaeyaman song genre
Joji	叙事	Narrative (song)
Jojōka	叙情歌	Lyrical song
Jūrukunitsï	十六日祭	Ancestor ritual on the 16th day of the 1st month
Kabuni (Kafuni) wan	嘉保根御嶽	Shrine in Kohama
kagai	燿歌	See *utagaki*
Kahi	歌碑	Song monument
Kakeuta	掛歌	Antiphonal singing style
Kakuon	核音	Nuclear tone
Kane	鉦	Gong
Kanfutsï	神口	Ritual song genre
Karī	嘉例	Auspiciousness
Kaze no Donan	風のどなん	Nishidomari Shigeaki song
Ken	県	Prefecture

Kettō	血統	Blood lineage
Kokkei	滑稽	Comical
Kōminkan	公民館	Community centre
Kōminkanchō	公民館長	Community centre leader
Konkūru	コンクール	Examination, grade test (cf. French *concours*)
Kōnōkai	興農会	Agriculture promotion group
Kontu-on	幸本御嶽	Taketomi shrine
Koten min'yō	古典民謡	Classical folk song
Koto/kutu	箏	13-stringed zither
Koyō	古謡	'Old' song
Kuduki/Kuduchi/ Kudoki	口説	Yaeyaman/Okinawan song genre
Kuigusuku bushi	越城節	*Fushiuta* title
Kumiodori	組踊	Ryūkyū musical drama
Kumōma bushi	小浜節	*Fushiuta* title
Kuniburi	国風（国振り）	Early Japanese genre of folk song
Kunkunshi	工工四	Okinawan tablature notation system
Kurushima kuduki (*kuduchi*)	黒島口説	Song title
Kyōdo geinō-bu	郷土芸能部	Local performing arts club
Kyōkunka	教訓歌	Educational song
Kyon'gin	狂言	Comical drama
Machi-okoshi	町興し	Town/village promotion
Maki-odori	巻き踊り	Ring/circle dance
Man'yōshū	万葉集	7th–8th century Japanese poetry collection
Menkyo	免許	Certificate
Michiyuki uta	道行唄	Processional song
Min'yō	民謡	Folk song
Miruku Munari	ミルクムナリ	Hidekatsu song title
Mīzïru	女弦	'Female' (highest) string of *sanshin*
Montō	問答	Question and answer (in *An'gamā* ritual)
Mukei	無形	Intangible
Mukei bunkazai	無形文化財	Intangible cultural asset
Nabi no koi	ナビの恋	1999 film by Nakae Yūji
Nakazïru	中弦	Middle string on *sanshin*

Nantō-ron	南島論	'Southern island theory'
Nama ni nukushōri	今に残しょーり	'Preserve in the present' (*Tubarāma* lyric)
Niagi	二上	Sanshin tuning
Nintōzei (Jintōzei)	人頭税	Poll tax
Nirai-kanai	ニライカナイ	Mythical other-world
Nmi	媼	'Old woman' role in Angama
Nungunjima	野国島	Non-rice-growing island
Nzō nenbutsu bushi	無蔵念仏節	Song title
Onkai	音階	(Musical) scale
Paka	パカ	Village division
Pūrï	穂利	Harvest festival (see *hōnensai*)
Raihōgami	来訪神	'Visiting' gods
Riyō	里謡	Early term for folk song in Japan
Ryo (scale/mode)	呂（音階・旋法）	do re mi sol la do
Ryūha	流派	Lineage/school
Ryūka	琉歌	Okinawan lyrical song with 8,886 syllable count
Ryūka Hyakkō	琉歌百控	*Late 18th century Okinawan lyric collection*
Saiyūshūshō	最優秀賞	Top prize (in *konkūru*)
Sakanayā	肴屋	Drinking house. Predecessor of folk song bar.
Sanshin/Shamisen/santi	三線・三味線（occasionally 三弦）	Okinawan three-stringed lute
Seigakufu-tsuki	声楽譜付	Including vocal melody (*kunkunshi*)
Seinenkai	青年会	Youth group
Senpō	旋法	Mode
Shakuhachi	尺八	End-blown bamboo flute
Shibubari sanshin	渋張り三線	Homemade *sanshin* using a paper membrane
Shika aza	四ヶ字，四箇字	The main settlement in Ishigaki island, comprising Ishigaki, Tonoshiro, Arakawa and Ōkawa villages
Shima (sïma) nu takara	島ぬ宝	Island treasures
Shimabagari	島別り	'Island splitting' – forced relocation of villages
Shimanchu nu takara	島人ぬ宝	Island people's treasures

Shimauta	島唄	Lit. 'island song'
shīmī-sai	清明祭	Ancestor ritual
Shimin kaikan	市民会館	City auditorium
Shinjinshō	新人賞	Elementary (newcomer) level (in *konkuru*)
Shūritsï yunta	首里子ユンタ	Song title
Sïma muni taikai	島むに大会	'Dialect' speech contest
Sōron	精霊	Ancestor festival (see *bon*)
Taiko/tēku	太鼓	Stick drum
Takashima	高島	'High' islands
Tanadui /Tanedorisai	種子取り祭	'Rice-planting' festival
Tangunjima	田国島	Rice-growing island
Tochi sanka	土地賛歌	Land praise song
Tō nu tsindami	唐ぬツィンダミ	'Chinese' tuning (*sanshin*)
Tōsï	とーすぃ	Fast second section of *yunta*
Tsimi/Chimi	爪	Pick for *sanshin*
Tsukasa	司	Female ritual specialist
Tsukï ya pama bushi	月夜浜節	*Fushiuta* title
Tsurukami bushi	鶴亀節	Song title
Tunimutu	殿元	Ancestral house
Ushumai	御主前（翁）	*'Old man' role in Angama*
Utakake/utagaki	歌掛け・歌垣	Practice of antiphonal singing, often between men and women
Utaki/On	（お）嶽	Shrine
Utsugumi no kokoro	うつぐみの心	Spirit of mutual cooperation (Taketomi)
Ūzïru	男弦	'Male' (lowest) string on *sanshin*
Yaeyama Kyōiku Jimusho	八重山教育事務所	Yaeyama Education Office
Yakunin	役人	(Shuri) government official
Yamabarē yunta	山原ユンタ	Song title
Yokyō	余興	Entertainment
Yubi ga yū jiraba	昨夜が夜ジラバ	Song title
Yugafu bushi	世果報節	Song title
Yukarupitu	ユカルピトゥ	Yaeyaman ruling class
Yūkei	有形	Tangible
Yūkui	世乞い	Lit. 'praying for the world'. Ritual at Taketomi *Tanadui*

Yuimāru	結い回る	Work 'rotation'
Yūmuchi utaki	世持ち嶽	Shrine in Taketomi island
Yunaha bushi	与那覇節	*Fushiuta* title
Yungutu	ユングトゥ	Song genre, often comical, with a relatively simple melody
Yūnkai	世迎え	Ritual greeting the gods from *Nirai kanai*
Yunta	ユンタ（詠歌・結い歌）	Yaeyaman song genre
Zen'yasai	前夜祭	'Night before' festival alternative *Tubarāma Taikai*
Zokuyō	俗謡	Early Japanese term for folk song
Zōuta	雑唄	Popular 'dance' songs

Appendix 2:
Glossary of Place Names

Readings follow the current standard Japanese place names. Dialect names are included in brackets. Where more than one dialect name exists the name used in the place concerned is written first, followed by the alternative name. For example Taketomi is known as 'Tēdun' in the Taketomi dialect, and as 'Takidun' in the Ishigaki dialect.

Amami	奄美
Aragusuku (Panari)	新城
Arakawa (Arakā)	新川
Hateruma (Patirōma)	波照間
Hatoma (Patuma)	鳩間
Hazama (Taketomi)	坡座間
Hirae (Pisai)	平得
Hokkaido	北海道
Iriomote (Irimuti)	西表
Ishigaki (Ishanagira)	石垣
Kabira (Kabïra)	川平
Kohama (Kumōma/Kubama)	小浜
Kuroshima (Safusïma)	黒島
Miyako (Myāku)	宮古
Miyara (Mēra)	宮良
Naha (Nafa)	那覇
Nakasuji (Taketomi)	仲筋
Ōkawa (Fukā)	大川
Okinawa (Ukïnā/Uchinā)	沖縄
Ryūkyū (in English Ryukyu)	琉球
Sakieda (Sakida)	崎枝
Satsuma (Kyūshū)	薩摩
Shiraho (Sabu/Shirafu)	白保

Sonai (Sunai)	組納
Shuri (Shui/Sui)	首里
Taishō ward (Osaka)	大正区
Taketomi (Tēdun/Takidun)	竹富
Tonoshiro (Tunusuku)	登野城
Tōrinji (temple, Ishigaki)	桃林寺
Tōzato	桃里
Yaeyama (Yaima/Yēma)	八重山
Yonaguni (Dunan/Yunōn)	与那国

Appendix 3:
Glossary of Personal Names

Ara Yukito (b. 1967, Ishigaki)	新良幸人	Leader of the band Parsha Club
Asato Isamu (b. 1937, Kuroshima)	安里勇	Owner of the *min'yō* club
Chin Kan	陳侃	Chinese envoy to Ryūkyū in 1534
China Sadao (b. 1945, Osaka)	知名定男	Okinawan musician
Daiku Tetsuhiro (b. 1948, Ishigaki)	大工哲弘	*Fushiuta* performer resident in Okinawa mainland
Haebaru Eiiku (b. 1924, Ishigaki)	南風原英育	Journalist for *Kainan Jihō* newspaper
Haeno Kisaku	南風野喜作	Kabira *fushiuta* performer
Hatoma Kanako (b. 1983, Ishigaki)	鳩間可奈子	*Fushiuta*/pop performer
Hatoma Takashi (b. 1944, Hatoma)	鳩間隆志	Father of Kanako. Owner of *min'yō* club in Ishigaki
Hidekatsu (b. 1961, Taketomi)	日出克	Singer/guitarist/composer
Iha Fuyū (1876–1947)	伊波普猷	Okinawan scholar
Iha Kōryō	伊波興良	
Iha Nantetsu (1902–1976)	伊波南哲	Ishigaki writer/poet
Ishigaki Hirotaka (b. 1937, Ishigaki)	石垣博孝	Folk song scholar resident in Ishigaki
Ishigaki Hisao	石垣久雄	President of the Taketomi *minzoku geinō hozonkai*
Ishigaki Shigeru (b. 1937, Ishigaki)	石垣繁	Folk song scholar resident in Ishigaki
Ishigaki Yasunobu (b. 1950, Kohama)	石垣安信	Kohama musician
Kadekaru Rinshō (1920–1999)	嘉手苅林昌	Okinawan musician
Kamei Yasunobu	亀井安信	Taketomi musician
Kina Shōkichi (b. 1948)	喜納昌吉	Okinawan musician
Kinjō Asao (Tomoyose Eishō)	金城朝夫	Yaeyaman journalist
Kishaba Eijun (1885–1972)	喜舎場永珣	Tonoshiro writer/teacher

Kohama Kōjirō (b. 1935, Hatoma)	小浜光次郎	Musician resident in Naha, author of Hatoma *kunkunshi*
Maehana Tomohiro (b. 1940, Ishigaki)	前花友宏	*Fushiuta* teacher in the YKMH
Miyara Jitsuan	宮良実安	Head of Miyara *koyō hozonkai*
Miyara Kōrin (1917–1959)	宮良高林	Ishigaki musician
Miyara Kōsei (b. 1940, Yonaguni)	宮良康正	Musician based in Naha
Morita Son'ei (1921–2008)	森田孫榮	Ishigaki writer/poet
Nakae Yūji (b. 1960, Kyoto)	中江裕司	Film director
Nakashima Tama (b. Ishigaki)	仲島タマ	Singer resident in Shiraho
Nane Misao (b. 1952, Iriomote)	那根操	Musician resident in Iriomote
Narai Chidori (b. 1958, Iriomote)	那良伊千鳥	Musician based in Okinawa
Nēnēs	ネーネーズ	Mainland Okinawa group
Nishidomari Shigeaki (b. 1969, Yonaguni)	西泊茂昌	Musician based in kinawa
Noborikawa Seijin (b. 1932, Hyōgo)	登川誠仁	Okinawan musician
Ōhama Anpan (Anhan) (1914–2001)	大浜安伴	Ishigaki musician
Ōhama Tsuro (1891–1970)	大浜津呂	Tonoshiro musician
Ōhama Yōnō (1841–1916)	大浜用能	Tonoshiro musician
Orikuchi Shinobu (1887–1953)	折口信夫	Japanese folklorist
Ōshima Yasukatsu (b. 1969, Ishigaki)	大島康克	Musician based in Japan
Ōsoko Choyo (b. 1934, Iriomote)	大底朝要	*Fushiuta* teacher in YKMH. Resident in Ishigaki
Ōta Shizuo (b. 1948, Ishigaki)	大田静男	Scholar and musician resident in Ishigaki
Ōtake Zenzō (b. Kohama)	大嵩善三	*Fushiuta* teacher, resident in Okinawa mainland
Oyake Akahachi (d. 1500)	遠弥計赤蜂	Yaeyaman chieftain
Ōyama Takeshi (b. Taketomi)	大山剛	Native of Taketomi, resident in Ishigaki
Sakieda Kiyo (born Ishigaki)	崎枝キヨ	*Tsukasa* and singer of *koyō*
Shimazu (clan)	島津	
Shimoji Isamu (b. 1969, Miyako)	下地勇	Miyako musician
Shinjō Kazuhiro (b. 1963, Naha)	新城和博	Okinawan editor/lyricist

Shinjō Wataru (b. 1948, Tonoshiro)	新城亘	*fushiuta* performer and scholar
Takamine Hōyū (b. Taketomi)	高嶺方祐	Yaeyaman school teacher
Takamine Mitsu (b. 1924)	高峰ミツ	*Sanshin* teacher in YKMH. Resident in Kabira
Takamine Zenshin (b. 1950, Ishigaki)	高峰善伸	*Fushiuta* teacher in YKMH
Takenaka Rō (1930–1991)	竹中労	Japanese journalist/writer
Tamashiro Kōichi (b. 1937, Hatoma)	玉城功一	*Fushiuta* teacher in YKOARH and scholar of Yaeyaman *koyō*
Tamayose Choden (b. 1917, Ishigaki)	玉代勢長傳	*Fushiuta* teacher and head of YKOARH
Tau Toki (b. Ishigaki)	田宇トキ	Singer resident in Shiraho
Teruya Rinken (b. 1949, Koza)	照屋林賢	Okinawan musician
Teruya Rinsuke (1929–2005)	照屋林助	Okinawan musician
Tominaga Hide (b. Ishigaki)	富永秀	Singer and leader of Tonoshiro *kayō no kai*
Tōyama Yoshitaka (Zendō)	富山善堂	*Sanshin* teacher in YKMH. Resident in Okinawa
Uehara Naohiko (b. 1938, Naha)	上原直彦)	Okinawan broadcaster
Uehara Shinkō	上原信考	Head of Youth group in Shimanaka, Yonaguni
Uesedo Tomoko	上勢頭同子	Singer and *koyō* scholar. Resident in Taketomi
Uesedo Yoshinori	上勢頭芳徳	Taketomi resident. Head of Kihōin museum
Yakabi Chōki (1716–1775)	屋嘉比朝寄	Okinawan musician
Yamazato Setsuko (b. Ishigaki)	山里節子	Singer and *min'yō* scholar Resident in Ishigaki
Yamazato Yukichi (b. 1925, Ishigaki)	山里勇吉	*Fushiuta* performer. Resident in Okinawa
Yanagi Muneyoshi (1889–1961)	柳宗悦	Japanese folk arts scholar
Yanagita Kunio (1875–1962)	柳田国男	Japanese folklorist

Bibliography

Akiyama, Hiroyuki. 1997. 'Matsuri ni miru aidentiti no hoji to denshō' [The maintenance and transmission of identity in festivals], *Okinawa Minzoku Kenkyū* 17: 1–40.

Allen, Matthew. 2002. *Identity and Resistance in Okinawa*. Lanham: Rowman & Littlefield.

Arai, Kiyoshi. 2000. *Taketomijima Hazama mura no Kyon'gin* [The *kyon'gin* of Hazama village, Taketomi island]. Ishigaki: Arai Kiyoshi.

Arakawa, Akira. 1987. *Shin nantō fudoki* [A New Account of Travels in the Southern Islands]. Tokyo: Asahi Bunkō.

Arakawa Kōminkan Bunkabu (ed.). 1986. *Arakawa mura koyō-shū* [Arakawa Village *koyō* Collection]. Ishigaki: Arakawa Kōminkan Bunkabu.

Arasaki, Zenjin. 1992. *Yaeyama min'yō no kōsatsu* [An Examination of Yaeyaman Folk Songs]. Ishigaki: Kankō Iinkai.

Arashiro, Kanzō (ed.). 2001. *Kaisetsu-tsuki Yaeyama koten min'yō kashishū* [Annotated Yaeyaman Classical Folk Song Lyric Collection]. Ishigaki: Yaeyama Koten Min'yō Hozonkai.

Atkins, E. Taylor. 2010. *Primitive Selves. Koreana in the Japanese Colonial Gaze, 1910–1945*. Berkeley and Los Angeles: University of California Press.

Attali, Jacques. 1985. *Noise – The Political Economy of Music*. Minneapolis: University of Minnesota Press.

Baily, John. 2001. 'Learning to perform as a research technique in ethnomusicology', *Ethnomusicology Forum* 10/2: 85–98.

Baranovitch, Nimrod. 2003. *China's New Voices: Popular Music, Ethnicity, Gender, and Politics, 1978–1997*. Berkeley and Los Angeles: University of California Press.

Barz, Gregory F. 2000. 'Politics of remembering: performing history(-ies) in youth *Kwaya* competitions in Dar Es Salaam, Tanzania', in Gunderson, Frank and Barz, Gregory F. (eds), *Mashindano! Competitive Music Performance in East Africa*, pp. 407–20. Dar es Salaam: Mkuki na Nyota Publishers.

Barz, Gregory F. 2003. *Performing Religion: Negotiating Past and Present in Kwaya Music of Tanzania*. Amsterdam; New York: Rodopi.

Beatty, Andrew. 1999. 'On ethographic experience: formative and informative (Nias, Indonesia)', in Watson, C.W. (ed.), *Being There – Fieldwork in Anthropology*, pp. 74–97. London: Pluto Press.

Befu, Harumi. 2001. *Hegemony of Homogeneity: An Anthropological Analysis of Nihonjinron*. Melbourne: Trans Pacific Press.

BEGIN. 2005. *Chimugukuru – BEGIN ON BEGIN*. Tokyo: Sony Magazines.

Berger, Harris M. and Carroll, Michael Thomas. 2003. *Global Pop, Local Language*. Jackson: University Press of Mississippi.

Biddle, Ian and Knights, Vanessa. 2007. 'Introduction: national popular musics: betwixt and beyond the local and global', in Biddle, Ian and Knights, Vanessa (eds), *Music, National Identity and the Politics of Location*, pp. 1–15. Aldershot: Ashgate.

Bise, Katsu. 1998. 'Sengo Okinawa ongaku-shi 1945–1998' [History of music in post-war Okinawa 1945–1998], in Fujita, Tadashi (ed.), *Uchinā no Uta*, pp. 183–92. Tokyo: Ongaku no Tomosha.

Blasdel, Christopher. 2005. *The Single Tone: A Personal Journey into Shakuhachi Music*. Tokyo: Printed Matter Press.

Bohlman, Philip V. 1992. 'Epilogue: musics and canons', in Bergeron, Katherine and Bohlman, Philip V. (eds), *Disciplining Music – Musicology and its Canons*, pp. 197–210. Chicago: University of Chicago Press.

Bourdieu, Pierre. 1984. *Distinction – A Social Critique of the Judgement of Taste*. Cambridge, MA: Harvard University Press.

Brocken, Michael. 2003. *The British Folk Revival 1944–2002*. Aldershot: Ashgate.

China, Sadao. 2006. *Utamāi – Shōwa Okinawa kayō o kataru* [Utamāi – Telling the Story of Okinawan Song in the Showa Period]. Tokyo: Iwanami Shoten.

Christy, Alan S. 1993. 'The making of imperial subjects in Okinawa', *Positions* 1/3: 607–39.

Cohen, Sara. 1994. 'Identity, place and the Liverpool sound', in Stokes, Martin (ed.), *Ethnicity, Identity and Music – The Musical Construction of Place*, pp. 117–34. Oxford: Berg.

Cohen, Sara. 1995. 'Sounding out the city: music and the sensuous production of place', *Transactions of the Institute of British Geographers* 20/4: 434–46.

Condry, Ian. 2006. *Hip-hop Japan: Rap and the Paths of Cultural Globalization*. Stanford: Duke.

Connell, John and Gibson, Chris. 2003. *Sound Tracks: Popular Music, Identity, and Place*. Abingdon: Routledge.

Danielson, Virginia. 1997. *The Voice of Egypt: Umm Kulthūm, Arabic Song, and Egyptian Society in the Twentieth Century*. Chicago: University of Chicago Press.

Dawe, Kevin (ed.). 2004a. *Island Musics*. Oxford and New York: Berg.

Dawe, Kevin. 2004b. 'Introduction: islands and music studies', in Dawe, Kevin (ed.), *Island Musics*, pp. 1–30. Oxford and New York: Berg.

Dawe, Kevin. 2004c. 'Island musicians: making a living from music in Crete', in Dawe, Kevin (ed.), *Island Musics*, pp. 65–75. Oxford and New York: Berg.

DeMusik Inter (ed.). 1998a. *Oto no chikara [Okinawa] Amami, Yaeyama, Gyakuryūhen* [The Power of Sound 'Okinawa' – Amami, Yaeyama, Back-flow Edition]. Tokyo: Impact Shuppansha.

DeMusik Inter (ed.). 1998b. *Oto no Chikara [Okinawa] Koza Futtō hen* [The Power of Sound 'Okinawa' – Koza Boiling Edition]. Tokyo: Impact Shuppansha.

Denoon, Donald and McCormack, Gavan (eds). 1996. *Multicultural Japan – Palaeolithic to Postmodern*. Cambridge and New York: Cambridge University Press.

Dinnie, Keith. 2008. *Nation Branding: Concepts, Issues, Practice*. Oxford: Butterworth-Heinemann.

Dujunco, Mercedes M. 2002. 'Hybridity and disjuncture in mainland Chinese popular music', in Craig, T. and King, R. (eds), *Global goes Local: Popular Culture in Asia*, pp. 25–39. Vancouver: UBC Press.

Durkheim, Émile. 1912/1926. *The Elementary Forms of the Religious Life*. London: Allen & Unwin.

Ferranti, Hugh de. 2008. 'The Kyushu *biwa* traditions', in Tokita, A. and Hughes, D. (eds), *The Ashgate Research Companion to Japanese Music*, pp. 105–26. Aldershot: Ashgate.

Ferranti, Hugh de. 2009. *The Last Biwa Singer – A Blind Musician in History, Imagination and Performance*. New York: Cornell University East Asia Program.

Fisher, Paul. 2002. 'Okinawa West' [interview with Ōshima Yasukatsu], *Froots*, April.

Fujita, Tadashi (ed.). 1998. *Uchinā no Uta* [Songs of Uchinā]. Tokyo: Ongaku no Tomosha.

Fujita, Tadashi. 2000. *Okinawa wa uta no shima – Uchinā ongaku no 500 nen* [Okinawa is the Island of Song – 500 Years of Okinawan Music]. Tokyo: Shōbunsha.

Fujita, Takanori. 2002. 'Continuity and authenticity in traditional Japanese music', in Provine, R., Witzleben, J.L. and Tokumaru, Y. (eds), *Garland Encyclopedia of World Music, Vol. 7: East Asia*, pp. 767–72. New York and London: Routledge.

Fujita, Takanori. 2008. '*Nō* and *kyōgen*: music from the medieval theatre', in Tokita, A. and Hughes, D. (eds), *The Ashgate Research Companion to Japanese Music*, pp. 127–44. Aldershot: Ashgate.

Fukui, Akifumi. 2006. *Yoku wakaru nihon ongaku kiso kōza – gagaku kara min'yō made* [An Easy Introduction to Japanese Music – from *Gagaku* to *Min'yō*]. Tokyo: Ongaku no Tomosha.

Gabriel, J. Philip. 1999. *Mad Wives and Island Dreams: Shimao Toshio and the Margins of Japanese Literature*. Honolulu: University of Hawaii Press.

Garfias, Robert. 1993/1994. 'The Okinawan kunkunshi notation system and its role in the dissemination of the Shuri Court music tradition', *Asian Music* 25/1/2: 115–44.

Geertz, Clifford. 1973. *The Interpretation of Cultures: Selected Essays*. New York: Basic Books.

George, Brian. 2007. 'Rapping at the margins: musical constructions of identities in contemporary France', in Biddle, I. and Knights, V. (eds), *Music, National Identity and the Politics of Location – Between the Global and the Local*, pp. 93–113. Aldershot: Ashgate.

Gibo, Eijirō. 1999. *Sanshin no hanashi* [Tales of the *sanshin*]. Naha: Hirugi-sha.

Gibson, Chris and Connell, John. 2005. *Music and Tourism: On the Road Again.* Clevedon: Channel View.

Giddens, Anthony. 1990. *The Consequences of Modernity.* Stanford: Stanford University Press.

Gillan, Matt. 2008a. 'Treasures of the island people: tradition and modernity in Yaeyaman pop music', *Asian Music* 39/1: 42–68.

Gillan, Matt. 2008b. 'Ryūkyū ongaku no senritsu ni okeru kakudai to shukushō – Chikuten-kei no kakyoku o chūshin ni' [Melodic expansion and contraction in Okinawan music: the Chikuten Song Group], *Ongakugaku – Journal of the Musicological Society of Japan* 54/1: 15–29.

Gillan, Matt. 2009: 'Imagining Okinawa – Japanese pop musicians and Okinawan music', *Perfect Beat* 10/2: 177–95.

Govers, Robert and Go, Frank. 2009. *Place Branding. Glocal, Virtual and Physical Identities, Constructed Imagined and Experienced.* Basingstoke: Palgrave Macmillan.

Gummere, Francis B. 1907. *The Popular Ballad.* Boston and New York: The Riverside Press.

Haebaru, Eiiku. 2002. 'Yaima Hakkutsu – Tobarāma Taikai Sōsetsu no Koro' [Yaeyama excavations – the time of the establishment of the *Tubarāma* competition], *Jōhō Yaima* 117: 28–31.

Hall, Stuart. 1991. 'Old and new identities, old and new ethnicities', in King, A. (ed.), *Culture, Globalization, and the World System*, pp. 41–68. Basingstoke: Macmillan Education.

Hanamaru, Mangetsu. 2007. *Okinawa o utsu* [Shooting Okinawa]. Tokyo: Shūeisha.

Hara, Tomoaki. 2000. *Minzoku bunka no genzai: Okinawa, Yonaguni-jima no minzoku e no manazashi* [Folk culture in the present: views of 'folk' in Yonaguni, Okinawa]. Tokyo: Dōseisha.

Hara, Tomoaki. 2007. 'Okinawan studies in Japan, 1879–2007', *Japanese Review of Cultural Anthropology* 8: 101–36.

Harker, Dave. 1985. *Fakesong: The Manufacture of British Folksong 1700 to the Present Day.* Milton Keynes: Open University Press.

Harnish, David. 2005. 'Isn't this nice? It's just like being in Bali: constructing Balinese music culture in Lombok', *Ethnomusicology Forum* 14/1: 3–24.

Harootunian, Harry D. 1998. 'Figuring the folk: history, poetics, and representation', in Vlastos, S. (ed.), *Mirror of Modernity – Invented Traditions of Modern Japan*, pp. 144–59. Berkeley and Los Angeles: University of California Press.

Harris, Rachel. 2008. *The Making of a Musical Canon in Chinese Central Asia: The Uyghur Twelve Muqam.* Aldershot: Ashgate.

Hateruma, Eikichi. 1992. 'Yaeyama – fūdo to rekishi soshite saishi shūzoku' [Yaeyama – environment, history, and ritual practice], in Amino, Y., Ōsumi, K. and Ozawa, S. (eds), *Oto to eizō to moji ni yoru Nihon rekishi to geinō, 11 rettō no kamigami*, pp. 36–68. Tokyo: Heibonsha.

Hateruma, Eikichi. 1999. *Nantō Saishi Kayō no Kenkyū* [Research on Okinawan Ritual Songs]. Tokyo: Sunakoya Shobō.

Hatoma Shōgakkō sōritsu Hyakushūnen Kinenshi Henshū Iinkai (eds). 1997. *Hatō o Koete* [Crossing the Waves]. Taketomi: Taketomi Chōritsu Hatoma Shōgakkō.

Hayashi, Hidemi. 2002. 'BEGIN Shimanchu nu Takara' [Interview with BEGIN], *Urma (Uruma)*, November.

Hein, Laura and Selden, Mark (eds). 2003. *Islands of Discontent – Okinawan Responses to Japanese and American Power*. Lanham: Rowman & Littlefield.

Henry, Edward O. 1989. 'Institutions for the promotion of indigenous music: the case for Ireland's Comhaltas Ceoltoiri Eireann', *Ethnomusicology* 33/1: 67–95.

Hesselink, Nathan. 1994. 'Kouta and karaoke in modern Japan: a blurring of the distinction between *Umgangsmusik* and *Darbietungsmusik*', *British Journal of Ethnomusicology* 3: 49–61.

Hirano, Kenji, Kamisangō, Yūkō and Gamō, Satoaki (eds). 1989. *Nihon Ongaku Dai-jiten* [Dictionary of Japanese Music]. Tokyo: Heibonsha.

Hirata, Daiichi. 2008. *Kimutaka*. Tokyo: Aspect (Asupekuto).

Hokama, Shuzen. 1995. *Nantō bungakuron* [Theory of Okinawan Literature]. Tokyo: Kadokawa Shoten.

Hook, Glenn D. and Siddle, Richard (eds). 2003. *Japan and Okinawa: Structure and Subjectivity*. London and New York: RoutledgeCurzon.

Howard, Keith. 2004. 'Chindo music: creating a Korean cultural paradise', in Dawe, K. (ed.) *Island Musics*, pp. 99–121. Oxford and New York: Berg.

Howard, Keith. 2006a. *Preserving Korean Music: Intangible Cultural Properties as Icons of Identity – Perspectives on Korean Music Volume 1. (SOAS Musicology Series)*. Aldershot: Ashgate.

Howard, Keith. 2006b. *Creating Korean Music: Tradition, Innovation and Discourse of Identity – Perspectives on Korean Music Volume 2. (SOAS Musicology Series)*. Aldershot: Ashgate.

Hughes, David. 1981. 'Japanese folk song preservation societies: their history and nature', *Proceedings of the Fourth International Symposium on the Conservation and Restoration of Cultural Property*, pp. 29–45. Tokyo: National Research Institute of Cultural Properties.

Hughes, David. 1985. *The Heart's Home Town: Traditional Folk Song in Modern Japan*. PhD Dissertation, University of Michigan.

Hughes, David. 2001. 'Japan: scales and modes', in Sadie, S. (ed.), *The New Grove Dictionary of Music and Musicians – Second Edition*, vol. 12, p. 818. London: Grove.

Hughes, David. 2008. *Traditional Folk Song in Modern Japan. Sources, Sentiment and Society*. Folkestone: Global Oriental.

Iha, Fuyū. 1938. *Wonarigami no Shima* [The Islands of the Protecting Gods]. Tokyo: Heibonsha.

Iha, Fuyū. 1975. *Iha Fuyū zenshū* [Complete Works]. Tokyo: Heibonsha.

Iha, Fuyū. 2000. *Ko Ryūkyū* [Old Ryukyu]. Tokyo: Iwanami Bunkō.

Iha, Nantetsu. 1957. 'Washi no tori kō' [Thoughts on *Basï nu turi*]. *Yaeyama Mainichi Shinbun*, 12–15 January.

Iha, Nantetsu. 1962. 'Futatabi "washi no tori bushi" ni tsuite' [Further thoughts on *Basï nu turi*]. *Yaeyama Mainichi Shinbun*, 2–3 March.

Ikegami, Eiichi. 1994. *Bagajima nu Panasu* [Stories of My Island]. Tokyo: Bungei Shunjū.

Ikegami, Eiichi. 1997. *Kajimayā*. Tokyo: Bungei Shunjū.

Ikema, Eizō. 1972. *Yonaguni no Rekishi* [Yonaguni history]. Yonaguni: Ikema Nae.

Iramina, Kōkichi. 2002. *Sanshin wa Uchū o Kanaderu* [The *Sanshin* Sounds in Outer Space]. Naha: Nirayakanaya Shuppan.

Iriomote, Shin and Ōta, Shizuo (eds). 1983. *Tubarāma kahi konryū jomakushiki* [*Tubarāma* Song Monument Unveiling Ceremony Program]. Ishigaki: *Tubarāma kahi konryū* kiseikai.

Ishigaki aza-kai koyō henshū iinkai (eds). 1985. *Ishigaki-mura koyō-shū* [Ishigaki Village *Koyō* Collection]. Ishigaki: Aza-kai.

Ishigaki, Shigeru (ed.). 1992. *Tonoshiro-mura koyō-shū* [Tonoshiro Village *Koyō* Collection]. Ishigaki: Tonoshiro Yunta Hozonkai.

Ishigaki, Shinchi. 2002. 'Intabyū – Ishigaki Shinchi waga Tubarāma' [Interview – Ishigaki Shinchi, my *Tubarāma*], *Jōhō Yaima* 117: 20–24.

Ishigaki, Takenobu and Agarie, Hachijurō. 1986. *Okinawa bun'gaku-hi meguri* [A Trip around Okinawa's Song Monuments]. Naha: Naha Shuppansha.

Ishigaki-shi Bunka Kyōkai (eds). 1999. *Tubarāma Kashū* [*Tubarāma* Lyric Collection]. Ishigaki-shi Bunka Kyōkai.

Ishigaki-shi Sōmu bu shishi henshūshitsu (ed.). 1990. *Ishigakishi-shi shiryō hen, kindai 6, Shinbun Shūsei I* [Ishigaki City Historical Reference Materials – Newspaper Collection]. Ishagaki: Shiyakusho.

Ishigami, Satoshi. 2005. '*Churasan* ron – Nihon hondo no uchinaru Okinawa' [Theory of *Churasan* – Okinawa in Japan in 2001], *Ōsaka Shōgyō daigaku ronshū* 1/2: 83–98.

Isoda, Ken'ichiro and Kurokawa, Shuji (eds). 1995. *Okinawan myūjikku gaido fō bigināzu* [Okinawan Music Guide for Beginners]. Tokyo: Tōa Ongakusha.

Itosu, Chōryō. 1990 [1974]. *Yaeyama Koten Min'yō, Koyō Zenshū* [Complete Yaeyaman *Koten Min'yō* and *Koyō* Collection]. Ishigaki: Uenoyama Insatsu-sho.

Johnson, Henry. 2001. 'Nationalisms and globalization in Okinawan popular music: Nēnēzu and their place in world music contexts', in Starrs, Roy (ed.), *Asian Nationalism in an Age of Globalization*, pp. 359–73. Richmond: Japan Library.

Johnson, Henry. 2004. 'To and from an island periphery: tradition, travel and transforming identity in the music of Ogasawara, Japan', *The World of Music* 46/2: 79–98.

Johnson, Henry. 2006. '*Tsugaru Shamisen*: from region to nation (and beyond) and back again', *Asian Music* 37/1: 75–100.

Johnson, Henry. 2008. 'Recontextualising Eisā: transformations in religious, competition, festival and tourism contexts', in Johnson, H. and Jaffe, J. (eds), *Performing Japan – Contemporary Expressions of Cultural Identity*, pp. 196–220. Folkestone: Global Oriental.

Johnson, Henry. 2010. *The Shamisen: Tradition and Diversity*. Leiden: Brill.

Kajiku, Shin'ichi. 1972. 'Yaeyama Kayō ni okeru Tubarama Bushi no Hassei' [The development of *Tubarāma* in Yaeyaman song]. *Bungaku* 40/4: 136–45.

Kakinoki, Gorō. 1969. 'Kōzōshiki ni yoru Nihon min'yō senritsu no hikaku bunseki-hō. Minami Nihon Min'yō no bunkaken-teki bunseki' [A new comparative method on tone-systems by structural formulae – an analysis of southern Japanese folk songs from the view point of culture circle], in Tōyō Ongaku Gakkai (eds), *Nihon, Tōyō Ongaku Ronkō*, pp. 133–56. Tokyo: Ongaku no Tomo-sha.

Kamei, Hideichi. 1990. *Taketomi-jima no Rekishi to Minzoku* [Taketomi Island, History and People]. Tokyo: Kadokawa Shoten.

Kaneshiro, Atsumi. 1987. 'Yaeyama Min'yō no Gakushiki' [Musical form of Yaeyaman *min'yō*]. *Okinawa Bunka Kenkyū* 13: 241–89.

Kaneshiro, Atsumi. 1990. '*Ryūkyū onkai saikō*' [A review of the *ryūkyū* scale], *Tōyō ongaku kenkyū* 55: 91–118.

Kaneshiro, Atsumi. 1997. *Yamatonchu no Tame no Okinawa Ongaku Nyūmon* [An Introduction to Okinawan Music for Japanese Mainlanders]. Tokyo: Ongaku no Tomosha.

Kaneshiro, Atsumi. 2006. '*Hana-fū bushi shinshaku*' [A review on 'Hanafu-bushi'], *Mousa – Journal of Musicology, Okinawa Prefectural University of Arts* 7: 1–9.

Kanō, Mari. 2002. 'Social groups and institutions in Japan', in Provine, R., Witzleben, J.L., and Tokumaru, Y. (eds), *Garland Encyclopedia of World Music, Vol. 7: East Asia*, pp. 755–62. New York and London: Routledge.

Karimata, Keiichi. 1999. *Nantō Kayō no Kenkyū* [Research on Okinawan Song]. Fujisawa: Mizuki Shobo.

Katō, Tomiko. 1986. '*Kohamajima no ketsugansai – sono geinō to gakushū kōzō*' [The Kohama *ketsugan* festival – its performing arts and learning structure], in Henshū Iinkai (eds), *Shominzoku no Oto – Koizumi Fumio Sensei Tsuitō Ronbun-shū*, pp. 51–69. Tokyo: Ongaku no Tomosha.

Kawamura, Kyōko. 1993. *Umi o wataru uta* [The Song that Crossed the Sea]. Tokyo: Takarajimasha.

Kawamura, Tadao. 1999. *Nanpō bunka no tankyū* [An Exploration of Okinawan Culture]. Tokyo: Kodansha.

Keister, Jay. 2004. *Shaped by Japanese Music – Kikuoka Hiroaki and Nagauta Shamisen in Tokyo*. New York and London: Routledge.

Kerr, George H. 2000. *Okinawa. The History of an Island People*. Boston, Rutland and Tokyo: Tuttle Publishing.

Kinenshi Henshū Iinkai (eds). 1987. *Kinenshi – Akebono* [Commemorative Book – Akebono]. Ishigaki: Kinenshi Henshū Iinkai.

Kinenshi Sakusei Iinkai (eds). 1993. *Utsugumi – Sōritsu hyakushūnen Kinenshi* [The Hundredth Anniversary Publication of the Taketomi Elementary School]. Taketomi: Kinenshi Sakusei Iinkai.

Kinjō, Asao. 1979. 'Kansei Tubarāma Taikai ni Omou' [Thoughts on the 'controlled' *Tubarāma Taikai*], *Yaeyama Mainichi Shinbun*, 6 October.

Kishaba, Eijun. 1962. 'Bashi yunta to bashi no tori bushi ni tsuite' [On *Bashi yunta* and *Basï nu turi bushi*], *Yaeyama Mainichi Shinbun*, 20–27 January.

Kishaba, Eijun. 1967. *Yaeyama Min'yō shi* [Yaeyaman folk song]. Naha: Okinawa Times Sha.

Kishaba, Eijun. 1970. *Yaeyama Koyō*. Naha: Okinawa Times Sha.

Kishaba, Eijun. 1974 (first published 1924). 'Yaeyama-jima Min'yō shi' [Yaeyama folk song collection], in *Nihon Minzokushi Taikei* 1. Tokyo: Kadokawa Shoten.

Kishaba, Eijun. 1975. *Yaeyama Rekishi* [Yaeyaman History]. Tokyo: Kokusho Kankōkai.

Kishaba, Eijun. 1977. *Yaeyama Minzoku-shi* [Yaeyaman Folklore, vol. 2]. Naha: Okinawa Times Sha.

Kishaba, Eijun. 1990. 'Shisen o Koete rekōdo no tabi e' [The journey to make a record], in Ishigaki-shi sōmu bu shi shi Henshūshitsu (eds), *Ishigakishi-shi shiryō hen, kindai 6, Shinbun Shūsei I*, pp. 519–25. Ishigaki: Ishagaki Shiyakusho.

Ko, Mika. 2006. 'Takamine Go: a possible Okinawa cinema', *Inter-Asia Cultural Studies* 7/1: 156–70.

Kobayashi, Kimie. 1986. 'Okinawa no Usudēku' [The Okinawan *usudēku*], in Henshū Iinkai (eds), *Shominzoku no Oto – Koizumi Fumio Sensei Tsuitō Ronbun-shū*, pp. 93–100. Tokyo: Ongaku no Tomosha.

Kobayashi, Yukio. 1986. 'Okinawa hontō onna-eisā no onkai' [The scales of the Okinawan mainland *onna eisā*], in Henshū Iinkai (eds), *Shominzoku no Oto – Koizumi Fumio Sensei Tsuitō Ronbun-shū*, pp. 101–18. Tokyo: Ongaku no Tomosha.

Kodansha. 1983. *Kodansha Encyclopedia of Japan*. Tokyo: Kodansha.

Koizumi, Fumio. 1981. *Okinawa min'yō saifushū 1 Yaeyama* [Transcriptions of Okinawan Folksongs 1 Yaeyama, 2 Volumes]. Tokyo: Tokyo Geijutsu Daigaku Minzoku Ongaku Zemināru.

Koizumi, Fumio. 1983. 'Ajia no Naka no Okinawa Ongaku' [Okinawan music inside Asia], *Shin Okinawa Bungaku* 58 *'Tokushū Okinawa Geinō – Hihan to teigen'*: 44–51.

Koizumi, Fumio. 1989 [1958]. *Nihon Dentō Ongaku no Kenkyū 1* [Japanese Tradition Music Research]. Tokyo: Ongaku no Tomosha.

Kojima, Tomiko. 1974. 'Yaeyama no ongaku – toku ni onkai ni tsuite' [On Yaeyaman music – particularly scales], *Jinrui Kagaku* 27: 161–73.

Kojima, Tomiko. 1976. 'Okinawa Ongaku no Shoyōsu – futatabi Onkai nado ni tsuite' [Various appearances of Okinawan music – once more concerning scales etc.], in Kyūgakkai Rengō, Okinawa Chōsa Iinkai (eds), *Okinawa – Shizen, bunka, shakai* [Okinawa – Nature, Culture, Society], pp. 247–62. Tokyo: Kōbundō.

Kojima, Tomiko. 1994. *Nihon no oto no bunka* [Japanese Sound Culture]. Tokyo: Daiichi Shobō.

Kojima, Tomiko. 2008. '*Watashi-tachi no ongaku* – Nihon ongaku' [Our music – Japanese music], in T. Kojima (ed.), *Nihon no dentō geinō kōza – ongaku* [Japanese Traditional Performing Arts – Music]. Tokyo: Tankōsha.

Kojima, Yoshiyuki. 1962. 'Washi no uta no Genryū' [Origins of the eagle songs]. *Ryukyu Shinpo*, 4–5 March.

Kokuritsu Kokugo Kenkyūsho. 1963. *Okinawa-go Jiten* [Okinawan Language Dictionary]. Tokyo: Ōkurashō Insatsusho.

Kondō, Ken'ichirō. 2008. *Hōgen fuda – Kotoba to shintai* [*Hōgen fuda* – Language and Body]. Tokyo: Shakai Hyōron-sha.

Kumada, Susumu. 1998. '90 Nendai Okinawa Poppu ni Okeru Minzoku-sei Hyōgen no Shosō' [Various aspects of the expression of ethnic identity in 1990s Okinawan pop music], *Okinawa Kenritsu Geijutsu Daigaku-in Geijutsu Bunka-gaku Kenkyū-ka*: 134–62.

Kumada, Susumu. 2007. '*Ryūkyū geinō ni okeru sho-gainen no keisei katei – Yaeyama geinō no "dai-san kai kyōdo buyō to min'yō no kai"* e no shutsuen o megutte' [The formation of academic concepts and 'folk terms' in the Ryukyuan folk performing arts: a case study on 'The 3rd Folk Performing Arts and Folk Songs Festival' of Yaeyama], *Okinawa Geijutsu no Kagaku* 19: 43–72.

Kyō, Nobuko. 2006. *Namii! Yaeyama no obā no uta monogatari* [Namii! The Story of the Songs of an Okinawan Grandmother]. Tokyo: Iwanami shoten.

Kyūjin Okinawa. 2004. *65 nin ga kataru Okinawa ijū* [Relocating to Okinawa – as told by 65 People]. Tokyo: Kabushikigaisha Janisu.

Lancashire, Terence. 1997. 'Music for the gods: musical transmission and change in Iwami *Kagura*', *Asian Music* XXIX/1: 87–123.

Lau, Frederick. 1998. 'Packaging identity through sound: tourist performances in contemporary China', *Journal of Musicological Research* 17: 113–34.

Lebra, William P. 1966. *Okinawan Religion – Belief, Ritual, and Social Structure*. Honolulu: University of Hawaii Press.

Lipsitz, George. 1990. *Time Passages: Collective Memory and American Popular Culture*. Minneapolis: University of Minnesota Press.

Lipsitz, George. 1994. *Dangerous Crossroads: Popular Music, Postmodernism, and the Poetics of Place*. London: Verso.

Lomax, Alan. 1968. *Folk Song Style and Culture*. Washington, DC: American Association for the Advancement of Science.

Machida, Kashō, Misumi, Haruo, Ōshima, Harukiyo, Miyao, Shigeo and Nakasone, Shōei (eds). 1975. *Nihon Min'yō Zenshū: (5) Kyūshū, Okinawa hen* [Complete Collection of Japanese *Min'yō* Vol. 5: Kyushu and Okinawa]. Tokyo: Yuzankaku.

Maeda, Giken, Misumi, Haruo and Minamoto, Takeo 1972. *Okinawa Bunka-shi Jiten* [Dictionary of Okinawan Cultural History]. Tokyo: Tōkyō-dō Shuppan.

Maehana, Tetsuo. 1976. 'Teisetsu ni tai suru gimon – Nirai-kanai Kō, Tubarāma Kō' [Doubts about the established theories – on *nirai kanai* and *Tubarāma*], in *Yaeyama Bunka Ronshū*, pp. 39–58. Ishigaki: Yaeyama Bunka Kenkyū-kai.

Makino, Kiyoshi. 1973. 'Tubarāma bushi ni Tsuite' [On *Tubarāma*], *Okinawa Bungaku* 40: 59–68.

Makino, Kiyoshi. 1988. *Matsukaze – Ōhama Yōnō Yaeyama-uta kunkunshi sakufu hyaku-roku shūnen Kinenshi* [*Matsukaze* – Commemoration of the 106th Anniversary of the Creation of Ōhama Yōnō's Yaeyaman *Kunkunshi*]. Ishigaki: Yaeyama Koten Ongaku Ōhama Yōnō-ryū Hozonkai.

Matayoshi, Shinzō. 1985. 'Okinawa no sanshin kō' [Thoughts on the sanshin]. Presentation handout, *Sanshin kaisetsu kai*, Okinawa prefectural museum.

Matsumura, Hiroshi. 2002. *Uta ni Kiku Okinawa* [Okinawa heard through its songs]. Tokyo: Hakusuisha.

McCormick, Lisa. 2009. 'Higher, faster, louder: representations of the international music competition', *Cultural Sociology* 3/5: 5–30.

Miki, Takeshi. 1963. 'Semento no bōryoku – washi no tori bushi ronsō to sono go no zannen na jijitsu' [The violence of cement – the debate over *Basï nu turi bushi* and the subsequent unfortunate reality], *Yaeyama Mainichi Shinbun*, 13–15 September.

Miki, Takeshi. 1980. *Yaeyama Kindai Minshūshi* [The modern people of Yaeyama]. Tokyo: San'ichi Shobō.

Miki, Takeshi. 1989. *Yaeyama kenkyū no hitobito*. Naha: Niraisha.

Miki, Takeshi. 1992. *Yaeyama kindai-shi no shosō* [Various aspects of recent Yaeyaman history]. Ishigaki: Bunreisha.

Misumi, Haruo. 1976. 'Okinawa Geinō no Denshō Kihan – Yaeyama no Pūri o chūshin ni' [The basis for Okinawan traditions of performing arts – with special reference to the puri festivals on Yaeyama island], in Kyūgakkai Ren'gō, Okinawa Chōsa Iinkai (eds), *Okinawa – Shizen, bunka, shakai* [Okinawa – Nature, Culture, Society], pp. 233–46. Tokyo: Kōbundō.

Miyagi, Fumi. 1982. *Yaeyama Seikatsushi* [Yaeyaman Life]. Naha: Okinawa Times-sha.

Miyara, Kentei. 1979. *Yaeyama Geinō to Minzoku* [Yaeyaman Performing Arts and People]. Naha: Nemoto Shobō.

Miyara, Takahiro. 1963. 'Yaeyama guntō ni okeru iwayuru himitsu kessha ni tsuite' [So-called secret societies in Yaeyama], *The Japanese Journal of Ethnology* 27/1: 13–18.

Miyara, Takahiro. 1973. 'Shūkyō 1 – Saishi Soshiki to Sonraku no Kōzō' [Religion 1 – ritual organizations and village structure], in Miyara, T. (ed.), *Yaeyama no Shakai to Bunka*, pp. 149–72. Tokyo: Kōbunsha.

Miyara, Tōsō (also Miyara, Masamori). 1980. *Miyara Tōsō Zenshū* [Miyara Tōsō Complete Works], vol. 11. Tokyo: Dai'ichi Shobō.

Miyara, Yasuhira. 1979. *Zoku Yaeyama Hōgen no sosei* [Elements of Yaeyaman Dialect, Further Edition]. Naha: Shinpō Shuppan Insatsu.

Morita, Son'ei. 1999. *Yaeyama Geinō Bunka-ron*. Ishigaki: Morita Son'ei sensei ronbun kankō Iinkai.

Murao, Tadahiro and Wilkins, Bernadette. 2001. 'Japan', in Hargreaves, D. and North, A. (eds), *Musical Development and Learning: The International Perspective*, pp. 87–101. London: Continuum.

Murphy, David. 2007. 'Where does world music come from? Globalization, Afropop and the question of cultural identity', in Biddle, I. and Knights, V. (eds), *Music, National Identity and the Politics of Location*, pp. 39–61. Aldershot: Ashgate.

Nagoya, Sagenta. 1984. *Nantō zatsuwa: bakumatsu Amami minzoku-shi* [Tales of the Southern Islands – Folklore of the Amami Islands]. Tokyo: Heibonsha.

Nakasone, Chōichi. 1993. *Yaeyama Kayō-shū* [Collection of Yaeyaman Songs]. Naha: Nakasone Chōichi.

Nakasone, Kōichi. 1998a. *Ryukyu Rettō Shimauta Kikō 2 – Yaeyama, Miyako* [Record of the *shimauta* of the Ryukyu Archipelago, vol. 2 – Yaeyama, Miyako]. Naha: Ryukyu Shinpō Culture Centre.

Nakasone, Kōichi. 1998b. *Shimauta o oikakete* [Chasing *Shimauta*]. Naha: Border Ink.

Narusaka, Kimie. 1979. 'Ongaku kara mita Okinawa Ongaku' [Okinawan music seen from its music], *Koku-bungaku kaishaku to kanshō* (*Tokushū Nansei Shotō no Ko-kayō*) 7: 37–44.

Nettl, Bruno. 1983. *The Study of Ethnomusicology, Twenty-nine Issues and Concepts*. Urbana and Chicago: University of Chicago Press.

Neuman, Daniel M. 1980. *The Life of Music in North India – The Organization of an Artistic Tradition*. Chicago: University of Chicago Press.

Nippon Hōsō Kyōkai (eds). 1990a. *Nihon Min'yō Taikan (Okinawa, Amami) Yaeyama Shotō hen* [Anthology of Japanese *Min'yō* (Okinawa, Amami) Yaeyama]. Tokyo: Nippon Hōsō Kyōkai.

Nippon Hōsō Kyōkai (eds). 1990b. *Nihon Min'yō Taikan (Okinawa, Amami) Miyako Shotō hen* [Anthology of Japanese *Min'yō* (Okinawa, Amami) Miyako]. Tokyo: Nippon Hōsō Kyōkai.

Nishihara, Yōko. 1995. *Yaeyama no kokoro – Tubarāma to jinsei* [The Soul of Yaeyama: Tubarāma and Life]. Tokyo: Kokubunsha.

Nishimura, Asahitarō. 1987. 'Kishaba Eijun to Kaiyō Minzoku-gaku' [Kishaba Eijun and ocean ethnology], in Kishaba Eijun Seitan Hyaku nen Kinen Jigyō Kisei-kai (eds), *Yaeyama Bunka Ronsō* [Papers on Yaeyaman Culture], pp. 1–52. Ishigaki: Kinen jigyō kiseikai.

Noborikawa, Seijin. 1970. *Buyōkyoku-shū kunkunshi* [*Kunkunshi* of Dance Pieces]. Okinawa: Noborikawa Seijin.

Noborikawa, Seijin. 2002. *Okinawa o utau – Noborikawa Seijin jiden* [Singing Okinawa – the Autobiography of Noborikawa Seijin]. Tokyo: Shinchōsha.

Ogawa, Hiroshi. 1995. 'Nihon no Popyurā Ongaku ni Arawareta Okinawa' [Okinawa as it appears in Japanese popular music], in Tōru, Fukazawa (ed.), *Oriento Gensō no Naka no Okinawa* [Okinawa within the Oriental Fantasy], pp. 149–73. Tokyo: Kaifūsha.

Ogawa, Hisao. 1988. *Uta no Minzoku – Amami no Utakake* [Songs and People – *Utakake* in Amami]. Tokyo: Yuzankaku.

Oguma, Eiji. 1998. *Nihonjin no kyōkai* [Boundaries of the Japanese]. Tokyo: Shin'yō-sha.

Ōhama, Anpan. 2004a/b. *Yaeyama Koten Min'yō Kunkunshi* (two volumes). Naha: Ōhama Anpan.

Ōhama, Tsurō. 1964. *Yaeyama min'yō kunkunshi jōkan* [Yaeyama *Kunkunshi* vol. 1]. Ishigaki: Ōhama Yōnō-ryū hozonkai.

Ohsuga, Takeshi. 1993. *Eijan poppu myūjikku no genzai – Asian Pop Music*. Tokyo: Shinjuku Shobō.

Okamoto, Tarō. 1996. *Okinawa Bunkaron – Wasurerareta Nihon* [Theory of Okinawan Culture – Forgotten Japan]. Tokyo: Chūō Kōronsha.

Orikuchi, Shinobu. 1995. *Orikuchi Shinobu zenshū* [Orikuchi Shinobu, Complete Works]. Tokyo: Chūō Kōronsha.

Orikuchi, Shinobu. 2003. *Kokubungaku no hassei* [The Birth of Japanese Literature]. Tokyo: Chūō kōron shinsha.

Ortolani, Benito. 1969. 'Iemoto', *Japan Quarterly* 16/3: 297–306.

Ōshima, Osamu. 1996. 'Kandō no Tubarāma – Ōhama Tsurō shi o shinobu' [A moving *Tubarāma* – remembering Ōhama Tsurō]. *Yaeyama Mainichi Newspaper*, 25 July, p. 3.

Ōshiro, Manabu. 1987. 'Yaeyama min'yō no *uragoe* ni tsuite' [On the use of *uragoe* in Yaeyaman *min'yō*]. In Kinenshi Henshū Iinkai (eds), *Kinenshi – Akebono*, pp. 97–113. Ishigaki: Kinenshi Henshū Iinkai.

Ōshiro, Tatsuhiro. 1985. 'Sanshin to Okinawa Bunka' [*Sanshin* and Okinawan culture], in Okinawa Prefectural Museum (eds), *Sanshin meiki hyakutei-ten* [Exhibition of 100 *Sanshin*s]. Naha: Okinawa Prefectural Museum.

Ōta, Ken'ichi. 1999. 'Sanshin ni matsuwaru hanashi' [About the sanshin], in Okinawa Prefectural Museum (eds), *Tokubetsu ten 'sanshin no hirogari to kanōsei' ten* [Special Exhibit, 'the Spread and Possibilities of the Sanshin'], pp. 62–4. Naha: Okinawa Prefectural Museum.

Ōyama, Nobuko. 2003. *Miyara Chōhō sakkyoku zenshū* [Miyara Chōhō complete compositions]. Naha: Ryūkyū Shinpō.

Peluse, Michael S. 2005. 'Not your Grandfather's music: *Tsugaru Shamisen* blurs the lines between folk, traditional, and pop', *Asian Music* 36/2: 57–80.

Rees, Helen. 2000. *Echoes of History: Naxi Music in Modern China*. New York: Oxford University Press.

Roberson, James E. (2001) 'Uchinaa pop – place and identity in contemporary Okinawan popular music', *Critical Asian Studies* 33/2: 211–42.

Roberts, Martin. 1992. '"World music" and the global cultural economy', *Diaspora* 2/2: 229–42.

Robertson, Jennifer. 1991. *Native and Newcomer: Making and Remaking a Japanese City*. Berkeley and Los Angeles: University of California Press.

Roseman, Marina. 1998. 'Singers of the landscape. Song, history, and property rights in the Malaysian rain forest', *American Anthropologist* 100/1: 106–21.

Ryūkyū Shinpō-sha. 2007. *2006 Okinawa kenmin ishiki chōsa hōkokusho* [Report of the 2006 survey of prefectural residents' opinions]. Naha: Ryūkyū Shinpō-sha.

Sakakeeny, Matt. 2010. 'Under the bridge: an orientation to soundscapes in New Orleans', *Ethnomusicology* 54/1: 1–27.

Sakihara, Kōshin. 1979. 'Yunta – Utau ba' [*Yunta* – performance context], *Kokubungaku kaishaku to kanshō – tokushū nansei shotō no kokayō* 7: 119–24.

Sakiyama, Saburō. 1997. *Taketomi-jima Min'yō Kunkunshi* [Taketomi island *min'yō kunkunshi*]. Ginowan: Sakiyama Saburō.

Schnell, Scott. 1999. *The Rousing Drum – Ritual Practice in a Japanese Community*. Honolulu: University of Hawaii Press.

Shigeno Yūkō. 1960. *Amami Man'yō renka Hishō* [The *Man'yō* love songs of Amami]. Tokyo: Shōshinsha.

Shikina, Chōei. 1979. *Yaeyama Min'yō Kunkunshi Gekan* [Yaeyama *min'yō kunkunshi*, Vol. 2]. Ishigaki: Yaeyama Ongaku Ōhama Yōnō-ryū Hozonkai.

Shinjō, Tadashi. 1982. '*Tubaryāma Yamato-yū*', *Murikabushi* 2 (September): 734.

Shima Editorial Board. 2007. 'An Introduction to Island Culture Studies', *Shima: The International Journal of Research into Island Cultures* 1/1: 1–5.

Shore, Cris. 1999. 'Fictions of fieldwork: depicting the "self" in ethnographic writing (Italy)', in Watson, C. (ed.), *Being There – Fieldwork in Anthropology*, pp. 25–48. London: Pluto Press.

Siddle, Richard. 1998. 'Colonialism and identity in Okinawa before 1945', *Japanese Studies* 18/2: 117–33.

Siddle, Richard. 2003. 'Return to Uchinā: the politics of identity in contemporary Okinawa', in Hook, G. and Siddle, R. (eds), *Japan and Okinawa: Structure and Subjectivity*, pp. 133–47. London and New York: RoutledgeCurzon.

Sklar, Deidre. 2001. *Dancing with the Virgin: Body and Faith in the Fiesta of Tortugas, New Mexico*. Berkeley and Los Angeles: University of California Press.

Slobin, Mark. 1993. *Subcultural Sounds – Micromusics of the West*. Hanover: Wesleyan University Press, University Press of New England.

Sogabe, Tsukasa. 2006. *Warau Okinawa – uta no shima no onjin Onaga Būten-den* [Okinawa Laughing – Onaga Būten, Benefactor of the Islands of Song]. Tokyo: Xknowledge.

Sparling, Heather. 2007. 'One foot on either side of the chasm – Cape Breton singer Mary Jane Lamond's Gaelic choice', *Shima: The International Journal of Research into Island Cultures* 1: 28–42.

Stevens, Carolyn. 2008. *Japanese Popular Music – Culture, Authenticity, and Power*. Abingdon: Routledge.

Stokes, Martin. 1992. *The Arabesk Debate – Music and Musicians in Modern Turkey*. Oxford: Clarendon Press.

Stokes, Martin (ed.). 1994. *Ethnicity, Identity and Music – the Musical Construction of Place*. Oxford: Berg.

Sugimoto, Nobuo. 1975 'Yaeyama no Uta no Ongakusei – yunta, jiraba, tubaruma, sunkani o chūshin ni' [The musicality of Yaeyaman songs – with emphasis on *yunta, jiraba, tubaruma, sunkani*], *Yaeyama Bunka* 3: 88–9.

Sugimoto, Yoshio. 1997. *An Introduction to Japanese Society*. New York: Cambridge University Press.

Sugimoto, Yoshio and Mouer, Ross E. 1989. *Constructs for Understanding Japan*. London and New York: Kegan Paul International.

Sutton, R. Anderson. 1991. *Traditions of Gamelan Music in Java: Musical Pluralism and Regional Identity*. Cambridge: Cambridge University Press.

Suwa, Jun'ichiro. 2007. 'The space of *shima*', *Shima: The International Journal of Research into Island Cultures* 1/1: 6–14.

Suzuki, Hideo. 1988. *Ine no michi, Uta no michi: Yunnan ni utagaki no rūtsu o motomete* [The Path of Rice and Songs: Looking for the Roots of *Utagaki* in Yunnan]. Tokyo: Hon'ami shoten.

Sweeney-Turner, Steve. 1998. 'Borderlines. Bilingual terrain in Scottish song', in Leyshon, A., Matless, D. and Revill, G. (eds), *The Place of Music*, pp. 151–75. New York and London: The Guilford Press.

Sweers, Britta. 2005. *Electric Folk – The Changing Face of English Traditional Music*. New York: Oxford University Press.

Szego, C. Kati. 2003. 'Singing Hawaiian and the aesthetics of (in)comprehensibility', in Berger, H. and Carroll, M. (eds), *Global Pop, Local Language*, pp. 291–328. Jackson: University Press of Mississippi.

Tada, Osamu. 2008. *Okinawa imēji o tabi suru – Yanagita Kunio kara ijū būmu made* [Travels of the Okinawan Image – from Yanagita Kunio to the Immigration Boom]. Tokyo: Chuokoron Shinsha.

Takahashi, Miki. 2002. 'Shimauta ni matsuwaru sho-gainen no seiritsu katei' [The process of formation of concepts regarding '*shimauta*'], *Okinawa Bunka* 37/2: 85–138.

Takahashi, Miki. 2006. 'Okinawa popyurā ongaku-shi no hensen – kaku janru no seisei o chūshin toshite' [The history of Okinawan popular music: a process of emergence of a new music genre], *Bulletin of Education, Kochi University* 66: 161–76.

Takamine, Hōyu. 1989. 'Kyōdō Geinō kurabu no 25 shūnen o furikaette' [A look back at the 25 years of the local performing arts club], in Yaeyama Kōtō Gakkō Sōritsu yonjūgo Shūnen Kinen-shi Henshū Iinkai (eds), *Sōritsu yonjūgo shūnen kinen-shi*, pp. 214–25. Ishigaki: Yaeyama kōtō gakkō sōritsu yonjūgo shūnen kinen jigyō kisei-kai.

Takenaka, Rō. 1975. *Ryūka genshi-kō – Shimauta no Sekai* [Ryūka Hallucinations. The World of *Shimauta*]. Tokyo: Tabata Shoten.

Takenaka, Rō. 2002. *Ryūkyū Kyōwakoku* [The Republic of Ryukyu]. Tokyo: Chikuma Shobō.

Tanabe, Hideo. 1976. 'Okinawa ni okeru Hondo Geinō no Teichaku – Kuduchi o Chūshin Toshite' [The arrival of Japanese mainland performing arts in Okinawa – with emphasis on *kuduchi*]. In Kyūgakkai Ren'gō, Okinawa Chōsa Iinkai (eds), *Okinawa – Shizen, bunka, shakai* [Okinawa – Nature, Culture, Society], pp. 225–32. Tokyo: Kōbundō.

Tanabe, Hisao. 1963. *Shamisen ongaku-shi* [History of Shamisen Music]. Tokyo: Sōshisha.

Tanabe, Hisao. 1968. *Nan'yō, Taiwan, Okinawa ongaku kikō* [Musical Research Trip to the South Sea Islands, Taiwan and Okinawa]. Tokyo: Ongaku no tomosha.

Tanaka, Kenji. 2003. *Hitome de wakaru Nihon ongaku nyūmon* [An Instant Introduction to Japanese Music]. Tokyo: Ongaku no Tomosha.

Tanaka, Yasuhiro. 2002. '*Media ni hyōshō sareru Okinawa bunka*' [Media representations of Okinawan culture], in Itō, M. (ed.), *Media bunka no kenryoku sayō* [The Power of Mediated Culture], pp. 175–97. Tokyo: Serika Shobō.

Tanaka, Yasuhiro. 2009. *Tasha no mezashi: Nantō-ron o megutte* [In the Eyes of the Other: On the Theories of Southern Island], *Japan Studies The Frontier* (International Christian University, Japan Studies Program), pp. 27–38.

Tanigawa, Ken'ichi. 2000. *Uta to Nihonjin* [Songs and Japanese People]. Tokyo: Kodansha.

Tatsumi, Masaaki. 2001. *Man'yōshū ni aitai* [Meeting the *Man'yōshū*]. Tokyo: Kasama shoin.

Taylor, Timothy. 1997. *Global Pop: World Music, World Markets*. New York: Routledge.

Teruya, Rinken and Matsumura, Hiroshi. 1995. *Nankuru-gurashi* [Living for the Moment]. Tokyo: Chikuma Shobō.

Teruya, Rinsuke. 1998. *Terurin Jiden* [Terurin's Autobiography]. Tokyo: Kabushiki Gaisha Misuzu Shobō.

Tōbaru, Yōei. 1970. *Yaeyama no Minshuka no tame ni* [For the Democratisation of Yaeyama]. Naha: Nansei Insatsusho.

Tōkawa, Seiichi. 1990. *Nihon no Onkai o Saguru* [Investigating Japanese Scales]. Tokyo: Ongaku no Tomosha.

Tokita, Alison. 1996. 'Mode and scale, modulation and tuning in Japanese shamisen music: the case of *Kiyomoto* narrative', *Ethnomusicology* 40/1: 1–33.

Tokita, Alison. 1999. *Kiyomoto-bushi – Narrative Music of the Kabuki Theatre*. Kassel: Bärenreiter.

Tokita, Alison and Hughes, David (eds). 2008. *The Ashgate Research Companion to Japanese Music*. Aldershot: Ashgate.

Tomiyama, Ichirō. 1990. *Kindai nihon shakai to Okinawajin* [Recent Japanese Society and Okinawans]. Tokyo: Nihon keizai hyōronsha.

Tsuchihashi, Yutaka. 1984. 'Utakake Bunka-kō no naka no Nantō' [Okinawa as a part of the *utakake* cultural region], *Bungaku* 6/52: 76–89.

Tubarāma Taikai Un'ei Iinkai Jimukyoku (eds). 1980. *Tubarāma Taikai Nenpyō* [Chronology of the *Tubarāma Taikai*]. Ishigaki: Ishigaki-shi.

Tuohy, Sue. 2001. 'The sonic dimensions of nationalism in modern China: musical representation and transformation', *Ethnomusicology* 45/1: 107–31.

Turino, Thomas. 1993. *Moving Away From Silence: Music of the Peruvian Altiplano and the Experiment of Urban Migration*. Chicago: University of Chicago Press.

Uchida, Ruriko. 1989. *Okinawa no Kayō to Ongaku* [Okinawan Songs and Music]. Tokyo: Daiichi Shobō.

Ueunten, Wesley. 2008. 'Okinawan diasporic identities: between being a buffer and a bridge', in Willis, D. and Murphy-Shigematsu, S. (eds), *Transcultural Japan: At the Borderlands of Race, Gender and Identity*, pp. 159–78. Abingdon: Routledge.

Umeda, Hideharu. 2001. '*Okinawa kankō ni okeru bunka o kangaeru*' [A study of 'culture' in tourism of Okinawa], *Mousa, Journal of Musicology, Okinawa Prefectural University of Arts* 2: 125–38.

Urahara, Keisaku. 1970. *Yaeyama Yunta-shū* [Collection of Yaeyaman *Yunta*]. Tokyo: Ongaku no Tomosha.

Urasaki, Eichō. 1935. 'Ongaku shūkan ni saishite Yaeyama Min'yōkai ni sasagu 2' [To the Yaeyaman *min'yō* world on the occasion of Music Week], *Kainan Jihō*, 20 November.

Wang, Yaohua. 1998. *Chūgoku to Ryūkyū no sangen ongaku* [Music of Chinese and Ryūkyūan Three-stringed Lutes]. Tokyo: Daiichi Shobō.

Willcox, Bradley J., Willcox, Craig and Suzuki, Makoto 2002. *The Okinawa Program*. New York: Three Rivers Press.

Yaeyama Koten Min'yō Hozonkai (eds). 1997. *Utagokoro Yutaka ni* [With a Rich Heart in Song]. (Yaeyama Koten Min'yō Hozonkai 20th anniversary concert programme.) Ishigaki: Yaeyama Koten Min'yō Hozonkai.

Yaeyama Kyōiku Jimusho (eds). 1976. *Kyōdo Ongaku Kyōzai-shū* [Local Music Educational Material]. Ishigaki: Yaeyama Kyōiku Jimusho.

Yaeyama nintōzei haishi hyakunen kinen jigyō kisei-kai (eds). 2003. *Nintōzei haishi hyakunen kinen-shi Asapana* [100th Anniversary of the Abolishment of the *Nintōzei* System]. Ishigaki: Nanzan-sha.

Yamashiro, Kenkō. 1988. *Nirai no Shimauta* [*shimauta* from *Nirai-kanai*]. Osaka: Sōgensha.

Yamazato, Setsuko. 1982. '*Tobaryāma*', *Murikabushi* 2 (September): 72–3.

Yamazato, Yūkichi (ed.). 1989. *Amuro-ryū Kunkushi Jōkan* [Amuro-*ryū Kunkunshi*, Vol. 1]. Ginowan: Yaeyama Ongaku Amuro-ryū hozonkai Yamazato Yūkichi Kenkyūjo.

Yamazato, Yūkichi (ed.). 1991. *Amuro-ryū Kunkushi gekan* [Amuro-*ryū Kunkunshi*, Vol. 2]. Ginowan: Yaeyama Ongaku Amuro-ryū hozonkai Yamazato Yūkichi Kenkyūjo.

Yamazato, Yūkichi and Ishigaki, Shigeru. 2002. 'Tubarāma, Izu su du Nusï' [*Tubarāma* – the singer is master], *Jōhō Yaima* 117: 25.

Yanagi, Muneyoshi. 1981. *Yanagi Muneyoshi Zenshū 15* [Yanagi Muneyoshi Complete Works, Vol. 15]. Tokyo: Chikuma Shobō.

Yanagita, Kunio. 1998. *Yanagita Kunio Zenshū* [Complete Works]. Tokyo: Chikuma Shobō.

Yang, Mu. 1994. 'On the Hua'er songs of North-Western China', *Yearbook for Traditional Music* 26: 100–16.

Yang, Mu. 1998. 'Erotic musical activity in multiethnic China', *Ethnomusicology* 42/2: 199–264.

Yano, Teruo. 1993. *Okinawa geinō-shi banashi* [Tales of Okinawan Performing Arts History]. Ginowan: Yōjusha.

Yonetani, Julia. 2003. 'Contested memories. Struggles over war and peace in contemporary Okinawa', in Hook, G. and Siddle, R. (eds), *Japan and Okinawa: Structure and Subjectivity*, pp. 188–207. London and New York: RoutledgeCurzon.

Discography

The discography contains a selection of the huge number of commercially available recordings by musicians mentioned in the text. Where possible I have included the serial number and original release date of the recording. Many are out of print, but sometimes turn up at second-hand book stores and Internet auction sites in Japan and Okinawa.

CD Recordings

Ara Yukito with Sandē: *Shunkashū chotto swing* (新良幸人： 春夏秋ちょっと酔ing) (Swing SW-0001).

Asato Isamu (安里勇):
1) *Uminchu – Yaeyama Nasake-uta* (海人・八重山情唄) (Respect Record Ltd. RES-12, 1996).
2 *Shiosai – Yaeyama Nasake-uta* (潮騒・八重山情唄) (Anima Music Ltd. AJCD-0011, 1999).

BEGIN (ビギン):
1) *BEGIN no Shimauta – Omoto Takeo* (ビギンの島唄-オモトタケオ) (Teichiku TECN-20647, 2000).
2) *BEGIN no Shimauta – Omoto Takeo 2* (ビギンの島唄-オモトタケオ2) (Teichiku TECN-20798, 2002).
3) *BEGIN no Shimauta – Omoto Takeo 3* (ビギンの島唄-オモトタケオ3) (Teichiku TECI-1284, 2010).

Daiku Tetsuhiro (大工哲弘):
1) *Uchinā jinta* (ウチナー・ジンタ) (Off Note ON-01, 1994).
2) *Daiku Tetsuhiro* (大工哲弘) (Off Note ON-5, 1995).
3) *Chibariyō Uchinā* (チバリョーウチナー) (Ongaku sentā CCD-760, 1997).
4) (with Tsundalers) *Agarooza* (Victor VICG-60098, 1998).
5) *Taborare – Yaeyama no Negai-uta* (賜・八重山の願いうた) (Akabana ASCD-2009, 1999).
6) *Gamelan yunta* (ガムラン-ユンタ) (DISC AKABANA SKA-3004, 2009).

Hatoma Kanako: *Yōn no Michi* (鳩間可奈子：ヨーンの道) (DIG Records DCA0002, 2000).

Hidekatsu (日出克):
1)   *Shinpi Naru Yoake* (神秘なる夜明け) (BMG VICTOR BVCR-679, 1994).
2)   *Mapirōma* (マピローマ) (BMG VICTOR BVCR-713, 1995).

Hosono Haruomi (細野晴臣): *Paraiso* (Sony Music Direct, 1978).

Iramina Kōkichi et al. (伊良皆高吉、他): *Yaeyama Utai* (八重山謡) (Victor VICG-60213, 1999).

Kawajo Masahiko (川門正彦): *Shima* (島) (HIKO-0002).

Miyara Kōsei (宮良康正):
1)   *Yaeyama nu Kukuru* (八重山ぬ心) (Kokusai Bōeki RMCA-0011, 1998).
2)   *Iwai Uta* (祝いうた) (Kokusai Boueki KOKU3-032, 2000).
3)   *Donan Uta* – two volumes (どなん歌) (Kokusai Boueki KOKU3-0044, KOKU3-0045, 2002).
4)   *Dunta* (どぅんた) (Kokusai Boueki KOKU3-0046, 2002).

Nagama Takao, Ayame band (長間孝雄・アヤメバンド):
1)   *Nantō Shōsetsu* (南島小説) (Kokusai Boueki NKCD1284, 1996).
2)   *Kaze no Matsuri* (風の祭) (Kokusai Boueki RMCA-0012, 1998).

Nishidomari Shigeaki (西泊茂昌):
1)   *Kaze ga Iyasu Uta wo Kike* (風が癒す唄をきけ) (OTV-0808, 1996).
2)   *Hibi Dandan* (日日淡淡) (OTV 88-02, 1997).

Ôshima Yasukatsu (大島康克):
1)   *Nishikaji Haikaji* (北風南風)   (Polystar PSCR-5066, 1993).
2)   *Arinutou* (東ぬ渡) (Victor VICG-60204, 1999).
3)   *Bagasïma nu uta* – *Songs of my Islands* (我が島ぬうた) (Victor VICG-60418, 2000).
4)   *Island Time* (島時間) (Victor VICG-60505, 2002).
5)   Ôshima Yasukatsu with Jeffrey Keezer (Victor VICL-61953).

Ōsoko Chōyō (大底朝要) *Yaeyama no hanazuna* (八重山歌の花綵) (Marufuku, FCD-1007, 2004).

Parsha Club:
1)   *Nada nada* (OPMC-0004, 2000).
2)   *Acoustic Parsha*: *Tsukiya Hama* (月夜浜) (OPMC-006, 2001).

Sakamoto Ryūichi (坂本龍一):
1)   *NEO GEO* (Sony, 1987).
2)   *Beauty* (Toshiba EMI, *TOCP*-53050, 1989).

Sakieda Hiroji (サキエダ・ヒロジ) *Hai nu yūshi Oyake Akahachi* (南ぬ勇士オ
　　ヤケ赤蜂) (KOKUSAI BOUEKI 1996).

Tamayose Chōden: *Yaeyama no Uta* – four volumes (玉代勢長伝：八重山の歌)
　　(Marufuku ACD-46).

Various:
Okinawa uta no Seizui (沖縄音楽精髄) (Columbia COCJ-30861~2, recordings
　　made in 1934–5).

Tiyumu Takidun – Tanedori-sai hōnō buyōkyoku (てぃゆむたきどぅん　種子取
　　祭奉納舞踊曲) (Kokusai Boueki KOKU3-0017~0018, 1999).

Yaeyama Koten Min'yō Hozonkai: *Yaeyama Koten Min'yō-shū* (八重山古典民謡
　　保存会：八重山古典民謡集) (Marufuku FCD-1003~1006, 1996).

Yamazato Yūkichi (山里勇吉):
1)   *Yaeyama Shosei bushi* (八重山書生節) (Akabana ASCD-2007, 1997).
2)   *Michi-uta, Asobi-uta* (道うた遊びうた) (Akabana ASCD-2006, 1997).

Cassette Tape Recordings

Nagama Takao (長間孝雄): *Nagama Takao* (長間孝雄) (OMK, n.d.).

DVD

Miyara Kōsei *Tubarāma no sekai* [The world of *Tubarāma*] (JCC-DVD-0002,
　　n.d.).
Nakae, Yūji (2004) *Shirayuri Kurabbu* [Shirayuri Club] (Tokyo: Prime Direction).

Index

agriculture 28, 35, 67, 72–3, 95
airport (Ishigaki) 127, 134
Akamata Kuromata 20, 71, 86–9
Akanma bushi 29, 79, 81, 113–14
America
    military bases 12–13, 154, 156, 164,
      174, 180
    post-WWII administration 1, 12–13,
      34, 63, 163–4, 169
ancestor 2, 6, 18, 35, 65–8, 77–82, 89, 151,
    171, 177
Angamā 77–82, 89, 177
antiphonal singing 23, 26, 54, 110, 132
Ara, Yukito 5, 35, 119, 152–3, 155, 159,
    161, 166–7, 174, 181
Aragusuku 18, 30–31, 86–7, 111, 177
Asadōya yunta 23, 26–7, 41, 62–3, 121,
    134, 149, 164
Asato, Isamu 14–15, 71, 92, 123–4
authenticity 7, 52, 83, 92–3, 120, 151, 160,
    172
    as primality 151
ayō 21, 65, 68, 107

Bali 4, 9–10, 44, 159
Basï nu turï 17, 37, 49, 104, 113–14, 118
BEGIN 2–3, 66, 121, 154–63, 166–7, 177,
    179, 181
bon festival 77–9, 121, 127, 174
Buddhism 66–9, 74, 77–8, 81, 177
Buena Vista Social Club 155, 179
bunkazai, see cultural asset

canon 48–50, 63, 107, 111–12, 128, 179
China (country) 10, 31–2, 35–7, 45–6,
    55–7, 80, 120, 150, 159, 181
China, Sadao 22, 88, 149–50

Churasan (television drama) 6, 12, 102,
    156–7, 170
classical (*koten*)
    folk song 21–2, 53
    vs. folk 51–3, 56–7
competitions 58, 96, 107–8, 115, 117,
    128–9, 141–8, 178
cultural asset 53, 65, 72, 98, 178
cultural distinction 22, 31, 37, 162

Daiku, Tetsuhiro 5, 8, 22, 29, 55, 66, 102,
    119, 141, 152–3, 158–9, 161–4,
    174, 179, 181
dance 9, 17, 52–4, 68–71, 75–83, 88–9,
    103–4, 115–21, 153, 174, 177
dialect (*hōgen*) see language

ethnic identity 11, 45–7, 59, 151, 158, 164,
    180

folk-song club, 121–5
fushiuta 13–14, 21–2, 29–31, 33, 37,
    39–40, 49–50, 53, 61, 65, 68, 75–6,
    79–82, 91, 109–10, 114–19, 123,
    128, 131, 136, 139–41, 144, 152–3,
    159, 162, 164, 169, 177–9, 181–2
    lessons 100–4
    lineages 39, 62, 91–100, 107, 114, 146,
    148, 179

gender 21, 23, 27, 52, 76, 86, 102–4, 108,
    110, 112, 116–17
generational differences 71, 76, 81–3, 88,
    107–10, 158
globalization
government official (Shuri) 19–20, 26,
    29–33, 62, 69, 93

grade tests, *see konkūru*

harvest festival 2, 65, 69–70, 86, 88, 109,
     117, 127, 174
Hateruma 17–19, 57, 77, 87
Hatoma 18, 59, 70, 77, 88, 114, 118–19
hayashi 23, 25, 27, 63, 76, 129, 133, 136,
     147, 153
Hidekatsu 152, 159, 165, 169–70, 174
history, representation in new music
     167–71
hōnensai, see harvest festival
hōnō geinō, see offertory performances
human race hall 46, 56–7

identity 1
     family 9, 67, 78, 80–82
     Okinawan 47, 51, 164
     village 85–8
iemoto 8, 97–8
Iha, Fuyū 17, 47–51, 132, 177, 179
island studies 9–10

Japan
     folklore movement 10, 47
     popular music in Yaeama 121, 153,
          161, 164–5
jinruikan, see human race hall
jiraba, see work songs
jūrukunitsï 80–81, 89, 177

Kadekaru, Rinshō 4, 55, 149, 155
kahi, see song monuments
Kina, Shōkichi 149, 159, 168
Kishaba, Eijun 19, 23, 37, 48–52, 62, 68,
     114, 130–31, 179
Kohama 18, 20, 23, 27, 30, 65, 69, 71,
     77–8, 81–2, 86–8, 156–7, 169
Koizumi, Fumio 40–44, 111
konkūru 100–106, 142, 162
koten, see classical
koto 21, 23, 48, 104, 153
koyō 21–9, 40, 71, 88, 108–12, 118
Kuigusuku bushi 41–2

kumiodori 53, 76
kunkunshi notation 21, 29, 33, 37–9, 76,
     93–7, 100–101, 105–6, 117, 131,
     136–9, 141, 144–5, 178
Kuroshima 17–19, 69, 71, 77, 123–4

language
     Okinawan/Yaeyaman 8, 20, 32, 57–64,
          78, 83, 88, 104, 116, 127, 130,
          136, 145–6, 154–5, 158, 164, 168,
          170–73, 180
     hōgen fuda (dialect board) 59
     hōgen ronsō (dialect controversy) 59
     standard Japanese 32, 57–64, 79, 134,
          145, 168, 171–3, 180
lineage (see also *fushiuta* lineages) 92,
     97–8
locality 7–11, 45, 68, 130, 150, 154, 171–2

Man'yōshū 55–6, 113
melodic variants 27, 106, 135–41, 145–8,
     178
minority 5, 9–10, 45–6, 180
min'yō 21–2, 51–3, 56, 95, 98, 111, 141,
     162, 178
min'yō sakaba, see folk-song club
min'yō scale 40, 42, 44, 165
miyako-bushi scale 40, 61
Miyara, Chōhō 60–62, 181
Miyara, Kōrin 139
Miyara, Kōsei 141
Miyara (village) 20, 27, 58, 72, 86–8,
     108–11, 114, 127, 143
mō-ashibi, see utagaki
mora structure 26, 29–30, 79, 140

Nabi no koi (film) 5–6, 12, 102, 155–6, 174
Nakae, Yūji 5, 155–6, 164
nantōron (Southern Island theory) 47–8,
     169
Nēnēs 4, 150, 159–60
Nichiryū dōsōron 47
Nihonjin-ron 11, 173
nintōzei, see taxation

Nirai-kanai 67–9, 73–5, 77–8, 82, 89, 177
Nishidomari, Shigeaki 35, 153–4, 159, 165, 171–2, 174, 180
Noborikawa, Seijin 4–5, 155

offertory performances 29–30, 65, 68–9, 71–2, 75–6, 82–5, 88–9, 118
Ōhama, Anpan 2–3, 7, 38, 91, 95–8, 104–6, 133, 139, 141–2, 177, 181, 192
Ōhama, Tsurō 35, 62–3, 95, 97, 104–6, 133–6, 164, 180–81
Ōhama, Yōnō 93–5
Orikuchi, Shinobu 52, 67, 77, 170
Osaka 3–7, 46, 56, 59, 62, 102, 141, 164
Ōshima, Yasukatsu 5, 119, 153–4, 159, 162, 174
Ōsoko, Chōyō 14, 91, 98, 100–103, 141, 182
Ōta, Shizuo 80–81
Oyake, Akahachi 18, 168–9
Ōyama, Takeshi 72, 74, 84

place
    branding 11–12
    performance of 68, 74–6, 81, 89, 130–31, 177
professional musician 11, 29, 66, 92, 119–20, 124–5, 152, 158, 174
pūrï, *see* harvest festival

record label 4, 55, 76, 123, 152–5, 169
ritsu scale 40–44, 61
ritual music 65–89
    and secret societies 71, 86–8
    social meaning 66, 70–72, 82–9
    and tourism 86–7
ryūka (structure) 29–30
Ryūkyū
    court 16, 18, 32, 37, 52–3, 66, 69, 76
    kingdom 1, 16, 18, 45, 67, 69, 168
    scale 39–44, 159, 165–7

Sakiyama, Yōnō 62, 139–40
sanshin 5–6, 13, 21–2, 29, 31–9, 61–2, 68, 75–6, 78, 81–2, 96–7, 102–3, 117, 119, 121–2, 124, 136, 140–43, 147, 150–61, 165–70, 178, 182

construction 35–6
    in Yaeyama 32–5
    social status 31–5, 59, 115–16
    tuning 36–7, 100
scales (musical) 4, 37, 39–44, 61, 154–5, 159, 165–7
shamisen (Japan mainland) 4, 11–12, 33, 36–7, 92, 104
shimauta (genre) 22, 161
Shimoji, Isamu 152, 172–3, 180
Shinjō, Wataru 139
Shimanchu nu takara (song) 2
Shin-asadōya yunta 62–3, 134
Shiraho 19, 27, 30, 34, 62–3, 118, 132–40, 143–7, 152–5, 164, 174
shrine 18, 50, 65–70, 75–6, 88, 110
social class 16, 18–22, 26, 29, 32–5, 51, 55, 59, 77, 93–5, 129–31, 146, 162, 178
social control 94
song monuments 112–14, 147
Sōron, see bon festival
spatial fixity 7–8
standardization (of variant forms) 93–4, 106–7, 111, 128, 140–45, 148, 178
strategic inauthenticity 160–63

Takamine, Hōyū 34, 116–18
Takamine, Mitsu 103, 138
Takenaka, Rō 4, 55–6, 153
Taketomi 17–18, 34, 57, 62, 65–6, 69–77, 82–6, 89, 110–11, 117–18, 121–3, 152, 165, 177–8, 181–2
Tamayose, Chōden 95, 98, 140
tanadui 65–6, 69–78, 82–8, 117, 177–8, 182
taxation 18–20, 23, 26, 94, 168
teaching licence 100, 104–5
teacher–student relationship 13–14, 92–3, 97, 100–103, 106–7, 110
Teruya, Rinken 149–50, 155–6, 159–60, 167
Teruya, Rinsuke 82
tetrachord 40–44, 111
Tominaga, Hide 72, 139, 145
Tonoshiro 19, 23–4, 27–8, 35, 41, 50, 63, 72, 93–8, 104, 106, 108–12, 117, 121, 130, 136, 138–9, 177, 182

tourism 10, 12, 15, 22, 65–6, 71–4, 86–7, 89, 91, 102, 114, 120–25, 134–5, 141–3, 157

Tōyama, Zendō (Yoshitaka) 96, 98

Tsukï ya pama bushi 37–8, 104

Tubarāma
lyrics 129–35
melodic variants 135–41
singing competition 96, 128, 141–7
song 2, 31, 91, 124, 127–48, 158, 162, 164, 177–8, 180–81
song monument 113–14

Uehara, Naohiko 22

utagaki 53–6, 132, 141

utakake, see utagaki

utinan-susanan 27–8

work song 20–21, 23–31, 34, 41, 49–50, 62, 91, 106–12, 118, 127, 129, 133, 139, 153, 159, 162, 178

preservation groups (*hozonkai*) 8, 29, 72, 106–12, 145, 178, 182

world music 4, 149–57, 160, 167, 179

WWII 12, 63, 96, 181

Yaeyama Mainichi newspaper 104–6, 114, 143

Yakabi, Chōki 33, 37

yakunin, see government official

Yamazato, Setsuko 103, 112, 143

Yamazato, Yūkichi 4–5, 14, 22, 34, 55, 92, 123, 132, 136, 141, 144–5, 149, 152–3, 155, 164

Yanagi, Muneyoshi 10, 47, 59, 146–7

Yanagita, Kunio 10, 47–8, 51–2, 56

Yonaguni 8, 17–18, 32, 35, 57–8, 65, 77, 117, 130, 141, 147, 153–4, 168–9, 171–2

Yūnkai ritual 73–5, 89, 117, 177

yunta, see work songs